DESERT

Between the

MOUNTAINS

ALSO BY MICHAEL S. DURHAM

The Mid-Atlantic States

The Desert States

Powerful Days

Guide to Ancient Native American Sites

Miracles of Mary

DESERT

Between the

MOUNTAINS

MORMONS, MINERS, PADRES,

MOUNTAIN MEN, AND THE OPENING

OF THE GREAT BASIN

1772–1869

MICHAEL S.

DURHAM

HENRY HOLT AND COMPANY

NEW YORK

Henry Holt and Company, Inc.
Publishers since 1866
115 West 18th Street
New York, New York 10011

Henry Holt ® is a registered trademark of
Henry Holt and Company, Inc.

Published in Canada by Fitzhenry & Whiteside Ltd.,
195 Allstate Parkway, Markham, Ontario L3R 4T8.

Library of Congress Cataloging-in-Publication Data
Durham, Michael S. (Michael Schelling), 1935–
Desert between the mountains: Mormons, miners, padres, mountain men,
and the opening of the Great Basin, 1772–1869 / Michael S. Durham. — 1st ed.
p.   cm.
Includes bibliographical references and index.
ISBN 0-8050-4161-3 (hardcover : alk. paper)
1. Great Basin—History.   2. Frontier and pioneer life—Great Basin.
3. Mormons—Great Basin—History.   4. Pioneers—Great Basin—History.   I. Title.
F789.D87   1997
941.07—dc21   97-13619

Henry Holt books are available for special promotions and premiums.
For details contact: Director, Special Markets.

First Edition 1997

Designed by Jessica Shatan

Printed in the United States of America
All first editions are printed on acid-free paper. ∞
1 3 5 7 9 10 8 6 4 2

For Carmile

CONTENTS

Acknowledgments

Until a decade or so ago, I had never set foot in the Great Basin; therefore, I am most grateful to those who introduced me to the region, particularly Kathleen Lubeck of the public information office of the Church of Jesus Christ of Latter-day Saints, as the Mormon Church is formally known. On her regular visits to New York City, where I was then an editor, she imbued me with the idea that Utah must be a fascinating place to visit. And so it turned out to be. On my first trip to Salt Lake City I met Esther Ruth Truitt Henrichsen, then garden designer for the Mormon Church, whose good-humored slant on Mormon history ignited my enthusiasm for the subject. With Esther as guide, I did Temple Square, visited Brigham Young's grave site, and toured Gilgal Gardens, a remarkable collection of folk sculpture hidden away in a backyard in central Salt Lake City.

My first visit to Nevada—the Great Basin's western half, vastly different from Utah but equally rich in history—came a year or so later, thanks to Henry Wiencek, series editor for the *Smithsonian Guide to Historic America*, who assigned me to write the volume that included both Nevada and Utah. I owe other trips to the Great Basin to assignments from Carla Davidson of *American Heritage* magazine and the staff of the now-defunct *Americana*. On these jaunts, I met and talked with curators, park rangers, professors, archaeologists, librarians, and guides, including the older folks who staff Mormon sites, often retired Latter-day Saints on missions. As I wrote for *American Heritage*, "Anyone who has heard that Mormons are reclusive, suspicious, aggressive, or just plain weird will think otherwise after meeting these gentle and friendly people."

While writing the book, I came to realize that it covered material that I first encountered long ago in college, particularly from the teaching of western historian Frederick Merk and Arthur Schlesinger, Jr., whose lectures introduced me to Mormons and other American religious groups. For current research, I was delighted to find that the libraries at Hartwick and SUCO, both colleges in nearby Oneonta, New York, had helpful staffs and large collections of western material. What they did not have I could usually unearth at larger repositories, such as Olin Library at Cornell and the public library in New York City.

I am grateful to my editor, Ray Roberts; his enthusiasm for my original proposal helped sustain me during the dark days of writing ahead. I thank my friend and agent, Maureen Graney, who has stepped in to salvage my adventure in freelance writing on more than one occasion. Jim Zihal of Zihal Design in New York City and photographer Mel Adelglass contributed greatly to the production of the illustrations for the book. Copy editor Patty O'Connell earned my gratitude for her fine fine-tuning of the manuscript. And, finally, I want to acknowledge the support, fellowship, and laughs I receive in abundance from my pals in and around Delaware County, New York. (You know who you are.)

INTRODUCTION

Outside my window a brook brimming with spring runoff rushes downhill. In the valley it joins a stream large enough to have a name—Bagley's Brook. This waterway cuts around the village of De Lancey, New York, and soon runs into a real river, the West Branch of the Delaware, which flows through the farmlands of the western Catskills until it is intercepted by a large reservoir. There, part of the water is siphoned off to New York City, but the rest moves on to the Delaware River and then to the sea. To me, this network of brook, stream, and river does just what flowing water is supposed to do: It moves in ever larger increments from headwater to ocean. Even children know that this is the natural order of things, that a stick thrown into a stream will eventually reach the sea.

I have since learned, however, that not all rivers run seaward. In the huge, arid region of the West known as the Great Basin, a brook might start out with vigor down the mountainside but end up—to go no farther—in a salty lake. Or, instead of getting ever larger, it might dwindle to a trickle, then disappear entirely in the desert floor. This puzzled early explorers, who did not understand that water evaporated; they could see that three major rivers ran into the Great Salt Lake but could find none running out. Where did the water go? Into a river that they somehow had missed in their explorations? Or did a giant whirlpool suck water through underground passages to the ocean, as some fur trappers believed?

This phenomenon of interior drainage repeats itself throughout the Great Basin. On the north, the region's most important river, the Humboldt, peters out in a marshlike sink. To the west, water pours out of the Sierra Nevada Range into lakes that Mark Twain described as "great sheets of water without any visible outlet . . . What they do with their surplus is only known to the Creator." Southern waters also run to the interior and stay, but there the climate is so dry that even a healthy Catskill brook would be considered a major waterway. It is exceptional, this desert basin that drains into itself; there is no other place like it in the United States, and few others in the world.

As a traveler, it took me years to get to the Great Basin. Once there, however, I could understand why the early entrants did not understand its true nature. The region is so vast, so intimidating, and so elemental and different from the rest of the continent that the mind can barely absorb what the eyes see, let alone understand the region as a whole. John Charles Frémont, the famed government explorer, was the first to comprehend the region's unique hydrology and to name it the Great Basin. But the mountain men, who were there before him, and the Mormons, who arrived later, cared little about which way the rivers ran. Simply surviving in an unfriendly climate was job enough.

This book is the story of the settlers, travelers, natives, and assorted bit players in the Basin from the entrance of the first Spaniard in 1772 to the coming of the railroad in 1869. It is a story as much about geography and landscape as it is about people and power and money and all the other engines that drive history. The Mormons proudly call themselves "a peculiar people."* It seems fitting, maybe preordained, that they chose an unusual and peculiar land to be their home.

Now, about that landscape . . .

---

* "Peculiar" in the biblical sense, meaning distinct from all others. From the New Testament, 1 Peter 2:9, "But ye are a chosen generation, a royal priesthood, an holy nation, a peculiar people."

DESERT

Between the

MOUNTAINS

Part One

FIRST INTO THE GREAT BASIN

Chapter One

A "Dead" and
"Rich" Land

The Great Basin is aptly named. It is like a bowl that has been wedged between two mountain ranges—the Sierra Nevada on the west and the Wasatch branch of the Rocky Mountains on the east, although the mid-nineteenth-century explorer James Hervey Simpson saw it as having "a triangular shape, nearly that of a right-angled triangle," with the Wasatch Range forming "the hypothenuse." As a region, it is vast—220,000 square miles. It takes in almost all of Nevada, the half of Utah lying west of the Wasatch, parts of southern Idaho and Oregon, a corner of Wyoming, and a thin slice of eastern California bordering on Nevada. It also reaches into southern California almost to the Pacific Ocean. From north to south, it is nearly 900 miles long at its longest point; east to west, its maximum distance is 570 miles. In all, the Great Basin covers one-fifteenth of the entire country, but, despite its great size, it was 1776, the year of American independence, before any white man made any significant attempt to explore it, and its unique character as a land of interior drainage would not be understood for another three-quarters of a century.

John Charles Frémont, "the Pathfinder," was the explorer who recognized the region's uniqueness and who named it the Great Basin. Frémont first saw the Great Basin on his expedition of 1843–1844, and his reports and memoirs, written in collaboration with his wife, Jessie Benton Frémont, are still among the best writings ever produced on the region. "It is a singular feature," he wrote, "a basin of some five hundred miles diameter in every way, between four and five thousand feet above the level of the sea, shut in all around by mountains, with its own system of lakes and rivers, and having no connexion whatever with the sea." Frémont did not realize it at first, but the Great Basin is really a series of basins and valleys—like cups arranged side by side within a bowl—many of them with their own drainage systems. They are formed by interior mountain ranges, between thirty and one hundred miles long, that trend (to use a word geologists favor) in a north-south direction. On a topographic map, these interior ranges look like the fingers of a hand stretching down over the region. Fifteen years after Frémont's expedition, Army explorer Simpson noted that the term *Great Basin* is misleading, since the region is neither concave nor "filled with lakes and rivers" as the term implies. "The truth is," he concluded, "this is only a basin so far as that the few lakes and streams that are found within it sink within it, and have no outlet to the sea."

Some of the interior mountains rise eight to ten thousand feet above sea level from valley floors that might themselves be four thousand feet high. The peaks are what geologists call block-faulted mountains, which eons ago tilted out of fault lines on the desert floor, leaving steep escarpments on one side, gentle slopes on the other, with eroded debris spreading out at the base in what are called alluvial fans. This "alluvion," Frémont explained in a rare, less-than-graceful passage, "may be called fertile, in the radical sense of the word, as signifying a capacity to produce, or bear, and in contradistinction to sterility."

The Great Basin

Garcés, 1776

Domínguez-Escalante, 1776–1777

Great Basin Boundary

Malheur River

Snake River

Humboldt River

Bear River

Great Salt Lake

Utah Lake

Sevier Lake

GREAT BASIN

SIERRA NEVADAS

WASATCH MOUNTAINS

Sevier River

Green River

Colorado River

Dolores River

Crossing of the Fathers

Santa Fe

Albuquerque

Pacific Ocean

Mojave R.

Needles

MOJAVE DESERT

Colorado River

Gila River

0   100   300

Scale of Miles

Jeffrey L. Ward 1997

Although the Great Basin is generally high—and, in winter, so cold that even the basin floors will briefly hold snow—it is also a land of extreme variations and contrasts. The basin's Death Valley, for example, is one of the most exotic areas in the United States and, at 282 feet below sea level, the absolute lowest. A mere eighty miles away in the Sierra Nevada, Mt. Whitney, the tallest mountain in the country outside of Alaska, rises to 14,494 feet. As Frémont made his way around the Great Basin in 1843–1844, he wrote of following the basin's "rim," but, as the geologist Nevin M. Fenneman has pointed out, there is no rim around the entire region; in places plateaus rather than mountains mark its boundaries. At best, the Great Basin is a leaky vessel; if it were filled with water, most of it would overflow into the sea.*

With its barren mountains, salty lakes, and vast stretches of sagebrush, the Great Basin's scenery is not to everyone's taste. In 1833, Zenas Leonard, clerk to one of the earliest exploring parties in the Great Basin, was appalled by his surroundings; the Humboldt River, he wrote, should be called the Barren, "as the country, natives, and everything belonging to it deserve the name," while twenty-six years later Horace Greeley, creator of the *New York Tribune*, exclaimed about the same waterway, "Here on the Humboldt famine sits enthroned, and waves his scepter over a dominion expressly made for him." Contemplating the waterless expanse he had just traveled through, another newspaper editor, Samuel Bowles, deemed the Great Basin "a region whose uses are unimaginable, unless to hold the rest of the globe together, or to teach patience to travelers, or to keep close-locked in its mountain ranges those mineral treasures that the world did not need or was not ready for until now."† Even admirers of the Great Basin often take a deprecating approach in describing its attractions. So the late Wallace Stegner wrote of the Great Basin:

> Its rivers run nowhere but into the ground; its lakes are probably salty or brackish; its rainfall is negligible and its scenery depressing to all but the few who have lived in it long enough to acquire a new set of values about scenery. Its snake population is large and its human population small. Its cli-

---

* In *Physiography of the Western United States* (1931), Fenneman wrote: "Nevada is like Minnesota in having many basins. If the latter had the arid climate of Nevada, she would have desert basins and lakes without outlet. If Nevada had the rainfall of Minnesota, all the basins would overflow to the sea."

† Bowles, the influential editor of the *Springfield (Mass.) Republican*, accompanied Speaker of the House Schuyler Colfax on a trip from Massachusetts to California in the spring and summer of 1865. His popular account of the journey, *Across the Continent: A Summer's Journey to the Rocky Mountains, the Mormons, and the Pacific States*, appeared later the same year.

mate shows extremes of temperature that would tire out anything but a very strong thermometer. It is a dead land, though a very rich one.

Frémont wrote of the trees found on the mountains of the interior Great Basin—the pine, cedar, and aspen—and of the excellent quality of the grass there, "equal to anything found in the Rocky mountains." He also pronounced the valleys between the mountains to be absolutely sterile—"no woods, no water, no grass; the gloomy artemisia [sagebrush] the prevailing shrub . . ." That is a common but inaccurate observation; there are sections of "absolute desert" in the Great Basin where nothing grows, but biologists know today that the region—even the valley floors—harbors a rich variety of plant life. Sagebrush, to Mark Twain "an imposing monarch of the forest in exquisite miniature," covers nearly half of the Great Basin like a gray-green carpet. But early travelers such as Frémont did not realize that there are a dozen species of sagebrush and that among sagebrush communities many different grasses flourish. Sagebrush is also mistakenly lumped together with two other important plants: shadscale, a prickly plant with a gritty name, which grows where it is too dry for sagebrush, and the desert-loving creosote bush, which thrives where it is too hot for shadscale.*

HYDROLOGY, BIOLOGY, GEOLOGY . . .

Not everyone agrees what the Great Basin is, although the common definition of it as a region that drains into itself is adequate for most purposes. With this in mind, even someone not familiar with the region can roughly follow the jagged "rim" of the Great

---

* In his *Sagebrush Ocean: A Natural History of the Great Basin*, Stephen Trimble noted that sagebrush should not be confused with the herb sage of the genus *Salvia*. He wrote: " 'Riders of the purple sage' ride through Salvia, not Artemisia. Woe to the creative camp cook who adds a few sagebrush leaves to the cookpot, again mistaking bitter Artemisia for the Salvia that flavors Thanksgiving turkey."

Basin on a map by figuring out which way the water flows and distinguishing between the inward- and the seaward-flowing rivers. Thus it is possible to trace a dividing line along the mountain peaks between, say, the upper reaches of the Great Basin's Bear River in the northeast, which feeds Great Salt Lake, and the nearby streams to the east, which run into the Green River. Or, in the north, it is easy to separate the tributaries of the Great Basin's Humboldt River and those of the Snake River north of it, or in the southeast, between the Gulf-of-Mexico-bound Virgin River and the Sevier, which ends up in a salty lake of the same name. And so in the west, the headwaters of the Great Basin's Truckee River and California's west-flowing American River are not far apart; together the two historic streams formed one of the earliest and most arduous crossings of the Sierra Nevada.

Biologists use criteria other than rivers to define the region; they do not include the Mojave Desert in the Great Basin because much of its plant life, such as the stately Joshua tree, is not found elsewhere in the region. Geologists think in terms of huge geophysical areas with similar landforms; to them, the Great Basin is just the northernmost part of the Basin and Range province, which extends south into Mexico and eastward across southern Arizona and into New Mexico. Some archaeologists include all of Utah and a thin slice of western Colorado in their Great Basin because the people of the Fremont culture lived throughout the Rockies in prehistoric times. Ethnologists interested in the distribution of historic tribes speak of a Great Basin Cultural Area that about doubles the size of the Great Basin as defined by rivers and includes most of Idaho and Colorado and half of Wyoming.

Aridity is the characteristic that defines the Great Basin. Samuel Bowles noted in 1865 that "rain is a rarity,—near neighbor to absolute stranger. . . ." Whatever precipitation occurs is deposited on mountaintops, often as snow. Westerly winds blowing in from the Pacific deposit their moisture on the western Sierra Nevada and then sweep down into the Great Basin as a hot, dry wind.* Western Nevada, therefore, is said to be within the "rain shadow" of the Sierra. In this shadow, however, there is little rain and few clouds. As Stephen Trimble pointed out in *The Sagebrush Ocean*, Nevada's yearly rainfall of nine inches is the lowest in the country, while Reno enjoys more sunny days than Miami, Florida. Storms that form within the Great Basin also move east and deposit their rain on the west slope of the Wasatch, producing the strip of verdure that sustained the Mormons, the first permanent settlers in the Great Basin.

The Great Basin's few lakes are all that remains of a time when one-fifth of the land of interior drainage was covered with water. In the Pleistocene epoch, a million or so years ago, there were some one hundred large lakes in the Great Basin. The largest of these were Lake Bonneville, whose waters would have covered today's Salt Lake City, in the eastern Great Basin and Lake Lahontan, whose western shore was the Sierra Nevada.† Lakes Bonneville and Lahontan were cut during the Ice Age by glaciers descending from the mountains. Bonneville, spreading westward from the foot of the Wasatch Range, covered 19,750 square miles and had an irregular shoreline 2,550 miles long. At its highest stage, its shoreline, which is etched on the slopes of the Wasatch today, was one thousand feet above the present Great Salt Lake. At that level, the Great Basin was no longer a basin, and Lake Bonneville overflowed through Red Rock Pass into the Snake River system. Great Salt Lake, Utah Lake (the freshwater body that flows, via the Jordan River, northward into the Great Salt

* Of the Washoe Zephyr, the name of the wind he encountered in Carson City, Nevada, in 1861, Mark Twain wrote: "It is a pretty regular wind, in the summer time. Its office hours are from two in the afternoon till two the next morning; and anybody venturing abroad during those twelve hours needs to allow for the wind or he will bring up a mile or two to leeward of the point he is aiming at."

† Lake Bonneville is named for the French-born Benjamin L. E. de Bonneville, a U.S. Army officer turned fur trader; Lake Lahontan for Louis-Armand de Lahontan, a French baron and deserter from the French army, whose 1703 account of his travels includes an imaginary account of a large salt lake somewhere in the West. Neither man ever saw the area named for him.

Lake), and Sevier Lake in southern Utah were all at one time under the waters of Lake Bonneville.

Less than half as large as Bonneville, Lake Lahontan at its height covered 8,422 square miles and encompassed such present-day landmarks of western Nevada as the Humboldt Sink, Walker Lake, and Pyramid Lake. High-water marks on the mountainside tell us that Lake Lahontan was once nearly nine hundred feet deep. From the west, Lake Lahontan was fed by rivers that still run out of the Sierra Nevada—the Truckee, the Carson, and the Walker. From the east, Lahontan was fed by the Humboldt, the Great Basin's only major river to rise from its interior mountains.* In the nineteenth century, the Humboldt became the famed Highway of the West, the route across the Great Basin for trappers, settlers, Mormons, miners, railroads, and, finally, the interstate highway. A million years ago the Humboldt entered Lake Lahontan to the east of where the town of Golconda is today, about a hundred miles west of its present sump, the historic Humboldt Sink.

First into the Basin

Human beings arrived in the Great Basin about 9,000 B.C.† Theirs was a difficult life; they left behind almost nothing in terms of permanent dwellings or cultural artifacts to fire the imagination of the general public, but the way they survived in the basin's

---

* In his *Trace of Desert Waters, the Great Basin Story*, Samuel G. Houghton speculated: "Long before the Pleistocene epoch began, the Humboldt may have flowed to the Pacific by way of the Pit or Feather River." This would make the Humboldt the prehistoric ancestor of the mythical Buenaventura River (see p. 16), which was thought to flow across the Great Basin to the Pacific Ocean. Belief in the Buenaventura persisted well into the nineteenth century.

† The Mojave Desert section of the Great Basin includes the controversial Calico Early Man Site, which, it has been claimed, was occupied by humans some two hundred thousand years ago. Many ancient artifacts have been recovered there, but most experts today believe they were produced by geological forces rather than by man. The eminent paleontologist Louis S. B. Leakey was a prominent supporter of the site and was the project's director when he died in 1973.

inhospitable environment has been of great interest to archaeologists. Out of necessity, most of the prehistoric people of the Great Basin were nomadic hunter-gatherers: Where food was scarce, they moved far and often just to sustain themselves; where sustenance was more abundant, such as the Humboldt Sink area, evidence suggests that they were more inclined to stay put and establish semipermanent communities.

The prehistoric people of the Great Basin often lived in caves, with lakefronts considered prime locations. At Hogup Cave in the Great Salt Lake region, studies showed that its residents between 6400 and 1200 B.C. relied heavily on small animals such as hares, rabbits, and rodents, while occasionally killing larger bison and deer. In the western Great Basin, archaeologists have concluded that prehistoric people used a site called Hidden Cave near Fallon, Nevada, for storing food and stockpiling projectile points.*

Technology is helping to change what we know about the prehistoric Great Basin. In 1996 a technique known as accelerator mass spectrometry was used to count the carbon atoms in the hair of an ancient mummy that was found in a cave near Fallon, Nevada, in 1940. At the time, experts thought the mummy was no more than two thousand years old, but the recent tests put its age at more than nine thousand four hundred years. The discovery has caused experts to begin the process of reevaluating what is known about the Great Basin's earliest inhabitants and their environment. In appearance, the male, who stood about five feet two inches, looks more like a Southeast Asian than a modern American Indian. The mummy, known to anthropologists as the Spirit Cave Man, was found with examples of extremely well preserved weaving so sophisticated that experts believe they must have been created on a loom.

---

* David Hurst Thomas, an archaeologist who examined the cave in 1979–1980, speculated that the Indians deliberately deposited feces containing undigested seeds in the cave so that the seeds could be consumed in times of famine. This survival technique, which archaeologists call second harvesting, is an indication of how difficult survival was for prehistoric people in the Great Basin.

The Fremont Indians of the eastern Great Basin, latecomers on the archaeological time scale, were the only prehistoric people in the region to practice agriculture—and that only on a limited basis, since hunting and gathering remained essential to their survival in the years A.D. 500 to 1400. They also lived in crude pithouses, which are the first signs of permanent settlements.

What happened to the Fremont after A.D. 1400 is uncertain; archaeologists do not believe there is any connection between them and the Utes, who were resident in the eastern Great Basin when white men first encountered them in the late eighteenth century. A small tribe in western Nevada, the Washo, are the only natives who might have ancestors among the prehistoric Indians of the Great Basin. They speak a dialect with linguistic roots different from other Great Basin Indian languages and could be descended from the people of the Lovelock culture, who lived in west-central Nevada between 2600 B.C. and A.D. 500 and left behind interesting decoys made of bulrushes over which they drew the feathered skins of real ducks.

There were three major tribes in the Great Basin when the white men arrived—Paiute, Ute, Shoshone—with the Bannock from the Snake River to the north making occasional forays into the region. Like their prehistoric predecessors, they were hunter-gatherers, and because part of their food came from digging for roots and grubs and insects, the whites lumped them together under the disparaging name of Diggers. The Paiutes were divided into two branches, northern and southern; the latter fought the Pyramid Lake War in 1860, one of the most serious conflicts in Great Basin history.

In the eastern Great Basin, Brigham Young, leader of the Mormon settlers, believed it was better to feed the Indians than to fight them, but there were still clashes, including some pitched battles. The raids of Ute Chief Joseph Walker, or Wakara, precipitated the 1853 Walker War with the Mormons, in which many Utes died. This was the same tribe that the Spanish explorer Father Escalante encountered on the shores of Lake Utah in 1776 and that won the admiration of the great American trapper and explorer Jedediah Smith during his swing around the Great Basin in 1825–1826. During the Civil War, the Shoshone, who lived around the Great Salt Lake, stepped up their raids on Mormon settlers and wagon trains, and, in retaliation, soldiers stationed at Salt Lake City massacred some 224 of them in 1863.

The attitudes of the first white men in the Great Basin toward Indians ranged from sympathy to disdain. On one occasion recorded in his notebook, Jedediah Smith went to great lengths to comfort and feed a hungry and frightened elderly Indian woman. On another, in a preemptive strike, he ordered his marksmen to gun down two defenseless Indian men. Of course, the trappers had to learn Indian ways to survive, and they learned these lessons so well that they were often indistinguishable from the natives. In his western classic, *The Adventures of Captain Bonneville*, Washington Irving wrote: "It is a matter of vanity and ambition with them to discard everything that may bear the stamp of civilized life and to adopt the manners, habits, dress, gesture, and even walk of the Indian."

Still, as a rule, the whites considered the Indians of the Great Basin to be barely human, to scrape along, in Frémont's words, "in the lowest state of human existence." In 1860, Dr. Garland Hurt, a former Indian agent in Utah, generalized in a report submitted to Congress, "Among all the tribes of this region there is the same indisposition to habits of industry, indolence being the rule and industry the exception, and nothing but the keenest impulses of necessity can impel them to action." Today anthropologists believe that the Indians of the Great Basin lived in harmony with their environment. If this is so, it was a harmony that depended on a precarious balance between man and nature that the arrival of the Europeans threw off forever.

RIVER OF MYTH, STRAIT OF FABLE

For reasons of geography and politics, recorded history (as opposed to unwritten prehistory) began late in the Great Basin, the last large region in the "lower forty-eight" of the United States to be explored by white men. In the mid-1770s, almost three centuries after Columbus, the Spanish, whose territory it was, made the first tentative *entradas*, or expeditions, into the region, across its southernmost tip and along its southeastern border. Their goal was to discover a direct route between the Spanish settlements of Sonora in Mexico and Spain's recently established presidios and missions in California. From there on in, the Great Basin remained an area of great interest to explorers, an interest, wrote James Hervey Simpson, an Army explorer of the late 1850s, that "has grown out of the circumstance of its reported inaccessibility from extended deserts, its occupancy by Indians of an exceedingly low type, and the laudable curiosity, which prevails in the minds of men, to know the physical characteristics of a country which has so long remained a *terra incognita*."

The Spanish ecclesiastics, who led the two most important early expeditions, also hoped that they might find an easier way—by water—to the coast, a hope that was a variation on the elusive dream of a Northwest Passage from the Atlantic to the Pacific. The route had several names, including the Strait of Anian.* It was also believed that there was a river, often called the Buenaventura, that flowed a great distance—at least from the Rockies to the Pacific. And some surmised that a long arm of the Pacific Ocean stretched inland.

The world's maritime powers had been searching for a Northwest Passage ever since Columbus—or at least since it was ascertained in the sixteenth century that America and Asia were separate land continents.† The discovery of such a passage not

---

* The Strait of Anian was named by a Venetian mapmaker, Giacomo Gastaldi. On a map he produced in 1546, Gastaldi placed the strait just about where the Bering Strait is located, but for the next two centuries mariners and explorers looked all over North America for it.

† It took a while for this idea to sink in: Columbus believed he had reached India; Magellan saw America as a peninsula of Asia; Verrazano, reporting on his voyage of 1524, depicted Asia and America as two different land masses, but he also believed that North America was a narrow barrier, no more than a mile wide in places, separating the Atlantic and the Pacific.

only would make it easier for Europe to trade with the Orient but would give whatever country controlled it a leg up in the exploitation of the North American continent. As an English commentator put it in 1789, "The Object of the English in the early attempts for the discovery of a NW Passage, was not only to facilitate the intercourse with the East, but to open a new branch of Commerce, in the Countries thro' which the Passage was expected to lead the adventurous Navigator."

Also, there were plenty of bogus reports of trips through the passage to help keep the idea alive. The predatory English admiral Francis Drake reportedly sailed through the North American continent in the late sixteenth century. A decade later, in 1588, a Spaniard, Lorenzo Ferrer Maldonado, claimed to have taken the Strait of Anian from the Atlantic to the Pacific and back, and reported seeing—and this in the Arctic—fruit trees growing on shore, just as they did in his native Spain. In 1596, another rogue, Juan de Fuca, announced that he had sailed through the Strait of Anian from the Pacific four years earlier. So great was the desire to believe him that, when the entrance to Puget Sound was discovered, it was named for him. In 1703, the previously mentioned French explorer and soldier/deserter, Louis-Armand, baron de Lahontan, published an account of his travels in North America in which he fantasized—but presented as fact—a river, la Rivière Longue, running from the Mississippi to a great inland sea on the shore of which lived natives with an ornate and elaborate culture. A later explorer, Captain Howard Stansbury of the U.S. Army Topological Corps, who was the first to circumnavigate the Great Salt Lake in 1849, dismissed Lahontan's account as "an imaginative voyage up this most imaginary river," but gave him credit for exciting, "even at that early day, the spirit of enterprise and speculation which has proved so marked a feature in the national character."

On July 12, 1776, a week and a day after the American colonies declared their independence from England, Captain James Cook set sail from Plymouth with two ships on his third and last voyage of discovery. His mission was to explore the western coast of North America to determine once and for all whether the Northwest Passage existed. Cook did not find the passage (and later in the voyage was killed by Hawaiian Islanders, not long after they had declared him a god), but the hope that such a strait existed lived on. There was also a variation on the idea: the so-called Sea of the West that was often depicted as a narrow extension of the Pacific Ocean piercing the continent. When a fur trader named Jim Bridger happened upon the Great Salt Lake in the 1820s and found it to be salty, it was assumed that he had discovered an arm of the Pacific Ocean.

Crossing the continent by river was not nearly so appealing as sailing through a broad, navigable channel, but it was the next best thing and far preferable to going overland through scorching deserts and over snow-covered mountains. In 1778, a mapmaker named Jonathan Carver (1710–1780) theorized in a widely read book, *Travels Through the Interior Parts of North America*, that all major North American rivers rose from a single fluvial hub, located, he believed, at the highest point of land on the continent, near the Minnesota River. If this were true, it might be possible to proceed up one river from the east and descend another to the Pacific. Even Thomas Jefferson hoped that America's rivers would become a highway across the continent. In instructing the Lewis and Clark expedition before it set out in 1804, he wrote: "The object of your mission is single, the direct communication from sea to sea formed by the bed of the Missouri and perhaps the Oregon. . . ."

As time passed, explorers continued to narrow down the places where a strait or a river could be found, until finally only the Arctic archipelago and the Great Basin were left. By the time Frémont set out to find it in 1843, the knowledgeable commander of the British trading post at Fort Vancouver was able to draw him a map showing him exactly where the Buenaventura had to be. Everywhere else had been explored, he told Frémont.

The irony is that the Great Basin, a land that drains into itself, was the least likely region on the continent to harbor such a water passage. Its rivers are few and unnavigable. They often dry up in the summer and, instead of flowing to the sea, end in salty lakes or sinks or disappear into the desert floor. During those first decades that the Great Basin was explored by white men, no one understood this, and the vision of a Strait of Anian or a Buenaventura River flowing to the Pacific was kept alive by fables, rumors, outright lies, and a number of imaginative maps that showed such a waterway.

Chapter Two

ENTER THE

WHITE MAN

The first party of Europeans to enter the Great Basin crossed the few miles of its southern tip south of the present Mexican border in 1774. The expedition was led by Juan Bautista de Anza, a Spanish colonial by birth with a considerable reputation as a soldier and Indian fighter. Anza left Tubac, south of Tucson, on January 8, 1774, with thirty-four men. Among them was Father Francisco Hermenegildo Tomás Garcés from mission San Xavier del Bac at Tubac, who would soon become more important than Anza in the opening up of the Great Basin.

Anza had been ordered to find a direct route from Sonora to California. Spain had, only a few years before, established its first missions in Alta, or Upper, California and needed to find a way to supply and defend them. Reaching Alta California by sea was dangerous and inefficient. The Spanish hoped that an overland route would put them in a better position to discourage the interest they believed both Russia and England were showing in the upper length of the sunny California coast. Although Anza successfully made it from Sonora to the mission at San Gabriel a few miles north of Los Angeles, Garcés came to the conclusion that the parched route across the desert was unnecessarily hard. In his diary, the friar cited "the extreme scarcity of water and pasturage and . . . the vast sand dunes" and became convinced that an easier route lay to the north, one that would link Monterey in California with Santa Fe.

Garcés was an experienced explorer and a curious combination of faith and worldliness. (The eminent—and quotable—Utah-born historian Bernard DeVoto called him "the saintly, desert-loving Francisco Garcés.") Between 1768 and 1771 he made three *entradas* to the Pima and Yuma Indians on the Gila and Colorado Rivers. Although Garcés was dedicated to converting the heathens he met on his travels, there was a strategic aspect to his work; Christian Indians, the Spanish hoped, would be peaceful Indians and less of an obstacle to Spanish expansion northward into the Great Basin and across it to California. On one occasion he entranced a group of Mojave Indians on the Colorado River by showing them a picture of the Virgin Mary: "It pleased them much," he wrote, "but they did not like to look at that of the lost soul." Father Pedro Font, a fellow explorer and diarist, provided an unforgettable picture of Garcés interacting with Indians.

Father Garcés is so well fitted to get along with the Indians . . . that he appears to be but an Indian himself. Like the Indians he is phlegmatic in everything. He sits with them in the circle, or at night around the fire, with his legs crossed, and there he will sit musing two or three hours or more, oblivious to everything else, talking with them with much serenity and deliberation. And although the foods of the Indians are as nasty and dirty as those outlandish people themselves, the father eats them with great gusto and says that they are good for the stomach and very fine. In short, God has created him, as I see it, solely for the purpose of seeking out these unhappy, ignorant, and rustic people.

Anza, after his first successful California expedition, was ordered, in 1775, to take a large party of colonists, some 240 people, back to California. Garcés again accompanied him, but this time he went only as far as the mouth of Gila River, where it enters the Colorado near present-day Yuma, Arizona.* Here he stayed behind, wrote LeRoy R. Hafen, historian of the Old Spanish Trail, "to labor among the Yumas and explore the surrounding country." Once on his own, with only a small group of men accompanying him, Garcés followed the Colorado to the Gulf of Mexico, then retraced his steps, passing Yuma again and proceeding farther up the Colorado to the Needles, named for the nearby needlelike mountains, where he became the first white man to enter the villages of the Mojaves. These natives pleased him, he wrote, because "they have great advantages over the Yumas and the rest of the Nations of the Rio Colorado; they are less molestful, and none are thieves; they seem valiant, and nowhere have I been better served."

MISSIONARY IN THE MOJAVE

Father Garcés left the Needles on March 4, 1776, and set out, with four Mojaves to guide him, to the west, in the direction of the Pacific coast. On the sixth of March, his party met a party of Mojaves returning from a trading trip to the coast. The Indians traveled light, carrying only the seashells they acquired in California, and so were able to cross the desert in just four days. "I was lost in wonder," Garcés wrote, "to see that they brought no provisions whatever on a route where there is naught to eat, nor did they carry bows for hunting." The encounter proved to Garcés

* Once he reached California, Anza proceeded up the coast to San Francisco Bay, where he founded a presidio and mission. In 1777, he was appointed governor of New Mexico.

that the desert could be crossed, although he realized that only an Indian could do it without food and water.

The next day, March 7, Garcés crossed the Providence Mountains and entered the Great Basin. The explorer, of course, had no way of knowing that he had entered a region of unusual drainage. Two days later he came to Soda Lake, a desert sink into which the Mojave River disappears, but if this phenomenon gave him cause for thought, it was not reflected in his diary.

The Mojave River rises in the San Bernardino Mountains, then, as Hafen described it, "wanders off into the desert, running north then east and south in great loups before it loses itself in the arid sands." Garcés followed the river, maybe to its source, before leaving the Great Basin on March 21 and descending the mountains to the San Gabriel mission. Along the way he had several encounters with Indians, including one where the women, in a gesture of submission, sprinkled both him and his mules with acorns. "I reciprocated these attentions as well as I could, and marveled to see that among these people so rustic are found demonstrations proper to the most cultivated, and a particular prodigality in scattering their greatest treasures, which are shells."

Garcés was a reluctant diarist. For him, wrote historian Herbert Eugene Bolton, "writing was a weariness. His hand was crotchety and his spelling bad." He was awkward and restrained in describing terrain—his discovery on March 9 of Soda Lake elicited these few words: "Here I encountered an arroyo of saltish water that I named (Arroyo) de los Martires. There is good grass."* On the other hand, his observations of the natives he encountered along the way are unforgettably vivid. Among the Pimas and Yumas he described their "affability and familiarity" and their "keen desire to touch us

---

* In retracing the father's route in the late nineteenth century, historian Elliott Coues, translator of Garcés's diary, provided a more detailed description of Soda Lake: "When I crossed it was nearly dry except in some reedy patches, and most of the surface was whitened with alkaline efflorescence; the water was bad, as Garcés says; the grass was poor, there was no wood, and myriads of mosquitos tormented us, though water had frozen half an inch on our buckets [the night before]."

and examine us, to satisfy their simplicity," behavior that others in his party found irritating. The Mojave, he wrote, "seem valiant . . . The female sex is the most comely on the river; the male very healthy and robust. The women wear petticoats. . . . The men go entirely naked, and in a country so cold this is well worthy of compassion. . . . They talk rapidly with great haughtiness. . . . During the harangues that they make they give smart slaps with the palms on the thighs."

From San Gabriel, Garcés went north through the San Fernando Valley, took the Tejon Pass into the San Joaquin Valley, and proceeded on to the Kern River above the site of present-day Bakersfield. At the Kern, Garcés, a nonswimmer, was taken across by four Indians, "whereupon I took advantage of the occasion to bathe at my pleasure in that water so limpid and beautiful," although, as befits a missionary, he disrobed only "down to shirt and drawers." About May 10, he passed into the Great Basin once more and traveled east until he again hit the Mojave River, which he followed, more or less retracing his steps, until he departed the Great Basin on May 25.

Once he was back at the Needles on the Colorado River, Garcés devised a bold plan to blaze a trail eastward to New Mexico, and set out alone except for his Indian guides. On the way, he became the first white man in 236 years to gaze on the Grand Canyon.* But once he was in the Hopi town of Oraibi in northeastern Arizona, he found the natives so hostile to the Spanish that—fearing his life threatened—he turned back to the Colorado and, from Yuma, returned to San Xavier del Bac.

Garcés had spent no more than a month in the Great Basin, but he had discovered the Mojave River segment of what was to become the Old Spanish Trail, described by Hafen as the "longest and crookedest mule trail in the world," from Santa Fe to Los Angeles. From what he observed, Garcés concluded that there must be a waterway through the Sierra Nevada to the Pacific. In California,

---

* One of Coronado's men, Garcia Lopez de Cardenas, was the first European to view the Grand Canyon, in 1540.

Garcés had crossed the west-flowing Kern River and heard from Indians about an even larger river, which would be the San Joaquin. Both rivers, he believed, must rise east of the Sierra Nevada, and he guessed it might be possible to follow the San Joaquin through the mountains to the Tulares, and then continue by boat to San Francisco. To someone who had crossed the Great Basin's southern parts and survived the punishment meted out by the waterless Mojave Desert, the prospect of reaching California by a water route must have had considerable allure.* It is no wonder, then, that the dream of a westward-flowing Rio Buenaventura stayed alive for so long in spite of increasing amounts of evidence that it could not possibly exist.

Garcés never entered the Great Basin again. From his home base at San Xavier del Bac, he returned to the junction of the Colorado and Gila Rivers where, on the invitation of the local chief, he founded two pueblo missions. Unfortunately he misread his host's intentions; the chief really wanted only the gifts that he thought the father would bring him. When these were not forthcoming, the Indians attacked the missions in July 1781, and Garcés was killed. So, in martyrdom, ended the life of one of the greatest of all the explorers of the Great Basin. Garcés was the first white man to blaze a trail across a significant portion of the Great Basin and the first to report on the native people who lived there. Except for his native guides, he was mostly alone in his explorations, and, wrote Bolton, he "furnished an example of physical endurance and human courage that have rarely been excelled."

FATHER ESCALANTE: "WITHOUT NOISE OF ARMS"

No sooner had Garcés finished his monumental voyage of discovery through the Great Basin than another one began. This one

---

* In *Exploring the Great Basin* (1963), Gloria Griffin Cline wrote of Garcés's conjectures: "It is obvious that the idea of a Northwest Passage and the Straits of Anian had not died, but was only lying dormant waiting for one spark of hope which would again ignite it."

bears the name of Father Francisco Tomas Velez de Escalante, a Franciscan missionary at Our Lady of Guadelupe at the pueblo of Zuni and, in the words of historian J. Cecil Alter, "an unusual person, a man of learning, fearless, undaunted, determined, a keen observer and a man of zeal . . ." Escalante heard the same call that Anza and Garcés did—for the discovery of a land route to California—and he responded enthusiastically. In a letter to his superiors written on October 28, 1775, he proposed a route that would detour around the hostile Indians on the Gila and lower Colorado Rivers by proceeding from Santa Fe northwest along established trading routes until it reached the latitude of Monterey. Then it would head west to the Pacific coast. The expedition would be accomplished peacefully "without noise of arms" and without having to make the daunting crossing of the canyons of the Colorado River. Escalante explained that his own function would be to accompany the others "in order to aid them in matters spiritual and keep a diary with the greatest exactitude."

Escalante's plan was approved, and with ten men, one of whom could speak the Ute language, he left Santa Fe "under the patronage of the Virgin Mary, Our Lady of the Immaculate Conception, and of the most holy patriarch Joseph her most happy spouse" on July 29, 1776. Although Escalante was outranked by two other members of the expedition—a cartographer and frontiersman, Miera y Pacheco, and his ecclesiastic superior, Father Francisco Atanasio Domínguez—the expedition bears his name. And justly so, wrote Bernard DeVoto: "There can be no question, he [Escalante] was the principal person of the expedition and its principal sustaining force."*

The group followed the paths of traders until they reached the Uncompahgre and Gunnison Rivers, at which point they headed east into unknown territory, apparently to find a Laguna Indian

---

*Walter Briggs, in his account of the expedition, *Without Noise of Arms*, expressed his belief that Domínguez's importance has been unfairly downplayed. "Let there be no mistake: Domínguez, not Escalante, led the expedition," he wrote.

(from the far side of the Wasatch Range) who had been visiting a band of Utes. With this Indian guiding them, they went farther to the northwest, crossing first the Colorado, then the White and Green Rivers, before moving west up the Duchesne and across the Wasatch Range. On September 21, they entered the Great Basin. As Escalante recorded the occasion: "We continued through the grove which became more dense the farther we went, and having traveled half a league west, we emerged from it, arriving at a high ridge from which the guide pointed out to us the direction of the Lake, and, to the southeast of it, another part of the sierra in which he said lived a great many people of the same language and character as the Lagunas."

Two days later, after descending the Wasatch by way of Spanish Fork Canyon, they were on the shores of Utah Lake, the largest freshwater lake west of the Mississippi and the home of the Laguna Indians, the tribe to which their guide belonged. It is not clear why Escalante went so far north; his plan was to reach the latitude of Monterey and then head west, but at Utah Lake he was far north of that point. DeVoto speculated: "Perhaps there was some idea they might reach the inland shore of the Strait of Anian, which, of course, would make the northern route to Monterey simpler and more valuable."

The approach of the Spaniards, which the Indians heralded with smoke signals, apparently caused the Laguna some anxiety, as they were under constant threat of attack from raiding Apaches. The voyagers responded "with our own signals, so . . . they would not take us for enemies or flee, or greet us with arrows." That night, when the party assumed it was being spied upon, the Indian guide spoke into the darkness, "giving them to understand that we were peaceful, friendly and good people." Once contact was made the next day, the Indian guide continued to sing his companions' praises, "telling them that only the Fathers tell the truth, that in their company one might travel all over the earth without risk, and that only the Spaniards were good people."

From the Lagunas, the explorers heard for the first time about the Great Salt Lake, which, it was explained, was connected to Utah Lake by "a narrow passage." Escalante referred to it as "the other lake," adding that it "covers many leagues and its waters are noxious and extremely salty, for the Timpanois assure us that a person who moistens any part of his body with the water of the lake immediately feels much itching in the part that is wet." The Indians also informed Escalante that a large river flowed from the west into the lake, a river that must have sounded to them very much like the water route to the Pacific that they were looking for. Why Escalante did not visit Great Salt Lake, a mere two days' travel away, was, to quote DeVoto, "inexplicable"; perhaps the onset of winter weather made them anxious to head south.

On September 23, after a three-day stay at Lake Utah, the party proceeded southwest in the company of Indian guides who had no more idea than they did how to get to Monterey. On September 29, they reached the Sevier River, where they encountered a band of bearded Indians, including one man "of venerable mien . . . [whose beard] was so thick and long he looked like one of the European hermits." These natives, Escalante noted, "look more like Spaniards than like the other Indians hitherto known in America . . . they have holes through the cartilage of their noses and they wear as an ornament a little polished bone of deer, fowl, or some other animal thrust through the hole."*

As they made their way through the Great Basin, the fathers did not neglect "matters spiritual." The Indians on and about the Sevier River seemed particularly receptive to their message, which was, in Escalante's words: "the Oneness of God, the punishment

---

* Spanish colonists had heard reports of unusual bearded Indians to the northwest, and finding them had been, for Escalante, one of the goals of the expedition; in his letter to his superiors he speculated that they were shipwrecked Europeans who had made their way inland from the California coast. He wrote: "This discovery would be very useful to the Religion and to the Crown, either to prevent any invasion of our kingdom if they are strangers, or to unite them with us if they are Spaniards as the Indians say." The encounter convinced him that they were, in fact, Indians.

He reserves for the wicked and the reward in store for the good ones, and the necessity of being baptized and understanding and obeying the divine law." The fathers also promised to return soon to the Indians, to baptize them and live among them. In taking their leave of some Indians on October 2, the party could hear "the sad lamentations of these poor lambs of Christ, strayed away only through lack of enlightenment. We were so moved that some of our companions could not hold back their tears."

On October 5, they reached Black Rock Springs, the point at which they believed they should start heading west to Monterey. But winter was threatening, and "all the sierras which we were able to see in all directions were covered with snow." Escalante proposed abandoning the mission and returning to Santa Fe, but he was vigorously opposed by Miera and others in the party who wanted to press on, as originally planned. So, in the spirit of harmony that marked most of their voyage, they drew lots on October 8. As Escalante recorded the decision:

> They all submitted in a Christian spirit and with fervent devotion they said the third part of the Rosary and other petitions, while we said the penitential Psalms and the litanies and other prayers which follow them. This concluded, we cast the lot, and it was decided in favor of [returning to Santa Fe]. Now, thank God, we all agreeably and gladly accepted this result.

So the explorers turned back. Five days later, on October 13, they passed out of the Great Basin near where Cedar City is today and headed toward the Colorado, which they first reached at present-day Lee's Ferry. To find a place to cross the fearsome river, wrote Bolton, "the wayfarers spent thirteen hard days, tried the river at three places, and zig-zagged along its western banks for fourteen leagues, or some forty fearful miles, before they could get across." They finally forded the Colorado at a place, now inundated by Lake Powell and known as the Crossing of the Fathers (although the padres themselves named it for the Most Holy Conception of the Virgin Mary). How they reached the river—by gingerly leading animals down steps they cut into the face of the canyon—is one of the great feats of western exploration. Once safely across the river, Escalante and his party celebrated, "praising God our Lord, and firing off a few muskets as a sign of the great joy which all felt at having vanquished a difficulty so great and which had cost us so much travail and delay."

The expedition reached Santa Fe on January 2, 1777. They had gone some two thousand miles in little more than five months of almost nonstop travel through unchartered deserts, over immense mountains, and across turbulent rivers. Through his careful journal, which, wrote Bolton, "gave the heroic odyssey its place in history," Escalante brought back a detailed account and description of a part of the Great Basin never before traveled by white men. Miera produced a superb map of the region they had traveled, but it contained three errors that kept reappearing in other maps and influenced opinions about the Great Basin for more than half a century. First, it showed Utah Lake and Great Salt Lake as one body of water (Laguna de los Timpanogos). It also showed a large river flowing into the Great Salt Lake from the west, and, finally, it had the Green River, an important branch of the Colorado, flowing right across the Wasatch Range into Sevier Lake. Miera named this river the San Buenaventura, possibly because he thought it might lead eventually to the Pacific Ocean.

The expedition never did find a way between New Mexico and Monterey, but it brought back a wealth of information on a region that was totally unknown to Europeans. In assessing the expedition, J. Cecil Alter wrote in 1941, "Escalante was the first white man to see buffaloes near the Green River, Utah; the first one to view Utah's magnificent Mount Timpanogos;* the first to view the beautiful Utah Valley and Utah Lake. He was the first white man to go among and describe many of the interior Indian

---

* At 12,008 feet, Mt. Timpanogos is the highest mountain in the Wasatch Range, which forms the southeastern border of the Great Basin.

tribes, and was the first white man to cross the great Colorado River. . . ." And the voyage was accomplished, as Escalante had wished, peacefully, with no exploitation of the natives the Spaniards met along the way, and without the vexing "noise of arms" reaching their ears.

THE OLD SPANISH TRAIL

In 1776, Escalante on the east and Garcés on the west pioneered portions of what would become known as the Old Spanish Trail from Santa Fe to Los Angeles, but the nineteenth century would be well under way before anyone linked all its parts together to provide the overland route that Spain had been looking for. There were other incursions into the Great Basin, but nothing to match the achievements of these two late-eighteenth-century padres. In 1813, for example, Spanish trappers Moricio Arze and Lagos Garcia crossed the Wasatch from the Green to trade with the Utes around Utah Lake. After conflict with the Indians drove them southward out of the Great Basin, they reported that they had fled to the Rio Seviro (Spanish for "severe" or "violent"), and so the Sevier River got its name.

Gradually the Old Spanish Trail began to take shape. In 1826, the American trapper Jedediah Smith extended the Old Spanish Trail westward when he made his swing through the Great Basin from the Great Salt Lake to Los Angeles. Three years later Ewing Young led trappers from Taos down the Salt River, eventually taking Garcés's trail across the Mojave. In 1830, Antonio Armijo took a trading party along the route of what would become the Old Spanish Trail, although his route differed in several respects from the final trail. Armijo was a trader dealing in the main currency of the Old Spanish Trail—California horses and mules for New Mexican wool blankets. (This trade was still in full swing in 1844, when Charles Frémont encountered two survivors of a Mexican horse-trading party that had been massacred by Indians.)

The man who put the finishing touches on the trail, in that his route became the one others followed for the next two decades, was an American, William Wolfskill, who, in 1830–1831, led a party of trappers over the entire length of the trail, from Taos to Los Angeles. Wolfskill was accompanied by George C. Yount, an experienced fur trapper, and some eighteen other men. Wolfskill did not keep a journal, but his ledger, which survived, shows the men, who were paid between $7 and $8 a month, were charged $1.50 a pound for tobacco and gunpowder. The party took a few nonessentials, such as Jews' harps, but no liquor, Wolfskill having learned, Hafen speculated in his 1954 classic, *The Old Spanish Trail*, that "a good way to avoid quarrels and trouble was to leave the Taos lightning at Taos."

Wolfskill and his men left in September, as winter approached, to take advantage of the fall trapping season. The search for beaver took them northwest, along the route that Escalante pioneered, to the bend in the Dolores River. They crossed the Colorado River near present-day Moab and the Green River near the town that today bears that name. After they forded the San Raphael River, the party turned to the southeast and entered the Wasatch Mountains.

Inside the Great Basin, the party had one memorable encounter with Ute Indians who had gathered on the Sevier River to mourn the passing of a chief. The Indians knew Yount from previous trips and assumed he was the leader of the party, so Wolfskill, who needed the Utes' permission to hunt in their territory, allowed Yount to play that role. If Yount's retelling of the event—to a Reverend Orange Clark in 1855—can be believed, he was an eloquent advocate for the trappers. Speaking of himself in the third person, Yount told the Indians that he represented the Big Chief in Washington, who was "vice regent and son of the Great Spirit who rolls the sun, and whose pipe when smoking makes the clouds." According to his own account, his words kept flowing until the Indians

fell flat on their faces, take earth from under his mockasins and sprinkle it on their heads; and as he closed [they] would rise upon their knees and worship him. Majestically would he raise them, or order Wolfskill to raise them upon their feet, bid them kiss his rifle, in token of respect for the Great Father at Washington and be seated at his side. The presents, which were the chief object of regard, after all, and to obtain which they would worship anything, were distributed, and Yount permitted them to taste a morsel from his dish.

Winter struck the party somewhere in the vicinity of Panguich, Utah, just on the edge of the Great Basin. Even if we allow for Yount's hyperbole, the severe weather was an ordeal, and his words reflect the despondency felt by other early parties of trappers, explorers, and settlers who had to contend with winter in the mountains. "As they pursued their journey," Yount told his chronicler, "all around them was soon wild wintry waste—the party encountered deep snows and solitary gloom. . . ." After one storm subsided, Yount recounted:

> Yount & Wolfskill ascended a lofty Peak of the mountains for observation— In the whole range of human view, in every direction, nothing could be discerned, in the least degree encouraging, but only mountains, piled on mountains, all capped with cheerless snow, in long and continuous succession, till they seemed to mingle with the blue vault of heaven and fade away in the distance— It was a cheerless prospect, and calculated to cause emotions by no means agreeable in the stoutest heart. . . .

The Wolfskill-Yount expedition survived its wintery ordeal, and once the storm had passed, the men made their way south to the Virgin River Valley. Here they encountered, in Yount's none-too-reliable words, a Disneyesque paradise where "the earth was bare of snow, & the evergreens waved in gentleness & calm serenity" and where they enjoyed the sight of elk, deer, and antelope "basking with their frolicsome fawns, unaware & unintimidated by the sight of man . . ." The party followed the Virgin River to its junction with the Colorado, which they traveled along, Ziba Branch, one of Wolfskill's men, later recorded, "till they reached the country of the Mohaves, a treacherous tribe of Indians, who, however, treated them kindly, and gave them bread which was made of pounded corn and baked in the ashes . . ."

The Wolfskill party broke up when it reached Los Angeles in February 1831; both Wolfskill and Yount stayed in California, where, as two of the first permanent American settlers in what was then Mexican territory, they became successful and outstanding citizens.* "They were to have no further important connections with the Old Spanish Trail," Hafen wrote, "but they had performed real service in first footing a route that for nearly twenty years was to be a link of commerce and travel between New Mexico and California." The Old Spanish Trail was used mostly during spring and fall. Wolfskill's experience in the mountains was proof enough that winter was no time to make the trip, and the desert was unbearable in the summer. It was also a difficult trail—as Hafen wrote, long, crooked, and arduous. It was never well suited for wagon travel, but still, in 1841, William Workman and John Rowland led an emigrant party over the Old Spanish Trail to California, providing an alternative to the route that by that time was already established along the Great Basin's Humboldt River and over the Sierra Nevada.

* Wolfskill (1798–1866) became a successful farmer and rancher and founded the first American school in California. Yount (1794–1865), one of the first settlers in the Napa Valley, established a large ranch and fort as protection against Indians in northern California.

Chapter Three

WESTWARD

AFTER BEAVER

The mountain men who opened up the Great Basin in the early 1800s are among some of the most compelling figures in the history of the American West. Independent, self-reliant, adventurous, courageous—the heroes of many a tall tale and dime novel—they captured the popular imagination in their day as cowboys and astronauts stirred later generations. They were trappers, not explorers, but it is hard to dismiss them as simple hunters. Some of them blazed trails through unknown territory that official U.S. government explorers such as John C. Frémont would later follow. Others became successful entrepreneurs; many, after the fur trade had died, put the skills they learned in the wilderness to use as guides for settlers and surveyors. In the American West, including the Great Basin, trappers were the vanguard of civilization. Wherever they went, settlers were sure to follow; it did not matter which nation claimed the land, what the international boundaries were, or how the treaties read, the flag followed their footsteps. So when the great American mountain man Jedediah Smith suddenly appeared, from the east, in California in 1826, it is not surprising that Mexican authorities panicked and almost clapped him in jail.

Trapping, under the best of circumstances, was hard work, a cold-weather occupation, in which the trapper had to wade through streams of freezing water for hours at a time. Spring and fall were the best time for hunting; beaver fur loses sheen in the summer, and, in the dead of winter when streams freeze, the animals hibernate. The danger to trappers was considerable—from Indians, grizzly bears, exposure, and other hazards—and many men died in the wilderness.*

There were never more than five or six hundred individual trappers at one time operating in the mountains during the short heyday of the western fur trade. They were a varied lot and included the educated and the illiterate, the law-abiding and the criminal, the God-fearing and the profane, although to survive they all had to be tough, smart, and resourceful—with a taste for adventure. The records they kept were poor or nonexistent, and their journals, wrote one scholar, "were made of small sheets of beaver skin often indifferently cured and tied with a thong; and [written] with a quill often under very uncertain conditions of weather or comfort." As a group, they had a reputation for telling tall tales, but even when they told the truth they were not believed. The legendary Jim Bridger, one of the more colorful characters ever to go after beaver, was indignant when his reports of hot springs, spouting geysers, and the geologic wonders of the present-day Yellowstone National Park were received with disbelief. "They said I was the damndest liar that ever lived," he groused. "That's what a man gets for telling the truth."†

* In the Far West, grizzly bears "were everywhere," the trapper George Yount reported, "upon the plains, in the valleys and on the mountains, so that I have often killed as many as five or six in one day, and it is not unusual to see fifty or sixty within twenty-four hours."

† Wrote historian John A. Hawgood in *America's Western Frontiers*: "A winter spent with Jim Bridger set up 'Ned Buntline' for the rest of a career as a dime novelist, and many of the stories he wrote about Jim were even true."

American Explorers

Legend:
- ·····: Jedediah Smith, 1826-1829
- ·–·–· John C. Frémont, 1843-1844
- ～～ John C. Frémont, 1845-1846
- ··–·· John C. Frémont, 1853-1854

Fort Vancouver
Malheur River
Ft. Boise
Snake River
Ft. Hall
From St. Louis
Ft. Laramie
CALIFORNIA TRAIL
Bear River
Ft. Bridger
Ft. Redding
Humboldt River
Great Salt Lake
Walker Lake
Green River
Dolores River
Moab
Ft. Sutter
Sevier River
Colorado River
Walker Pass
Crossing of the Fathers
Monterey
Taos
Santa Fe
Albuquerque
Mojave R.
Pacific Ocean
Los Angeles
Colorado River
San Diego
Gila River

0   100   300
Scale of Miles

Jeffrey L. Ward 1997

But it was the mountain man's appearance that inspired western artists and writers alike. Painters Carl Bodmer, Frederic Remington, Arthur Fitzwilliam Tait, and O. C. Seltzer all tried their hand at capturing the eccentric look of the fur trapper with his fringed buckskin garments, his outlandish head gear, and rifle always at the ready. Numerous written accounts confirm the portrait. George Frederick Ruxton, a precise chronicler of the era, described the trapper's "hunting shirt of dressed buckskin, ornamented with long fringes; pantaloons of the same material, and decorated with porcupine quills and long fringes down the outside of the leg. A flexible felt hat and moccasins clothe his extremities."* Rufus Sage, in his 1846 account, *Scenes in the Rocky Mountains*, described the entire mountain man, "fully equipped":

> His skin, from constant exposure, assumes a hue almost as dark as that of the Aborigine, and his features and physical structure attain a rough and hardy cast. His hair, through inattention, becomes long, coarse, and bushy. . . . His head is surmounted by a low crowned wool-hat, or a rude substitute of his own manufacture. His clothes are of buckskin, gaily fringed at the seams with strings of the same material, cut and made in a fashion peculiar to himself and associates. The deer and buffalo furnish him the required covering for his feet which he fabricates at the impulse of want. His waist is encircled with a belt of leather, holding encased his butcher-knife and pistols—while from his neck is suspended a bullet-pouch securely fastened to the belt in front, and beneath the right arm hangs a powder-horn traversely from his shoulder. . . . With a gun-stick made of some hard wood and a good rifle placed in his hands, carrying from thirty-five balls to the pound, the reader will have before him a correct likeness of a genuine mountaineer when fully equipped.

To survive, the trappers had to become familiar with Indians and their ways. In this unusual relationship, the whites and the Indians were enemies at times and allies at others. To the white man, the Indian was without question a savage, but, wrote Hiram M. Chittenden, he still "found much to his taste in the wild, free life of the Indian [as] amply proven by the willingness with which so many abandoned the blessings of civilization for the hardships of the wilderness." The flamboyant black mountain man Jim Beckwourth, who was born a slave, lived with the Crow Indians

---

* "The deerskin shirt, when soaked, wrung out, and dried, "became a veritable buckskin coat of mail that only the hardest driven Indian arrow would penetrate," Robert Glass Cleland wrote in *This Reckless Breed of Men*.

for six years, and, in his autobiography, claimed that as a Crow chief he participated in raids and war parties: "If I chose to become an Indian while living among them, it concerned no person but myself; and by doing so I saved more life and property for the white man than a whole regiment of United States regulars could have done at the same time."

Beckwourth married a succession of Blackfoot, Snake, and Crow women; a trapper with a squaw in tow was not an uncommon sight in the mountains.* A work by the Baltimore artist Alfred Jacob Miller shows the renowned mountain man (and Great Basin explorer) Joseph Walker proceeding through the wilderness on horseback with "his squaw" riding a respectful distance to the rear. While admitting that his Indian wife was not "exactly fitted to shine at the head of a nobleman's table," Charles Ross of the Hudson's Bay Company pointed out in a letter to his sister that "she suits the sphere [in which] she has to move much better than any such toy—in short she is a native of the country, and as to beauty quite as comely as her husband."

The mountain man also had to know how to fight Indians and, if he survived, to spin a good tale about it, preferably one that proved the treachery of all Indians. A good one involved a Ute chief with an ominous name, Mauvais Gauche, or Bad Left-Handed One, who, in 1824, invited Etienne Provost and his men to "smoke the calumet of peace." After persuading the whites to lay down their arms, the Indians set upon them with knives and tomahawks they had hidden under their robes. Provost ("a very athletic man," according to a contemporary writer) and a few others managed to escape, but the rest of the fifteen men were slaughtered.

Often the unexpected appearance of a party of trappers would terrify Indians and they would flee, but at other times they were a lurking presence and a constant danger. One of Jedediah Smith's expeditions was harassed by Indians who, from a distance, shot

---

* Abstemious Jedediah Smith was a notable exception; "There is no suggestion," Dale L. Morgan wrote in his *Jedediah Smith and the Opening of the West*, "that he ever admitted a squaw, no matter how lovely or eager, into his bed."

arrows into the sides of their horses and mules. On Frémont's 1843–1844 expedition, a man who dropped behind to tend a lame pack animal was killed by Indians, the only fatality of the entire trip. And near the Humboldt Sink in 1833, Joseph Walker turned his well-armed men loose on a band of Indians who, he felt, were menacing him and his trappers. In the massacre that followed, thirty-nine Indians (and no whites) died.

"Hos and Blaver"

Americans came to the fur trade late—in its waning days in the early nineteenth century. By then it was necessary to go farther afield for furs—into unexplored land, sometimes controlled by the warlike Indians who lived west of the Mississippi. The fur trade had been the most important economic activity in colonial America; the exploration and settlement of the continent were driven by the quest for pelts to be shipped to Europe, where most of the fur was used to make hats. All the important powers were involved— the Dutch and English in New York; the French in Canada and throughout the Mississippi Valley; and the English. The English chartered the Hudson's Bay Company in 1670 and, in the far north, moved rapidly westward. The profits from the fur trade were enormous, but there were other rewards. As the trappers and traders spread across the continent, they also extended power and influence. In this, the French were particularly adept until their defeat in the French and Indian War.

The American Revolution freed Americans to pursue the fur trade on their own, independent of the colonial powers. In 1803, the Louisiana Purchase gave Americans an uncontested right to some of the best trapping grounds on the continent, and the Lewis and Clark expedition (1804–1806) demonstrated that western rivers could carry furs to market. In 1807, a St. Louis trader named Manuel Lisa established the first American trading post on the upper Missouri. In 1809, Lisa and several other entrepreneurs formed the Missouri Fur Company, also out of St. Louis, a city that owed its rapid growth entirely to the fur trade. Beginning in 1823, the politician and entrepreneur William Ashley began sending young trappers west from St. Louis. Their epic trailblazing would open up the South Pass through the Rocky Mountains, thereby making possible an overland route to California and Oregon, and establish for the first time an American presence in the Great Basin.

Unlike the British, who ventured out after beaver in large brigades, Americans preferred to hunt in small groups or even alone. This made for better hunting but left them vulnerable to attack by Indians, hence their high casualty rate. The innovative Ashley understood that his trappers, if properly supplied and provided with one good get-together a year, were often content to stay in the wilderness for years at a time. To accommodate them and, not incidentally, increase his own profits, Ashley held, at a prearranged time and place, an annual rendezvous at which trappers would gather to sell their pelts (for about half what they would get in St. Louis) and buy (for exorbitant prices) traps, ammunition, and whatever other supplies they would need for the upcoming year.

Like the western fur trade itself, the rendezvous system was short-lived but impressive in the impact it had on the historical imagination. The first, at Green River in 1825, was a modest, decorous affair, perhaps because Ashley neglected to bring rum to the gathering, an oversight he was careful not to make again. The get-togethers that followed were more along the lines of orgies: Trappers would carouse, gamble, cavort with Indian women, and, in the process, routinely squander all the profit they received from selling their furs. As George Frederick Ruxton described the scene:

> The rendezvous is one continued scene of drunkeness, gambling, and brawling and fighting, as long as the money and the credit of the trappers last. Seated, Indian fashion, round the fires, with a blanket spread before them, groups are seen

with their "decks" of cards, playing at "euker," "poker," and "seven-up," the regular mountain games. The stakes are "beaver," which here is current coin; and when the fur is gone, their horses, mules, rifles, and shirts, hunting packs, and breeches, are staked. Daring gamblers make the rounds of the camp, challenging each other to play for the trapper's highest stake,—his horse, his squaw (if he has one), and, as once happened, his scalp. There goes "hos and beaver!" is the mountain expression when any great loss is sustained; and, sooner or later, "hos and beaver" invariably find their way into the insatiable pockets of the traders.

In 1810, the German-born fur entrepreneur John Jacob Astor moved directly to the West Coast and established a trading post and fort, Astoria, on the Pacific at the mouth of the Columbia River, to ship beaver and other fur to China.* The British, who controlled the Oregon country, responded to this affront by buying out Astor in 1812. The British, at that time, were too busy competing among themselves to worry much about American trappers and fur companies in the trans-Mississippi West. However, when the two British rivals, the Hudson's Bay Company and the Canadian North West Company, merged in 1821, the British turned their attention to the beaver-rich Snake River region, the unexplored Great Basin, and the upstart Americans encroaching from the east.

Sir George Simpson, governor of the Hudson's Bay Company, understood the big picture: American settlers would follow American trappers. To keep the trappers away, he set out to get rid of the beaver west of the Rocky Mountains. It was a feasible policy based on the biological fact that beavers reproduce slowly

---

* In 1811, five of Astor's men, who were heading west to found Fort Astoria, left their main party on the north fork of the Snake River and headed south to trap beaver on the Bear River in southern Idaho and northern Utah. That puts them among the earliest whites to enter the Great Basin.

and on the simple reality that intensive, systematic trapping will soon wipe them out. In a letter, Simpson explained the strategy:

> The greatest and best protection we can have from opposition is keeping the country closely hunted as the first step that the American Government will take towards Colonization is through their Indian Traders and if the country becomes exhausted in Fur bearing animals they can have no inducement to proceed thither. We therefore entreat that no exertions be spared to explore and Trap every part of the country. . . .

Simpson, an innovator, instituted the brigade system, sending large numbers of men out together on expeditions.* Some of these were employees, others were free-trappers, dependent on the brigade for supplies and security but free to sell pelts to whomever they pleased. He was also among the first to realize that in the West horses, rather than boats and canoes, were a superior mode of transportation. To carry out the extermination, Simpson turned to a tough Canadian-born trapper, Peter Skene Ogden, and put him in command of the Snake River brigade. His mission was to enter the Great Basin, search out new trapping grounds, and keep the Americans at bay. Although the territory was vast, both Ogden and the Americans were drawn to the Bear River, a beaver-rich stream that loops through southern Idaho and empties into the Great Salt Lake, and it soon became inevitable that they would meet and confront each other there, in the northeast corner of the Great Basin.

---

* The brigades were often heterogeneous in an interesting way. The expedition that John Work of the Hudson's Bay Company took to the Great Basin's Humboldt River in 1830 was composed of 114 people, including 1 slave, 29 women, 45 children, 26 Canadians, 2 Americans, 6 half bloods, 2 Iroquois, and 1 Nipissing Indian.

"Enterprising Young Men"

On February 13, 1822, William H. Ashley placed an advertisement in St. Louis's *Missouri Gazette & Public Advertiser* that has become one of the most famous documents in the history of the western fur trade. "To Enterprising Young Men," it read. "The subscriber wishes to engage ONE HUNDRED MEN, to ascend the river Missouri to its source, there to be employed for one, two or three years. . . ."

Ashley was an important man in Missouri; the year before, Missouri had been admitted to the Union as a state with Ashley as its elected lieutenant governor. For his new fur trading enterprise, Ashley and his partner, the veteran fur trader Andrew Henry, had no trouble attracting men. The eighty to one hundred he sent up the Missouri in 1823 were, wrote Robert Glass Cleland, "more disreputable in appearance than Falstaff's tatterdemalion battalion," but they included a nucleus of a dozen or so men whom historian Dale Morgan has called "the most significant group of continental explorers ever brought together." Among them were several who went on to play major roles in the exploration of the Great Basin. James Bridger and Etienne Provost, for example, have both been given credit for being the first white man to discover the Great Salt Lake. Thomas "Broken Hand" Fitzpatrick, after an active career as a fur trader, led the first emigrant train to the Great Basin and guided Frémont in his second expedition (1843–1844). Other soon-to-be-famous names included James Clyman, Hugh Glass, Milton and William Sublette, but, above all of them, there was Jedediah Strong Smith, then in his early twenties, who would, before the decade was out, establish himself as the foremost explorer of the last great undiscovered territory in the country, the mysterious Great Basin.*

* Because he was killed before he had a chance to publish accounts of his adventures, Jedediah Smith was, for many years, the forgotten man of western history. The writings of his biographer, historian Dale Morgan, and others (among them, John G. Neihardt, who in 1941 published *The Song of Jed Smith*, an epic poem

Smith did not fit the popular image of the mountain man. As a young man with strong religious convictions, Smith is popularly pictured as roaming the West with a rifle in one hand and a Bible in the other, and "the mild teachings of the one never diminished in any way the vigor with which he used the other," wrote Hiram Chittenden in his turn-of-the-century classic, *The American Fur Trade in the Far West*. Born in Bainbridge, New York, on January 6, 1799, Smith had an unusually clear idea of why he went west and what he hoped to accomplish there: "I started into the mountains with the determination of becoming a first rate hunter, of making myself thoroughly acquainted with the character and habits of the Indians, of tracing out the sources of the Columbia River, and following it to its mouth, and of making the whole profitable to me."

Whereas other explorers and mountain men had probed the edges of the Great Basin, Smith plunged right in. He was the first non-Indian to cross from the Great Salt Lake to southern California, the first to cross the Sierra Nevada (and, once this was accomplished, to travel, west to east, right across the middle of the Great Basin), and the first white man on record to pass from southern California to the Columbia River in Oregon. He is given credit for discovering the entrance to the West through the Rocky Mountains known as South Pass, and the information he brought back from his travels contributed greatly to the understanding of the Great Basin and other unknown regions of the West. He was brave, upright, a natural leader, and an astute businessman and entrepreneur. Ashley, who immediately singled him out as a group leader, made him a partner in 1825 and the following year sold the business to him and two others.

On his first trip up the Missouri River, Smith distinguished himself when, in early June 1823, a trading party led by Ashley came under a surprise attack by Arikara Indians, and Smith coolly

---

celebrating the mountain man) have helped to rectify the situation, but, even today, Smith is less well known than many lesser lights of the fur trade.

extracted his men, who had been pinned down by rifle fire, from an exposed sandbar in the river. As Morgan points out, the attack, in which more than a dozen whites were killed, was the worst disaster in the history of the western fur trade. To bury the men, the expedition also turned to Smith. In a letter to the parents of one of the fallen men, a trapper named Hugh Glass wrote: "Mr. Smith, a young man of our company, made a powerful prayer which moved us all greatly, and I am persuaded [your son] died in peace."

Ashley rewarded his young employee by putting him at the head of a party of about a dozen men with the mission of finding new beaver territory south of the Yellowstone.* The men left Fort Kiowa in late September and proceeded west to the Dakotas. Somewhere west of the Black Hills, Smith was attacked and nearly killed by a grizzly bear that had, according to trapper James Clyman, "taken nearly all his head in his cap[a]cious mouth . . . and laid the skull bare to near the crown of the head . . . one of his ears was torn from his head out to the outer rim." Under Smith's calm direction, Clyman stitched him up and reattached his ear. In ten days, Smith, his reputation for courage and sangfroid enhanced by the incident, was ready to travel again. The party wintered in Wyoming's Wind River Valley, where Crow Indians told them of an easy way to get across the Rockies to a river filled with beaver. The river was the Green,† a tributary of the Colorado River, and the opening in the mountains would soon become famous as South Pass.

The discovery of the South Pass alone would be enough to guarantee Smith's place in history.‡ This opening through the Rockies threw open the Great Basin and the entire West to fur-

---

* The hostility of Indians on the upper Missouri convinced Ashley to look farther south for routes west. This probably brought the Americans to the Great Basin somewhat sooner than if they had been free to trap the Missouri and its tributaries.

† Bernard DeVoto writes of the Green River: "It should be called the Colorado for it is the parent stream but governmental edict has bestowed that name on the Grand [former name for the Colorado, from its source to its junction with the Green]. . . ."

‡ Smith was not even the first white man to use South Pass; Robert Stuart led a party returning from John Jacob Astor's Astoria on the Pacific coast through it

ther exploration, trapping, and settlement. Between 1841 and 1853, 150,000 people, among them Mormons, gold hunters, and explorers, would make use of South Pass on their way west. Finally a railroad went across the Rockies at this point. Smith did not just stumble on the pass: Indians showed him where it was and how to get to it on a crude topographical map made of sand spread out on a buffalo robe. And, unlike most of his other deeds, "discovering" South Pass involved no derring-do. The pass, twenty miles wide, rises to a height of seventy-five hundred feet in such gentle stages that westward travelers were not aware of crossing the Continental Divide until they saw west-flowing streams on the far side.

It was mid-March, still winter, when Smith and his men went through South Pass, arriving on the Green River on March 19. There he split his small party in two for the spring hunt, sending Fitzpatrick and some men upstream, while he moved down to Blacks Fork. After the two groups rendezvoused on the Sweetwater River in July, Smith sent Fitzpatrick with the furs back to St. Louis, while he headed west through South Pass intending to conduct a hunt on the Columbia River in the heart of British territory. In mid-September he stumbled across a beleaguered band of Iroquois that had detached itself from the Hudson's Bay Snake River brigade to hunt alone. They in turn had come under attack by Blackfoot Indians, and they begged Smith to escort them back to the British post in the Flathead region of Montana. Smith agreed, on the condition that the Indians turn all their beaver over to him—105 pelts that otherwise would have gone to the Hudson's Bay Company.

As he guided the Indians back to Flathead Post, Smith met the Hudson's Bay Snake River brigade, also on its way to the post for the winter. The commander, Alexander Ross, was not at all happy to see the Americans, whom he regarded more as "spies

on his way east in 1812, but the world did not take note. Historians, therefore, usually call Smith the "effective" discoverer of South Pass, a weak way of saying that, while not the first, this was the discovery that put it on the map.

than trappers." Ross tried to buy the furs that the seven Americans had cached along the way, but they were not interested in selling. In his journal for that day, Ross noted gloomily: "They intend following us to the fort."

For the British, the unwelcome appearance of the Americans at Flathead Post in November 1824 was evidence that the "scorched earth" policy of trapping out the country west of the Continental Divide was not working. If Smith had managed to come this far into British territory, surely more Americans were on the way. For Smith, meeting the Indians in the wilderness was fortuitous. Not only did he acquire more beaver from them, but they provided him with an excuse to get inside the British post, where he could observe what his rivals were up to. Dale Morgan speculated that Smith and his small party had already killed as many beaver as they could transport out of the mountains: "He could very well break off his hunt for the sake of some firsthand information about British operations."

Faceoff with the British

We can only guess why the British allowed their competitor to spend almost a month in their midst as they prepared for the spring hunt: Either it was the rude etiquette of the frontier or they wanted Smith where they could keep an eye on him. At Flathead Post, Smith crossed paths with Peter Skene Ogden, the Canadian who would become second only to Smith himself in the early exploration of the Great Basin. Five years older than Smith, Ogden originally worked for the North West Company, but his methods were so ruthless that his employer banished him to the Columbia River and then dropped him when the company merged with the Hudson's Bay Company in 1821. He was hired back two years later when the company felt some ruthlessness was needed in the competition with the Americans. In 1824 Simpson put Ogden in charge of the Snake River expedition. He replaced the hapless Alexander Ross, the man who led Jedediah Smith into the British camp.

With Ogden at its head, the huge British expedition—some 60 men, 268 horses, and 352 traps—took off on December 20, 1824, with Smith and his 6 men not far behind. The two parties traveled more or less in tandem for three months, the Americans relying on the formidable British presence to protect them from Indians. On March 19, when the parties were out of hostile Indian territory, the British and the Americans parted. William Kittson, journal-keeper for the British, recorded their departure and his impressions of Smith: "About noon they left us well satisfied I hope with the care and Attention we paid them. For since we had them with us no one in our party ever took any advantage of or ill treated them. One Jedidiah [*sic*] S. Smith is at the head of them, a sly cunning Yankey. . . ."

Although they were now traveling separately, the Americans and British were keeping an eye on each other as they began the serious business of the spring hunt. As the two parties approached the Great Basin's Bear River, Ogden noted on April 17, 1825, that, although the Americans had camped only three miles ahead, "this will avail them naught as independent of our party we have traps 12 Miles a head." It was not long afterward that Smith learned of a party of Americans who had wintered on the Bear River and were now trapping its lower portion. Assuming that they were Ashley's men, Smith turned down the Bear River to meet them.

Among the trappers Smith found on the Bear River was the legendary Jim Bridger, who the previous winter had, on a bet, built a bullboat out of buffalo hide and willow sticks and floated down the Bear to the Great Salt Lake, thereby becoming—or so many believe—the first white man to see the Great Salt Lake.* Once he reached the lake, Bridger noticed that his boat was floating unusually high in the water, so, out of curiosity, he tasted it and found it to be salty. When he told the story back in camp, his companions responded, according to Stanley Vestal's spirited biography, "Hell, Jim, you done found the Pacific Ocean!" The men might have

---

*Another great mountain man, the portly Etienne Provost, also has a claim to being the white discoverer of the Great Salt Lake; he might have come upon it in the fall of 1824.

been joking, but the conclusion—that the Bear River emptied into the ocean—was not totally absurd in view of how little these mountain men really knew about the geographic void soon to be called the Great Basin.

Another American camped on the Bear River was an aggressive trapper named Johnson Gardner, whose resentment of the British presence on what he considered American territory came to a head on the afternoon of May 23. Waving the American flag, Gardner led a contingent of twenty-two of his countrymen into the British camp and denounced their competitors as trespassers. Gardner also offered to buy pelts from Ogden's trappers at $3.50 a pound, eight times what the Hudson's Bay Company was paying. Whatever hold Ogden had on his men, he could not compete with $3.50 a pound; twenty-three of his men deserted to the Americans.

The next morning Gardner was back, warning Ogden that he remained in American territory "at your own peril" and chastising him for taking advantage of his trappers, "treating them as slaves, selling them goods at high prices and giving them nothing for their skins." Tension mounted when Ogden tried to prevent the deserters from taking horses and goods with them, and the Americans advanced with their weapons at the ready but then withdrew without firing a shot. The next day, May 25, as Ogden and his remaining men prepared to break camp, Gardner and his men returned and, as Ogden recorded the incident, "like all villains appeared to exult in their Villany." Gardner delivered some more threats, telling Ogden, "you will See us shortly not only in the Columbia but at the Flat Heads & Cootanies as we are determined you Shall no longer remain in our Territory." In reply, Ogden said, "When we Should receive order from our Government to leave the Columbia we would but Not before. . . ."

There was something almost comical about the episode—the representatives of two nations talking tough deep in the American wilderness. (If shots had been fired, it would have been many weeks before word reached either Washington or London.) Even more unusual was the fact that the clash occurred on territory that belonged to neither nation. The men did not know it, but they were south of the forty-second parallel, on Mexican soil. And while Gardner's aggressiveness did succeed in driving Ogden from the Great Basin, it was the high prices the Americans were paying, not the threat of force, that turned Ogden around and sent him back to the Snake River. As he wrote (with characteristic lack of punctuation) in his journal:

> Here I am . . . Surrounded on all Sides by enemies & our expectations & hopes blasted for returns this year, to remain in this quarter any longer it would merely be to trap beaver for the Americans for I Seriously apprehend there are Still more of the Trappers who would Willingly join them indeed the tempting offers made them independent the low price they Sell their goods are too great for them to resist. . . .

Jedediah Smith played no direct role in the conflict. While Gardner was blustering his way into the British camp, Smith was back in camp some eight miles away. But Smith apparently was the one who informed his fellow Americans of the British presence. At least, that is how Ogden viewed the situation. In a letter, Ogden rued "the unfortunate day Mr. Ross consented to allow the 7 Americans to accompany him to the Flatheads, for it was these fellows that guided and accompanied them [Gardner and company] to our Camp."

That July Smith met Ashley at the first rendezvous held on Henry's Fork of the Green River. Ashley, accompanied by his new partner, Jedediah Smith, left the first rendezvous for St. Louis with 8,829 pounds of beaver worth some fifty thousand dollars, which the *Missouri Advocate* called "one of the richest cargoes of fur that ever arrived at St. Louis." Smith and Ashley arrived in St. Louis on October 4, 1825; in less than a month, on October 30, Smith was headed back to the mountains at the head of a party of seventy men, 160 horses and mules, and supplies and equipment worth twenty thousand dollars.

After following a route west that would become the Oregon

Trail, Smith and his men wintered inside the confines of the Great Basin—at the mouth of the Bear River where it empties into the Great Salt Lake. After breaking camp in the spring, Smith moved around the northern end of the lake and partway down its western shore. Smith was certainly hoping to discover a river running from the Great Salt Lake to the Pacific Ocean; when he did not find it, he dispatched four men in bullboats to explore further, while he headed north out of the Great Basin to the beaver-rich Snake River.* After a successful spring hunt, Smith returned to the Great Basin and the 1826 rendezvous in the Cache Valley; there he and his two partners, William Sublette and David E. Jackson, bought out Ashley, and Jedediah Smith became, at age twenty-seven, the dominant partner in the most important firm in the American fur trade.

---

* Even their successful circumnavigation of the Great Salt Lake did not end speculation that there was an outlet from the lake to the sea; they later reported that they passed a bay that looked to them like a beginning of a westward-flowing river.

Chapter Four

THROUGH "A COUNTRY OF STARVATION"

The Great Basin had now been probed—by Garcés, Escalante, Wolfskill, Bridger, Provost, Smith, Ogden, and others—but not explored. The next step was to penetrate its forbidding interior and to cross it, one side to the other. The first to take on this challenge was, not surprisingly, Jedediah Smith. In August 1826, after the July rendezvous, Smith's two new partners headed north to the Snake River region, where they knew they would find beaver. Smith and sixteen men went in the opposite direction, into "a Country of Starvation—Sandy plains and Rocky hills . . ." It was the start of a journey that would make him famous. His ostensible goal was to find new waters to trap beaver, but this passage in his log shows that there was in Smith something of the romantic—a "strong inclination," as he called it, to press on into unchartered lands.

What that great and unexplored country might contain we
knew not but hoped to find parts of the country as well
stocked with Beaver as some the waters of the Missouri which
was perhaps as much as we could reasonably expect. In taking
the charge of our S western Expedition I followed the bent of
my strong inclination to visit this unexplored country and
unfold those hidden resources of wealth and bring to light
those wonders which I readily imagined a country so extensive might contain. I must confess that I had at that time a full
share of that ambition (and perhaps foolish ambition) which
is common in a greater or less degree to all the active world. I
wanted to be the first to view a country on which the eyes of a
white man had never gazed and to follow the course of rivers
that run through a new land.

Only a few days out, somewhere in the vicinity of present-day
Provo, Utah, Smith's Southwest expedition, as it was called, came
across a Ute Indian village of thirty-five lodges. In his journal,
Smith complimented the Indians for their cleanliness, dignity, and
honesty: "As Stealing and Begging are the most degrading features in the Indian character and as their prevalence is almost uni-
versal so to be exempt from them is no ordinary merit." A month's
travel south brought them to a river, now known as the Virgin,
that Smith named after the president of the United States, John
Quincy Adams. With their provisions running low, the expedition
was delighted to encounter some Paiutes who, in exchange for
some "small presents," provided them with corn and pumpkins.
Commented Smith: ". . . as indifferent as this may seem to him
who never made his pillow of the sand of the plain or him who
would consider it a hardship to go without his dinner yet to us
weary and hungry in the solitary desert it was a feast . . . that made
my party in their sudden hilarity and Glee present a lively contrast
to the moody desponding silence of the night before."
Smith hit the Colorado River where Lake Mead is now and followed it downstream until he reached the Mojave villages in the

vicinity of today's Needles, California. It is not certain what Smith had in mind when he set out—whether he intended to go on to California or, at some point, turn back whence he came. The following passage from his journal indicated that it was circumstance that drove him on:

> Believing it impossible to return to the deposit at this season and in my present situation I determined to prepare myself as well possible and push forward to California where I supposed I might procure such supplies as woul[d] enable me to move on north. In that direction I expected to find beaver and in all probability some considerable river heading up in the vicinity of the Great Salt Lake.* By this route I could return to the deposit.

Smith was two hard weeks crossing the Mojave Desert. His relief at nearing the San Gabriel mission in the San Bernardino Valley was tempered by foreboding; he realized the authorities "might consider me a spy imprison me persecute me for the sake of religion or detain me in prison to ruin of my business . . ." Smith was not being paranoid; the Mexican governor of California, alarmed at the sudden appearance of the Americans out of the desert, summoned Smith to San Diego for questioning. Smith took the position that, "far from being a spy," he wanted only to procure supplies in California and then he would be on his way. Finally, it took the intervention of Captain William Cunningham of the American ship *Courier* to convince the governor that Smith was not in California on some nefarious political or military mission.

Smith promised the governor that he would leave California by the same route he came, and, on January 10, 1827, Smith and his men departed. Once he was over the San Bernardino Mountains, however, he veered off his earlier path, left the Mojave River

* By "considerable river" Smith obviously meant the Buenaventura River, which he still believed he would find.

about the point where Victorville is today, and headed across the Tehachapi Mountains and into California's San Joaquin Valley. It is generally assumed that Smith ignored the order to leave California as soon as he was safely away from the coast, but Dale Morgan suggested that California was "a territory narrowly delimited—at this time the settled belt along the coastal plain . . ." and that by crossing the San Bernardino Mountains he had obeyed the governor's orders.

By the end of April, the expedition reached the American River. Trapping in the San Joaquin Valley had been so good that Smith was now worried about getting the fur back to the rendezvous. An attempt to take the group over the Sierra Nevada by way of the American River was blocked by snow. During this venture the expedition found itself surrounded by hostile Indians. Smith, realizing that the Indians were not familiar with firearms, decided to strike first. While "wishing them as little harm as possible and yet consistent with my own safety," he ordered two of his best marksmen to fire at the Indians: "I preferred long shots that it might give them the idea that we could kill at any distance." When two Indians fell dead, the rest "stood still and silent as if a thunder bolt had fallen among them then a few words passed from party to party and in a moment they ran like Deer." A second confrontation, Smith noted matter-of-factly, had a similar outcome "except that more guns were fired and more Indians killed."

The attempt to take the party across the mountains ended when Smith, standing on a high peak, could see nothing ahead but more mountains and an endless expanse of "freezing desolation." But before he gave the order to turn back, Smith had a moment of reflection: "I thought of home and all its neglected enjoyments of the cherfull fireside of my father house of the Plenteous harvest of my native land and visions of flowing fields of green and wide spread Prairaes of joyous bustle and of busy life thronged in my mind to make me feel more strongly the utter desolateness of my situation. . . ."

The leader led his men back to the Stanislaus River, then, on

May 20, 1827, accompanied by Robert Evans and Silas Gobel, Smith, in his own words "took leave of my small but faithful party and started on an enterprise involved in great uncertainty." Smith intended to cross the Sierra Nevada and the Great Basin and reach Great Salt Lake in time for the July rendezvous. He must have known, however, that in trying to cross the mountains in winter he was taking a desperate gamble. Before leaving, he promised his men he would return in four months; if he did not, they could consider him dead.

Smith and his two companions became the first white men to cross the formidable Sierra Nevada. It took them eight days to pass through Ebbetts Pass on hard-packed snow four to eight feet deep. They descended from the mountains into the Great Basin, which was at that point, Smith observed, "a waste of sand with a few detached mountains some of which are in the region of perpetual snow." The only inhabitants were a few Indians "scattered over the land, the most miserable objects in creation."

A journey of unbelievable hardship followed:

With our best exertion we pushed forward, walking as we had been for a long time over the soft sand . . . worn down with hunger and fatigue and burning with thirst increased by the blazing sands . . . it then seemed possible and even probable we might perish in the desert unheard of and unpitied. . . . My dreams were not of Gold or ambitious honors but of my distant quiet home, of murmuring brooks of Cooling Cascades.

On June 25, Robert Evans collapsed, and Smith and Gobel left him behind "with feelings only known to those who have been in the same situation." Three miles farther on they found water. "Gobel plunged into it at once," Smith wrote, "and I could hardly wait to bath my burning forehead before I was pouring it down regardless of consequences." The two men returned with water to where Evans lay, by now "far gone being scarcely able to speak." Putting "the kettle to his mouth he did not take it away until he had drank all the water of which there was at least 4 or 5 quarts and then asked me why I had not brought more."

The men recuperated the rest of the day at the spring. Two more days' travel brought them around the Stansbury Mountains to the "joyful sight" of the Great Salt Lake. In his journal, Smith acknowledged that the reader might find it difficult to understand that "the sight of this lake surrounded by a wilderness of More than 2000 Miles diameter excited in me those feelings known to the traveler who, after long and perilous journeying, comes in view of his home. But so it was with me for I had traveled so much in the vicinity of the Salt Lake that it had become my home of the wilderness."

Although now on familiar ground, the men were not home free. As they made their way around the southern end of the Great Salt Lake, game was hard to find, and, in crossing the flooded Jordan River on June 28, Smith almost strangled and drowned while swimming a raft across with the tow rope in his teeth. The next day, the men supped on the last of their horse meat and "talked a little of the possibility of our suffering being at an end. I say we talked a little for men suffering from hunger never talk much but rather bear their sorrows in moody silence which is much preferable to fruitless complaint."

On the thirtieth, the men revived after they dined on a buck that Smith had shot, and three more days' travel took them to Bear Lake on the Utah-Idaho border, where Smith's partners and other men of the mountains were assembled for that year's rendezvous. Smith, terse and understated as usual, noted at his journey's end: "My arrival caused a considerable bustle in camp for myself and party had been given up as lost. A small Cannon brought up from St Louis was loaded and fired for a salute."

The Return to California

In ten days Smith, with eighteen men, was off again for California to relieve the party he had left on the Stanislaus River in the Sierra

Nevada. His recent eastward journey across the Great Basin had convinced him "that it would be impossible for a party with loaded horses and encumbered with baggage ever to cross it," so he set off in the same general direction he had gone the year before—along the southeastern edge of the Great Basin. Along the way, he encountered the same band of Ute Indians with whom he had concluded a treaty the previous year, and when he reached the Colorado in mid-August, he was again welcomed into the Mojave villages. He was not aware, however, that a clash with traders from Santa Fe had turned the Indians against whites. The Indians concealed their hostility until Smith, about August 18, began crossing the Colorado. Then, with his party divided, the Mojaves attacked those left on shore, killing ten of Smith's eighteen men, taking all of their horses and most of their provisions. The massacre left Smith and the eight other survivors alive on the other side of the river but in a tight spot. As Smith later noted, "not far off were some hundreds of Indians who might in all probability close in upon us and with an Arrow or Club terminate all my measures for futurity."

The Americans, who had only five guns among them, barricaded themselves on the river behind some hastily cut brush and awaited "the charge of four or five hundred Indians whose hands were yet stained with the blood of their companions." As the Mojaves closed in around them, Smith ordered his best marksmen to fire upon a few Indians who had come out into the open from behind cover. The shots killed two and wounded another; the rest, Smith recorded, "ran off like frightened sheep and we were released from the apprehension of immediate death."

When it was dark, the party slipped away from the Colorado and began making its way west across the southern spur of the Great Basin. Without Indian guides, Smith had to rely on his memory of the year before and on what historian Dale Morgan called his "ability to find water when life depended on it." At other times, Smith wrote, the party "found some relief from chewing slips of the Cabbage Pear, a singular plant . . . verry juicy although frequently found growing on the most parched and Barren ground." On August 28 the expedition left the Great Basin, passing through the Cajon Pass and into the San Bernardino Valley.

Here Smith's contribution to the exploration and history of the Great Basin ends. But his story—although it has not many years to run—is far from over. Smith rendezvoused with the party he had left on the Stanislaus River on the eighteenth, two days before the deadline he had set for himself when leaving earlier that year. But troubles continued to plague him. The Mexican government of California, suspicious as always of his presence in their territory, took him to Monterey, put him under house arrest, and threatened to send him to Mexico for trial. While waiting to be released, Smith managed to sell his beaver skins to the skipper of a Yankee ship and, with the proceeds, buy 250 horses, which he hoped to sell at a large profit at the rendezvous the following year. After a series of frustrating delays, Smith, on December 30, 1827, "returned again to the woods, the river, the prairae, the Camp & the Game with a feeling somewhat like that of a prisoner escaped from his dungeon and his chains."

Headed north, his destination the Columbia River, Smith led his party to the coast, but his progress was slowed by time spent crossing swamps and rivers and navigating difficult coastlines. In late June 1828, the party of nineteen men crossed into what is now Oregon. As they proceeded north, the Indians became increasingly hostile and troublesome, frequently shooting arrows into the sides of the valuable horses and mules. At Oregon's Umpqua River, while Smith and two others were scouting the route ahead, the rest of the party was attacked by Kelawatset Indians. Only one of the sixteen men survived the massacre.* Smith, his two companions, and the lone survivor made their way on foot to the Hudson's Bay Company's Fort Vancouver on the Columbia River. There his competitors cordially received him and aided him in a partially successful attempt to recover some of his property from the Indians.

---

* Two days earlier, Smith had disciplined a Kelawatset chief for stealing an ax by tying him to a tree. It was to avenge this humiliation that the Indians attacked.

Smith went from the Columbia to Montana, where he and his partners spent 1829–1830 trapping the upper Missouri and the Yellowstone and its tributaries. He returned to St. Louis on October 7, 1830, almost five years to the day since he had last seen civilization. Historians wish that he had stopped traveling long enough to publish his memoirs, but instead, in April 1831, he joined a trading caravan headed for Santa Fe. While crossing a waterless plain south of the Arkansas River, Smith, on May 27, rode on ahead to look for a spring. He was never seen again. According to stories that eventually reached Santa Fe, Smith was ambushed by Comanches who had been stalking buffalo at a watering hole.

Smith was thirty-two years old when he died, "a man whom none could approach without respect," a magazine writer noted shortly afterward, "or know without esteem. And though he fell under the spears of the savages, and his body has glutted the prairie wolf, and none can tell where his bones are bleaching, he must not be forgotten. . . ."

"Truly a Barren Country"

While Jedediah Smith was at Fort Vancouver, he once again encountered his British counterpart, Peter Skene Ogden, leader of the Snake River expedition of the Hudson's Bay Company. Ogden had stayed out of the Great Basin since his unfortunate encounter with Johnson Gardner near Mountain Green, Utah, but now, in the fall of 1828, he was preparing to enter it again by taking his fifth expedition south into the unexplored region that is now northern Nevada.

Ogden left Fort Nez Perce on September 22, 1828. On November 9, he reached an east-west flowing river where "the

---

Before he left on the scouting mission, Smith had warned his clerk of danger from the Indians, but the man, who apparently believed that all Indians in the territory of the Hudson's Bay Company were peaceful, permitted a large number into the camp.

first thing that presented itself was a Beaver House apparently well stocked a most pleasant sight to me and I hope it will repay us for all the trouble and anxiety it has caused me to reach it." This was the Humboldt River, a three-hundred-mile-long waterway within the Great Basin and, as Gloria Griffin Cline pointed out, "the only stream that has its source and terminus well within the area of interior drainage." The river had many names— the Unknown River, Mary's River (after Ogden's Indian wife), and Ogden River—before the explorer John Charles Frémont renamed it the Humboldt, after the German geographer and scientist Baron Alexander von Humboldt in 1843.* No matter what its name, it was a significant discovery. A decade or so after Ogden first saw it, the river became the so-called "highway of the west," a well-defined segment of the trail to California.

Ogden's men trapped the Humboldt and its tributaries until snow began to fall, then they followed the river upstream. The eastward journey was slowed by the illness of the trapper Joseph Paul. Finally Ogden left the man with two others to care for him and proceeded on without them. On December 26, the party came to within a "distant view" of a fog-bound Great Salt Lake, and two days later, as the party proceeded around its northern end, Ogden wrote that "having this Season explored the half of the North Side of it and can safely assert as the Americans have of the South side that it is truly a barren country." On New Year's Day 1829, the two men left to care for Joseph Paul rode into camp reporting that he had died. The news caused Ogden to reflect that "for a country so lately discovered it is almost incredible the numbers that have fallen in it."

From the Great Salt Lake, Ogden moved to the Bear River of northern Utah and southern Idaho. Here again, as they had in 1825, the British found themselves camped in close and nervous

---

* Humboldt never saw the river. Historian Hiram Chittenden indignantly called Frémont's naming of the river "an instance of the violence so often done by explorers to existing geographical nomenclature without justifiable cause. The river should have retained its original name, Ogden."

proximity to the aggressive Americans, who immediately induced Ogden's Indian trappers to trade their furs for whiskey. Ogden's brigade was still smarting from this loss when several of their horses stampeded into the American camp. One horse, belonging to Ogden's Indian wife, had their infant strapped to the saddle; the other was a pack horse loaded with beaver pelts. According to the story, as it was later written by mountain man Joseph Meek, Ogden's Indian wife, on foot, chased the horses into the American camp, mounted hers, grabbed the pack horse by the halter and began to lead it back to the British side. Some Americans, who considered the pelts to be a spoil of the beaver war and rightfully theirs, urged that she be shot, but others, admiring her spunk, let her ride away. True or not, the story is interesting, not only because it illustrates the potentially explosive nature of the British-American rivalry, but because it focuses on an Indian woman. Native-born trappers' wives and camp-followers accompanied most trapping parties, wrote historian Ted Warner, "and endured all the hardships, fatigue, famine, and drudgery of the journey but . . . are rarely mentioned in the journals or official records."

That spring, Ogden sent most of his party back directly to Fort Nez Perce and, with fourteen men, made his way back to the Humboldt River. On this trip he followed the stream to its end, the Humboldt Sink, which he described as "a large lake," and noted with the following entry in his diary for May 29: "The river is not half the size it was, no doubt spreading in the swamp we have passed. It is 2½ ft. deep and only 10 yds wide."* While at the Humboldt Sink, Ogden's brigade discovered Indians, some of them well armed, camped in the surrounding hills. Ogden appeased them by giving them tobacco, but he noticed that they had "pieces of Rifles, Ammunition Arms and other articles,"

---

* The Humboldt, not a large river, often floods with the spring runoff but can be no more than a trickle in the summer. Mark Twain wrote that a man could jump back and forth across Humboldt, until he worked up a thirst; then he could drink the river dry.

which, he suspected, had been taken from Jedediah Smith's men after the Umpqua Massacre. In early June, Ogden began his return home, reaching Fort Nez Perce a month later.

Jedediah Smith, whom Ogden described as "an American adventurer," was the inspiration for his sixth expedition, the first north-south crossing of the Great Basin. Ogden's diaries and papers were lost in a boating accident at the end of the trip, so not many details are known; even his route across the Great Basin is uncertain: whether, from the Humboldt Sink, he went southeastward across the Great Basin to the Sevier River or he proceeded directly south past Walker Lake and into the Sierra Nevada. Either way, after passing through "country as barren as Christians ever traversed," Ogden reached villages on the Colorado, inhabited by Mojave whom he suspected were the same who massacred Smith's men the year before. So, when the Indians indeed attacked, the party was ready and, in Ogden's vivid words ("now grown trite and flavorless by over use," wrote Cleland), twenty-six Mojaves were "made to lick the dust."

After crossing the Mojave Desert, Ogden left the Great Basin and passed into California, where he trapped the Sacramento, then returned to Fort Nez Perce and the Columbia. On the return to Fort Vancouver by water, nine of his men drowned and he nearly lost his life when his boat capsized in a whirlpool. On his arrival, Ogden found that he had been replaced as brigade leader by John Work, of whom Ogden wrote in a letter: "It is an unpleasant situation he fills I wish him every success but it is all a Lottery."

As a pathfinder, the Irish-born John Work was not his predecessor's equal, but in three expeditions, Work visited parts of the Great Basin that no white man had ever seen before. In the spring of 1831, he retraced Ogden's route from the Great Salt Lake to the Humboldt River but came closer to the river's source in the Ruby Mountains than Ogden ever had. Later that season he followed the river for about one hundred miles downstream to the site of present-day Winnemucca, and on his two subsequent expeditions, he crisscrossed the northern Great Basin that falls within modern-day Oregon. He also blazed a trail across the northern Great Basin from Malheur Lake west to California's Sacramento Valley. His large brigades, which often numbered more than one hundred people, also successfully implemented the "scorched earth policy" of the Hudson's Bay Company by deliberate overtrapping, which was designed to halt the American advance into the region. The policy, of course, failed; the Americans came anyway. But, by trapping out the waters of the northwest, it accelerated the decline of the fur trade.

"Unknown Regions . . . His Chief Delight"

The Humboldt River was also a path west for another of the Great Basin's preeminent mountain men/explorers. This was Joseph R. Walker, a native Tennessean, a man, in the words of his clerk, "well hardened to the hardships of the wilderness— understood the character of the Indians very well—was kind and affable to his men, but at the same time at liberty to command without giving offense—and to explore unknown regions was his chief delight."* Walker was thirty-four years old and a respected frontiersman when he signed on as guide and chief lieutenant for an expedition formed by one of the most controversial and colorful figures in the history of the West, Benjamin Louis de Eulalie de Bonneville, who was immortalized by Washington Irving in his 1837 *Adventures of Captain Bonneville*.†

* Many authors refer to him by his full name, Joseph Reddeford Walker, but his biographer, Bil Gilbert, argues convincingly that his real middle name was Rutherford. Walker has been confused with the thieving and warlike Ute Indian chief Walkara. Gilbert points out that Walker once did the chief a service and suggests that Walkara "often went among whites as not only Walker but Joe Walker. This may have been a mark of honor at the time, but it had an adverse effect on the historical reputation of the white man."

† Because of the fame Irving's book gave Bonneville, many landmarks in the West are named after him, among them a dam on the Columbia River, a mountain in Idaho, a prehistoric lake and salt flats in Utah, and towns in Idaho, Oregon, and Wyoming.

Born in France in 1796, Bonneville came to America as a child, graduated from West Point in 1815, and in the 1820s was posted at several locations in the West, where he saw firsthand just how profitable the fur trade could be. For all his alleged faults, Bonneville has to be given credit for enterprise. In 1830, he devised plans for his own expedition, and after obtaining financing in New York and a leave of absence from the Army, he departed Fort Osage, Missouri, on May 1, 1832, with 110 men and twenty wagons pulled by oxen and mules and followed the Platte and the Sweetwater Rivers west. Bonneville was the first man to take wagons, via South Pass, across the Continental Divide; within the decade, overland pioneers, inspired by his example, would follow in wagon trains. Once on the Green River, Bonneville built a fort, a misguided effort that came to be known as "Fort Nonsense" or "Bonneville's Folly." The outpost was soon abandoned, and Bonneville moved his entourage to the Salmon River for the winter of 1832–1833.

The next spring Bonneville divided his troop into three groups, putting Walker in charge of the so-called Bonneville-Walker expedition. Bonneville, however, accompanied it only as far as the Great Salt Lake before he returned to the Salmon River, and there is considerable confusion and disagreement over Walker's next move. According to Washington Irving, Bonneville gave Walker only one mission:

> To have this lake [Great Salt Lake] properly explored, and all its secrets revealed, was the grand scheme of the Captain for the present year; and while it was one in which his imagination evidently took a leading part, he believed it would be attended with great profit, from numerous beaver streams with which the lake must be fringed.

Walker, however, never explored the Great Salt Lake.* Instead he headed west to the Humboldt River. According to a narrative written by Zenas Leonard, Walker's clerk, Walker was following

---

* In telling his story to Irving, whom he met in the drawing room of a Hudson River estate, Bonneville evidently was trying to blame Walker for the failure of his

Bonneville's orders "to steer through an unknown country towards the Pacific and to return to the Great Salt Lake the following summer in case he failed to find beaver in the 'unknown country.' "

Although well supplied, Walker's party had a rough crossing to the Unknown, or Humboldt, River, which it found to be mostly trapped out. The men were also harassed by Indians, who stole their traps and threatened them constantly, especially when the trappers and hunters were out alone. When his men disobeyed his orders and killed a few Indians, Walker disciplined them, but the Indians, now apparently intent on revenge, became more numerous and aggressive. Finally, as the party arrived in the vicinity of the Humboldt Sink, Walker decided to strike the first blow, "saying," according to Leonard's account, "that there was nothing equal to a good start in such a case." When one hundred or so Indians, "who appeared more saucy and bold than any others," drew near, Walker's men opened fire, killing thirty-nine, while the rest of the Indians ran "into the high grass in every direction, howling in the most lamentable manner."

No whites were killed in the clash, which since has been described as both a justifiable response on Walker's part and a heartless slaughter. Irving, who was consistently critical of Walker, wrote, "We feel perfectly convinced that the poor savages had no hostile intentions, but had merely gathered together through motives of curiosity." Even Zenas Leonard, in his account, suggested that the whites might have overreacted, but otherwise tried to put the incident into perspective:

> The severity with which we dealt with these Indians may be revolting to the heart of the philanthropist; but the circumstances of the case altogether atones for the cruelty. It must be borne in mind, that we were far removed from the hope of any succor in case we were surrounded, and that the country

---

venture by claiming that the frontiersman had disobeyed orders. Irving termed the Walker expedition "disgraceful," a judgment no longer held by historians.

we were in was swarming with hostile savages, sufficiently numerous to devour us. Our object was to strike a decisive blow. This we did—even to a greater extent than we had intended.

For the next six weeks, the Walker expedition traveled in a southwesterly direction, through a part of the Great Basin never before trod by any white man, past Carson Sink and Walker Lake and up the Walker River to the vicinity north of Mono Lake, where, according to Bil Gilbert, Walker's biographer, "they caught their first impressive glimpse of the east wall of the Sierra." It is uncertain exactly where the party left the Great Basin and began its attempt to find a crossing of the Sierras, but Leonard provided a vivid picture of the suffering from hunger and cold they endured in the mountains. When some of the men urged turning back, Walker persuaded them that their salvation lay in pressing on. To bolster their morale, he allowed them to kill two horses for food, and, Leonard wrote, they ate "as much of this black, tough lean horse flesh as if it had been the choicest piece of beef steak."*

To the West's "Extreme End"

During their time in the mountains, the men had a splendid view of the Yosemite Valley—Walker always considered this his greatest discovery—but the steep slopes kept them from climbing down into it. On October 26, they were encouraged by a sight of the plains to the west and, a day later, began their descent into a region that, to them, must have been a veritable paradise of

---

* When supplies ran out or dangerously low, trapping parties regularly killed horses for food; the Walker party killed seventeen before it emerged from the mountains. Zenas Leonard appears to be one of the few mountain men who gave the practice a second thought. He wrote: "It seems to be the greatest cruelty to take your rifle, when your horse sinks to the ground from starvation, but still manifests a desire and willingness to follow you, to shoot him in the head and then cut him up and take such parts of their flesh as extreme hunger alone will render it possible for a human being to eat."

warm temperatures, lush vegetation, and plentiful game. By mid-November they were trapping the San Joaquin River when one night they heard "a loud distant noise similar to that of thunder," which some of the men feared was an earthquake. Walker, a trusted authority on all subjects to his men, assured them that what they heard was simply the noise of ocean waves breaking against the shore. Leonard wrote:

> The idea of being within hearing of the *end* of the *Far West* inspired the heart of every member of our company with a patriotic feeling for his country's honor, and all were eager to lose no time until they should behold what they had heard. We felt as if all our previous hardships and privations would be adequately compensated, if we would be spared to return in safety to the homes of our kindred and have it to say that we had stood upon the extreme end of the great west.

The Walker expedition stayed in California until April of the next year (1834), when, by turning eastward on the Kern River, they crossed over the southern Sierra Nevada back again into the Great Basin via a pass that Indians had told them about. This opening in the mountains, soon to be known as Walker Pass, was to become an important gateway to California for emigrant trains. By taking this pass, Walker and company were able to avoid crossing the Mojave Desert farther south, always an arduous and life-threatening ordeal for white adventurers, beginning with Garcés nearly sixty years before.

Not that the route Walker chose offered them easy passage or much in the way of sustenance. As they proceeded up the Owens Valley, they cut into the desert in hopes of shortening the distance to the Humboldt and the way back to the Great Salt Lake, but in a few days they were out of water and, Leonard wrote, their thirst "so intense, that whenever one of our cattle or horses would die the men would immediately catch the blood and greedily swallow it down." Finally, as they turned back toward the grassy slopes of the Sierras, their thirsty horses caught the scent of water and, in a stampede, led them to a river. Soon, in early June, they were back on their trail to the Humboldt, buoyed by the thought that the worst of their journey was over. As they came to the Humboldt Sink on June 8, they again were confronted by large numbers of Indians, and Walker, after efforts to pacify them failed, again gave his men the order to attack. This time, fourteen Indians died. The expedition continued up the Humboldt and reunited with Bonneville camped on the Bear River in July.

In Irving's version of the reunion, Walker's account of his expedition left Bonneville "so deeply grieved by the failure of his plans, and so indignant at the atrocities related to him, that he turned, with disgust and horror, from the narrators . . . The failure of the expedition was a blow to his pride, and still a greater blow to his purse. The Great Salt Lake still remained unexplored. . . ." Irving added that Bonneville sent Walker back to St. Louis in disgrace, but Leonard, as usual, weighed in with a different version: He reported that the two remained partners, with Bonneville heading off to the Columbia River and Walker to the Missouri for the fall hunt. "After the usual ceremony of parting on such occasions," Leonard wrote, "which is performed by each one affectionately shaking hands all round—we separated, each division taking off in a separate direction."*

Walker did not bring many furs to his reunion with Bonneville; instead the importance of the expedition lies in the view that he gave other Americans, as historian William H. Goetzmann has put it, "of California as a land of abundance that was potentially the province of the American settler." In his account, Zenas Leonard, Walker's faithful scribe, put into words the sentiments of many Americans, who were just beginning to learn about the lands the explorers and mountain men found west of the Continental Divide:

---

* Leonard's account, *Narrative of the Adventures of Zenas Leonard,* was published in 1839, two years after Irving's book, and might have been as biased in Walker's favor as Irving's book was in Bonneville's.

Much of this vast waste of territory belongs to the Republic of the United States.* What a theme to contemplate its settlement and civilization. Will the jurisdiction of the federal government ever succeed in civilizing the thousands of savages now roaming over these plains and her hardy free-born population here plant their homes, build their towns and cities, and say here shall the arts and sciences of civilization take root and flourish? . . . But this is left undone by the government, and will only be seen when too late to apply the remedy. The Spaniards are making inroads on the south—the Russians are encroaching with impunity along the sea-shore to the north, and further northeast the British are pushing their stations into the very heart of our territory, which even at this day more resemble military forts to resist invasion than trading stations. Our government should be vigilant. She should assert her claim by taking possession of the whole territory as soon as possible—for we have good reason to suppose that the territory west of the mountains will some day be equally as important to a nation as that on the east.

* Not a true statement; Mexico did not cede the Great Basin and California to the United States until the Treaty of Guadalupe Hidalgo was signed in 1848, ending the Mexican War.

Chapter Five

"WEST, EVER WEST"

A fter leaving the employ of Bonneville, Walker traveled throughout the Great Basin as an independent trapper. During this time, the latter half of the 1830s, the fur trade was in a serious and permanent decline. Throughout the decade the price of beaver pelts fell steadily—from four to six dollars a pound in the early years to one or two dollars a pound at the end. The main cause was fashion: Beaver hats were out; hats made from silk brought from the Orient were the popular new style. At the same time, the beaver were disappearing, a depletion due to over-trapping and the beaver's low birth rate. Greed also helped end the fur trade. In 1834, the debt-ridden Rocky Mountain Fur Company was squeezed out of business by one of its partners. The surviving American Fur Company held the last rendezvous on the Green River in 1840. By then no more than one hundred trappers remained in the mountains; early in the previous decade, there had been close to six hundred of them.*

But there was a need for the mountain men and their hard-learned skills in the 1840s, an era that was marked, William Goetzmann writes, by "the whole massive impulse that started the caravans of white topped wagons on the trail to Oregon and California and a hundred other places in the American West." The emigrants or overlanders who made the trip in the 1840s, particularly those who crossed the Great Basin to California, were a courageous and adventuresome lot. They were also green, inexperienced in the way of the wilderness, disorganized, quarrelsome, prone to panic, unreasonably afraid of Indians, often too young or too old for the rigors of the overland trail, and desperately in need of experienced leadership. And it was guidance, experience, and knowledge acquired from years in the wilderness that the ex-trappers could provide.

Many names from the fur trade appear again in the pioneer era—Jim Bridger, Caleb Greenwood, Joseph Walker, Thomas Fitzpatrick, James Clyman, among many others. Accounts by those trappers who had actually been to Oregon and California also inspired would-be settlers to make the trip. In 1840, for example, a young schoolteacher in Kansas Territory named John Bidwell was so moved by the stories of a well-traveled mountain man, Antoine Roubidoux, that he organized the first overland trip through the Great Basin to California. Bidwell later recalled Roubidoux's words:

> His description of California was in the superlative degree favorable, so much that I resolved if possible to see that wonderful land, . . . Roubideaux described it as one of perennial spring and boundless fertility, and laid stress on the countless thousands of wild horses and cattle. . . . He said that the Spanish authorities were most friendly, and that the people

---

* The surest sign that the heyday of the fur trade was over came in 1834, when shrewd John Jacob Astor read the handwriting on the wall and got out of the business.

were the most hospitable on the globe; that you could travel all over California and it would cost nothing for horses or food. Even the Indians were friendly. His description of the country made it seem like a Paradise.

The sixty-nine-person wagon train that Bidwell put together left Sapling Grove, Missouri, in May 1841, under the leadership of John B. Bartleson, an odious man who joined the company on the condition he be elected captain; the company agreed to his demand because it did not want to lose the eight hired men who came with him. As the Bartleson-Bidwell party set out, Bidwell wrote, "Our ignorance of the route was complete. We knew that California lay west, that was the extent of our knowledge."* Fortunately it was not long on the trail when it joined a party led by mountain man Thomas Fitzpatrick, who was guiding the Jesuit missionary Father Pierre Jean de Smet to the Pacific Northwest. Bidwell later concluded: "It was well we did [meet Fitzpatrick] for otherwise probably not one of us would ever have reached California. . . ."

Fitzpatrick got the Bidwell-Bartleson party as far as Soda Springs, located where the Bear River makes its north-south bend in present-day southern Idaho. There half of the pioneers, Bidwell wrote, "becoming discouraged, now decided not to venture without path or guide into unknown and trackless regions toward California . . ." and went on with Fitzpatrick to Oregon. The others, Bidwell and Bartleson among them, "remained firm, refusing to be diverted from our original purpose of going direct to California." The two groups parted company on August 11, 1841; Fitzpatrick's advice must have been disquieting, it was so vague: "Find the Mary's [Humboldt River], follow it to its end, then push west, ever west."

Now on its own, without a mountain man to guide it, the Bidwell party skirted the northern end of the Great Salt Lake and

---

* Some of the maps Bidwell consulted showed a long narrow lake in the vicinity of Great Salt Lake "with two outlets, both running into the Pacific Ocean, either apparently larger than the Mississippi River." He was also advised that he could make canoes to float down one of those rivers to the Pacific.

Pioneers

Donner Party Route

Fort Vancouver

OREGON TRAIL

Malheur River

Ft. Boise

Snake River

Ft. Hall

South Pass

OREGON TRAIL

Ft. Laramie

Platte River

CALIFORNIA TRAIL

Bear River

Great Salt Lake

Ft. Bridger

Ft. Redding

Humboldt River

Weber Canyon

Donner Pass

HASTINGS CUTOFF

Sacramento R.

Ft. Sutter

San Francisco

Sevier River

Colorado River

Green River

Moab

Dolores River

Monterey

Taos

Santa Fe

Albuquerque

Pacific Ocean

Mojave R.

Los Angeles

0   100   300

Scale of Miles

San Diego

Colorado River

Gila River

Jeffrey L. Ward 1997

headed west. Crossing the desert, its members displayed grit and determination that made them the equal of any party to venture into the Great Basin. After they left the Great Salt Lake, the emigrants were immediately lost and soon had to abandon their wagons in order to survive the brutal stretch of desert to the Humboldt River. Once they found the Humboldt, the way was easier, but there were still crises. On October 7, Bartleson and his men deserted the rest of the group in an effort to get across the mountains before winter. The rest continued on at a slower pace, and by the time they reached the Walker River, Bartleson and company were back. They had not found a pass across the mountains, he reported, and it must have given the others satisfaction to see him and his men "crest-fallen and weak with dysentery brought on by pine nuts and fresh fish given them by the natives."

As they started into the mountains, Bidwell wrote, "a frightful prospect opened before us: naked mountains whose summits still retained the snows perhaps of a thousand years. The winds roared—but in the deep dank gulf which yawned on every side, profound solitude seemed to reign." From the Walker River, the party crossed the Sierra Nevada by way of Sonora Pass, followed the Stanislaus River downstream, and came into the valley near present-day Sonora. The Bidwell-Bartleson company was half-starved when it reached California, but it was lucky: No one had died on the trek. They made history by being the first party of emigrants to cross the Great Basin and the Sierra Nevada. The only other non-Indians to make such a crossing—Jedediah Smith in 1826 and Joseph Walker in 1833—were experienced men leading other experienced men. The members of the Bartleson-Bidwell party were all greenhorns. Included among them were Nancy Kelsey and her infant daughter, the first two white females to enter the Great Basin and to cross the Sierra Nevada. Their heroic voyage was an inspiration to other overlanders coming on behind: if Nancy Kelsey and child could do it, they could too.

The emigrants continued coming; in 1843 nearly a thousand overlanders came across the country, but most of these skirted the Great Basin and ended up in Oregon. The exception was a party organized by Joseph Chiles, a member of the Bidwell-Bartleson party, who had returned to Missouri to organize another expedition. Chiles had the good fortune to retain Joseph Walker as a pilot, but even with this veteran to lead them, the fifty-person group was dangerously short of food when it reached Fort Hall, a Hudson's Bay Company post on the Snake River.* In des-

---

* Fort Hall, an important way station on the Oregon Trail, was built in 1834 by the Boston ice merchant Nathaniel J. Wyeth, whose efforts to establish a fur

peration, the leader and the pilot split up. Chiles took thirteen men on horseback in a dash ahead along the Snake in an attempt to get supplies; Walker with the remaining families and wagons veered southward into the Great Basin to the Humboldt River. When Chiles did not show up with provisions, Walker continued on—to the Humboldt Sink, past Walker Lake, and into the Great Basin's Owens Valley. Here, on the eastern edge of California, he abandoned his wagons to ease the passage over the Sierra Nevada. He crossed Walker Pass in early December, just days before a blizzard closed it. He had cut it close, but even more important, he had succeeded in bringing families across the Great Basin into California.

Walker's ultimate fate was unknown when the group led by Elisha Stevens, a former hunter and trapper and "probably the ugliest man ever to cross the plains," left Council Bluffs on May 18, 1844.* The large, well-prepared party included several large family groups, a doctor, a blacksmith, a gunsmith, and veterans of the fur trade, including the indestructible Caleb Greenwood, then eighty-one years old.† After an uneventful crossing to Fort Hall, Stevens followed Walker's trail to the Humboldt Sink, then crossed fifty miles of desert to where a river flowed out of the Sierra Nevada, which they named the Truckee after the Indian who told them about the river by drawing a map in the desert sand.

———

trading company and other enterprises in the Oregon country all failed. Wyeth sold the post to the Hudson's Bay Company in 1836. Wyeth brought the first scientists and missionaries to Oregon, and his efforts helped to bring attention to the region.

* In his popular history, *Men to Match My Mountains*, Irving Stone continued: "He [Stevens] is described by members of the party as courteous but silent to the point of taciturnity, a lean turkey-necked man with a long, narrow, misshapened head and a huge beaked nose which looked like a caricature of an eagle."

† Greenwood remained celibate until he was sixty-three years old, then married a woman who was half Indian and sired five children.

At first, following the river west into the mountains was easy going with plenty of grass and game, but the way soon turned into canyon so narrow that the emigrants had to take the wagons right up the rocky riverbed. When they reached a lake with good pasturage, the settlers could see the summit in the distance, but to navigate a sheer cliff blocking the way, they had to lead their animals up a narrow ledge and then, with the animals pulling from above, wrestle the wagons up the narrow incline. Once they were past this obstacle, the worst was over. An advance party reached Sutter's Fort in mid-December; the rest wintered over safely on the Yuba River and descended into the valley when the snows abated. Whereas the Bartleson-Bidwell party left their wagons in the Salt Lake Desert and the Chiles-Walker company abandoned theirs on the western edge of the Great Basin, the Stevens group was the first to bring the vehicles over the mountains. And the Truckee River route, via what would soon be known as Donner Pass, soon became the preferred trail to California.

"Put Your Spurs to Your Mules . . ."

Stevens pioneered a direct route across the Sierra Nevada; still the flow of emigrants to California was a mere trickle compared to the numbers—three thousand in 1845—who traveled the Fort Hall route into Oregon the same year. The next year only three hundred settlers reached California, but, wrote western historian Ray Allen Billington, "the new arrivals more than made up in drama what they lacked in numbers." Most of the drama could be attributed, directly and indirectly, to one man, Lansford W. Hastings, an opportunistic former lawyer and California booster who, in 1845, published his *Emigrants' Guide to Oregon and California*.

Hastings had grandiose dreams of becoming a kingpin in California, and he schemed about ways of establishing a base of support by attracting settlers to the land. Including Oregon in the title of his book was deceptive: its true purpose was to divert Oregon-bound emigrants to California. His book filled a void; there were very few sources of information on the Far West. Hastings contended that emigrant trains could shorten the journey to California to 120 days by leaving the Oregon Trail at Fort Bridger and "thence bearing southwest, to the Salt Lake; and thence continuing down to the Bay of San Francisco." The route did look shorter on a map. Following it, however, involved grappling with both the Wasatch Mountains and the Great Salt Desert, two formidable obstacles that Hastings, when he wrote the book, had never seen.

In the spring of 1846 Hastings did use his cutoff to go from California to Fort Bridger, but he was traveling light, on horseback, and was accompanied by two experienced mountain men, James Clyman, one of Ashley's enterprising young men and a cohort of Jedediah Smith, and the durable Caleb Greenwood. They made it, but Clyman could see that the route would be nearly impassable for wagon trains, and he did his gallant best to persuade emigrants to ignore Hastings and stick to the known trail to California.

Hastings, however, was more persuasive. Despite Clyman's warnings and protests, three emigrant parties took his cutoff. The first was the Bryant-Russell party: nine men riding mules and horses. One of Hastings's employees guided them across the Wasatch to the south end of Great Salt Lake, where he pointed to Pilot Peak across the eighty-mile desert and told them: "Put your spurs to your mules and ride like hell." Under the circumstances—eighty miles of blistering desert to cross—it was good advice, and, riding as advised, the mounted men made the trip in seventeen hours.

The next party over the Hastings Cutoff did not fare as well. Led by George W. Harlan and Samuel C. Young, it consisted of forty wagons and two hundred people, among them the first Mormons to enter the Salt Lake Valley. Hastings himself took them through the Wasatch Range, improvising as he went along. (He had no idea how to get wagons through the mountains, his only trip having been on horseback.) In Weber Canyon, they had to blast their way through rock and winch their wagons up the sides of cliffs. In the Salt Lake Valley, Hastings blithely assured them that the desert they had to cross was only forty miles wide; in actuality, it was twice that. With just enough hay and water for a day and a night, the party made it through to the Humboldt River only by abandoning in the desert thirst-crazed animals and wagons, which their owners later retrieved after they had recuperated on the Humboldt. From there, the Harlan-Young party made it safely to California, but, Billington wrote in *The Far Western Frontier*, "Some say that the blue haze noted on Utah's hills since that day is the last remnant of the curses against Hastings that they scattered along the trail."

"A Nigher Route"

The third and last party to try the Hastings Cutoff in 1846 was the ill-fated Donner-Reed party, whose tragic saga, DeVoto wrote, "has been a favorite story of historians and novelists because it is concentrated, because the horror composes a drama." The company was formed by the Donner brothers, George and Jacob, and their younger friend, James Frazier Reed, a furniture manufacturer in Illinois. Whereas other emigrant parties were lucky, the Donner-Reed party was plagued with misfortune; it was also quarrelsome, disunified, inexperienced, and poorly led. Unfortunately for others, its leaders were affluent men, and the company was slowed down by extra wagons filled with comforts and luxuries that had no place on the trail. There were heroes in the ranks of the Donner party, but the company had trouble coming together for a common purpose; in the end, petty differences became more important than survival.

Bickering on the trail was not unusual; wagon trains were always breaking up and re-forming because of disputes among the emigrants. As DeVoto pointed out, "No part of the tragedy is unique. . . . The Donners were not the only emigrants who disintegrated in panic, and the fact which the public chiefly remembers about them, their cannibalism, was no novelty in the West." This is all true, but they were more than ordinarily unlucky.

The emigrants' way across the plains was slow and onerous,

with quarrels, wagon breakdowns, and illness slowing them down from the start. Just east of Fort Laramie, they met James Clyman, whom Reed had known before. The frontiersman did his best to convince these greenhorns to stick to the established trail that went through Fort Hall. "It is barely possible to get through if you follow it," he told them, "and may be impossible if you don't." This was not what the emigrants wanted to hear. They were travel-weary and running short on supplies and time. Besides, Hastings had written this guidebook.... "There is a nigher route," James Reed told Clyman, "and it is no use to take so much of a roundabout course."*

At Fort Bridger, they discovered that Hastings, who had promised by letter to guide them, had gone ahead with the Harlan-Young party. The fort's proprietor, the veteran trapper Jim Bridger, also recommended the Hastings Cutoff. Certainly he knew better, but he had his reasons: A new shortcut, Sublette's Cutoff, farther east on the Oregon Trail, threatened his business by diverting traffic around his establishment.† After resting four days at Fort Bridger, the party continued on to the head of Weber Canyon. There they found a note from Hastings advising them to wait so he could show them a better route through the mountains. The party waited for eight precious days, then, on their own, struggled their way through the mountains, spending three weeks to go thirty-six miles. They arrived, exhausted and depleted, in the valley south of the Great Salt Lake on September 9.

Again, the only sign of Hastings was another note: "Two days and two nights of hard driving to reach the next grass and water." The dreadful desert crossing took six days and nearly the lives of everyone in the party. Then there was another week spent resting

---

* The Donner-Reed company also met Joseph Walker on the trail but, when he too advised against the Hastings Cutoff, the emigrants dismissed him as "a Missouri Puke," although, biographer Gilbert points out, "probably not to his face."

† Bridger established the fort in 1843. "They [the emigrants], in coming out, are generally well supplied with money," he wrote a friend, "but by the time they get here are in want of all kind of supplies."

and retrieving animals and supplies they had abandoned in the desert.* They reached the Humboldt River on September 30; the few of their companions who had opted for the longer route through Fort Hall had passed this point a month to six weeks earlier.

"Forlorn Hope"

On the trip down the Humboldt, which should have been easy and uneventful, the party continued to disintegrate. In trying to break up a fight, James Reed knifed and killed a man and was banished from the party. Soon afterward, a German named Wolfinger, believed to be carrying a large sum of money, suspiciously disappeared while lagging behind the rest; the two men with him reported Indians had killed him. At Truckee Meadows at the foot of the Sierra Nevada, the party was reinforced with supplies, then, confident they were ahead of the snows, rested for four days. An advance party made it to the summit but found it blocked with snow. Then an eight-day blizzard made it clear to them that they were stranded on the Great Basin side of the Sierras for the winter.

On December 16—four men had died by then—a little band known as the "Forlorn Hope," comprised of eight men, five women, and two Indian guides, started across the summit to get help. Their story is one of extraordinary suffering and terror. Cannibalism, the element for which their story is most remembered, was a measure of their desperation. On Christmas day, their food gone, they drew lots to select one to be killed for food, but no one wanted to kill the loser. Two days later, four people died and their flesh was roasted and eaten. The survivors, who could not bear to look at each other, wept as they ate. Later on the trail, the two Indians, who had refused to eat human flesh, weak-

* The Donner party's frequent delays on the trail are important to the outcome of their story; if they had been only a few days faster, they would have made it over the Sierra Nevada before the first blizzard.

ened and were shot and eaten. Finally, on January 10, 1847, the survivors staggered into an Indian village.

The relief parties found the survivors at the Donner Lake camp in deplorable shape. They had come so close to starvation that they too had resorted to cannibalism. Among those the rescuers found at Donner Lake was Tamsen Donner and her three daughters.* Tamsen refused to go on with the relief party; instead she left her daughters in their hands and went back to the camp at Alder Creek where her husband, George, lay dying. She too was dead by the time another party of rescuers reached her.

Only forty-five—just over half—of the eighty-nine emigrants who left Fort Bridger with the Donner-Reed party made it to California. The story endures not because of the fatalities or the cannibalism, but because it displays the whole range of human conduct—from base to exalted. The story also challenges modern-day readers to consider how they would react in similar circumstances, particularly when confronted with the dreadful prospect of consuming human flesh to save human life, a choice that is anything but morally clear in the context of the Donner story. The Donner tragedy tends to drive writers to rhetorical excess, as they try to find meaning in a story that might illustrate only what happens when bad luck coincides with human frailty. Irving Stone's attempt to put the Donner story in focus had eloquence, if nothing else:

> The Donner Party has mystical meaning in the settlement of the Far West; it is Greek tragedy, moving one to pity and terror, the bloodletting *par excellence*; the ultimate cup of grief

---

* Tamsen Donner was one of the few members of the party who doubted Hastings and his cutoff. Jesse Thornton, an Oregon-bound traveler who met the Donner party on the trail, observed that they "were generally much elated and in fine spirits, with the prospect of a better and nearer road to . . . their destination," but that "Mrs. George Donner was . . . an exception. She was gloomy, sad, and dispirited, in view of the fact that her husband and others could think for a moment of leaving the old road and confide in the statement of a man of whom they knew nothing but who was probably some selfish adventurer."

into which all of the tears avoided by former parties are shed. . . . It is the ultimate tragedy without which no distant frontier can be conquered; and which gives a structural base of blood and bone and suffering and sacrifice and, in a sense, of redemption to a new people creating a new life in a new world.

MORE TRAGEDY ON THE TRAIL

There would be many more deaths on the way west, but those individuals—and the routine and mundane ways that they died—are largely forgotten. Accurate figures are hard to come by, but the estimates, which historians revised time and time again, put the number of deaths between 1842 and 1859 at ten thousand, although figures as high as thirty thousand have been put forward. Pioneering was dangerous work, particularly for the inexperienced, which most emigrants were, but the question remains whether the death rate among them was higher than among the population at large. One thing is certain, wrote John D. Unruh, Jr., in his intriguing *Plains Across*: "The actual dangers of the overland venture have been considerably misrepresented by the mythmakers' overemphasis on Indian treachery." Fewer than four hundred emigrants, he reported, were killed by Indians.

Nine out of ten emigrants who died succumbed to disease, particularly cholera, and most of those died on the early stages of the overland trail, before they reached Fort Laramie. There were all sorts of accidents on the trail. Many involved children and were the result of the mishandling of wagons and livestock. Of all the accidents, deaths by drowning occurred most often. The fording of the Platte River near Fort Laramie was particularly treacherous. Nearer the Great Basin was the Green River; at least thirty-seven people drowned at that crossing in 1850.

Another hazard was firearms. The nervous emigrants went forth heavily armed and untutored in the use of weapons. Several deaths occurred from accidental firings when immigrants tried to pick up or take a loaded gun from a wagon muzzle first. Observing a Mormon party on the Mormon Trail, the English writer Sir Richard Burton in his enduring *City of the Saints* observed: "The greater part of the men were armed, but their weapons were far more dangerous to themselves and their fellows than to the enemy. There is not on earth a race of men more ignorant of arms as a rule than the lower grades of English; becoming an immigrant, the mechanic hears that it may be necessary to beat off Indians, so he buys the first old fire-arm he sees, and probably does damage with it."

Within the Great Basin, the Humboldt River became a highway that took increasing numbers of lives. The rich grasses that Hastings described were usually consumed by the livestock of the first parties to pass through each year. Indians along the Humboldt, the despised Diggers, grew increasingly hostile, probably because many overlanders took to shooting them on sight. By 1857, the situation had become so serious that Brigham Young complained, "It is hard to make an Indian believe that the whites are their friends, and the Great Father wishes to do them good, when, perhaps, the very next party which crosses their path shoots them down like wolves."

Banditry also became a problem on the trail, particularly along the Humboldt River. Often the culprits were whites disguised as Indians or Indians conspiring with white traders to rob the emigrants of their valuables. The attacks inspired an Army officer to submit an ironic report of "a tribe of Indians who have blue eyes and light hair, who wear whiskers, and speak good English." On August 6, 1857, a party of ten emigrants was attacked along the Humboldt by so-called Indians who killed six, including a two-year-old child, and scalped one, a plucky woman known only as Mrs. Holloway, who later retrieved her missing hair and had a wig made out of it.*

---

* This bizarre detail and many other fascinating accounts of the overland trail are found in John D. Unruh's *Plains Across: The Overland Emigrants and the Trans-Mississippi West, 1840–1860* (1979).

Another overland tragedy occurred within the Great Basin in 1849. Like the misfortune that plagued the Donner party, this disaster was also the result of misjudgment, inexperience, incohesiveness among the emigrants, and a willingness to take uncalculable risks by people in a hurry. The incident also gave a name to one of the Great Basin's most formidable stretches of desert, Death Valley.

The emigrants who lost their lives in Death Valley were on their way to California along a route that had opened up after the Mormons established themselves in the Great Basin in 1847 and that went southwest from Salt Lake City to California after joining the Old Spanish Trail in southern Utah. The route was appealing to gold rushers who arrived too late in the season to take the more northerly route along the Humboldt and across the snowy Sierra Nevada. So, in October 1849, the owners of one hundred emigrant wagons gathered in Provo, a new Mormon community sixty miles south of Salt Lake City, for the southwesterly journey. Their leader was a Mormon packer named Jefferson Hunt, who was paid ten dollars per wagon to take the contingent to California.

Although wagons had never been taken over the route before, Hunt organized the group in efficient Mormon fashion, and the trip was proceeding uneventfully until one of the packers, named O. K. Smith, came up with a map that showed a shortcut over Walker's Pass. Smith claimed that the route would save them five hundred miles of travel and bring them to the California gold mines in just twenty days. Hunt advised against the shortcut, but only seven wagons opted to proceed on with him as planned. They reached California just before Christmas.

Of those who headed off on the shortcut, most—over seventy wagons—soon changed their minds and turned back to the Old Spanish Trail and followed Hunt to California. The eighty-five people who were left proceeded blindly on, and seven of them died before they blundered out of the desert. They spent four months of incredible suffering to reach California on a shortcut that was supposed to take only twenty days.

In September 1857, another tragedy of the overland trail occurred in southwestern Utah, on the very edge of the Great Basin. There, in a grassy clearing 120 emigrants from Arkansas were massacred in cold blood by a band of Mormons and Indians, who had persuaded their victims to lay down their arms. Only 17 very young children were spared. The Mountain Meadows Massacre, as it is called, occurred at a time of great tension in Utah and was a prelude to the invasion of Utah by federal Army troops in 1858. (Both the massacre and the invasion, the so-called Mormon—or Utah—War, are discussed in chapter 11.)

At the time, the slaughter was blamed on the Indians and mostly covered up. And so it remained, a half-hidden secret, until 1950. In that year a courageous amateur historian, Juanita Brooks, published a book on the Mountain Meadows Massacre that spelled out Mormon responsibility for and participation in the bloody event, including that of her own grandfather. The publication forced Mormons to acknowledge their ancestors' responsibility for the crime and started a process of reconciliation that culminated in 1990 when descendents of both sides came together in an emotional ceremony at Mountain Meadows. There a descendent of one of the survivors from Arkansas read a passage from the Book of Mormon: "I, the Lord, will forgive whom I will forgive. But of you it is required to forgive all men"; and together the Mormons and Arkansans dedicated a memorial at the site.

Chapter Six

FRÉMONT: UNDERSTANDING

THE GREAT BASIN

In American history, there are few characters as interesting, as controversial, or as enigmatic as John Charles Frémont. Frémont made his mark as an explorer of the West, but in his lifetime he played in many arenas. On the trail during his exploring days, he was at once a leader, scientist, soldier, and writer; his reports of his expeditions were best-sellers in their day and are still among the best and most readable descriptions of the territory he traveled through, including the Great Basin. In the public realm, he was a U. S. senator, a Civil War general, a presidential candidate, and a governor of the Arizona Territory.* As an entrepreneur, he took a fortune out of a mine in California, but, in the end, he failed, not

* Frémont ran for president on the ticket of the newly formed Republican Party in 1856. In *Epic of America* (1931), James Truslow Adams wrote: "Frémont, the inadequate candidate of the new party, carried most of the North and West but Buchanan, Democrat, carried the South and won the election."

having a good head for business. He brought zeal to everything he did, and he had a genius for self-promotion, which backfired on him; his enemies made much of the fact that his exploits were never as heroic or extraordinary as he made them out to be in his reports and writings.

In his day, Frémont was known as the "Pathfinder," but as his biographer Allan Nevins first observed, he is better described as a "Pathmarker," since wherever he went, with a few notable exceptions, others had been before. Nonetheless, his achievements were many: He was the first to map and describe the unknown country of the West, and, through his maps and writings, he gave the nation its first accurate idea of what lay between South Pass and the Pacific Ocean. He was also the first to understand and communicate how the geography of this region was like a "Great Basin"—he was the first to use that descriptive term—into which the region's rivers and streams flowed. During his second expedition of 1843–1844, he traipsed around the edge of the Great Basin, weaving back and forth, in and out of its boundaries, until he came to understand that none of the Great Basin's rivers had an outlet to the sea, that they all ended in salty lakes or desert sinks, and that there was no Buenaventura or any other river running from the Rocky Mountains or the Great Salt Lake to the Pacific Ocean.

Unlike the mountain men who had gone before him, Frémont was able to understand and interpret what he was seeing. His mentors had taught him, Nevins wrote, "how to make an expedition into a new country scientifically profitable—to take accurate astronomical observations at every halt, record topography, observe botany, soils, and minerals, and draught careful sketch maps." Frémont also benefited from the presence of his melancholy German cartographer, Charles Preuss, whose masterful maps and sketches contributed greatly to the popular reports. There are many accounts of how Frémont, while his men slept, stayed up through the night to record his stellar observations.

In his travels, Frémont relied heavily on the former mountain men and trappers he hired to guide and accompany his expeditions. Etienne Provost, one of the first white trappers to penetrate the Great Basin, was an early mentor. Christopher "Kit" Carson, who was with Frémont on two expeditions through the Great Basin, owes his fame to the national exposure Frémont gave him in his writings.* Frémont also depended on the judgment and common sense of Thomas "Broken Hand" Fitzpatrick, whose name keeps cropping up in the Great Basin story—as one of Ashley's young trappers, an associate of Jedediah Smith, and the man who guided the Bidwell-Bartleson party as far as Idaho. Joseph Walker, trailblazer along the Humboldt, also contributed his expertise to Frémont's Great Basin explorations. The men who served with him frequently disagreed—just as historians do today—on what kind of man Frémont was. Walker ended up despising the Pathfinder, calling him in an interview "morally and physically the most complete coward I ever knew."

Carson, by contrast, was loyal to the end. In 1856, the year Frémont ran for president, Carson paid him this tribute:

> I was with Frémont from 1842 to 1847. The hardships through which we passed, I find it impossible to describe, and the credit which he deserves I am incapable to do him justice in writing. . . . I have heard that he is enormously rich. I wish to God that he may be worth ten times as much more. All that he has or may ever receive, he deserves. I can never forget his treatment of me while in his employ and how cheerfully he suffered with his men when undergoing the severest of hardships.

Born poor and illegitimate in Savannah, Georgia, Frémont overcame the circumstances of his birth to lead a young man's charmed life. A turning point came in 1838, when, through a

---

* Historian Harvey Carter described Carson as "a typical but undistinguished trapper . . . singled out by adventitious circumstances." Certainly it seems unfair that Carson is so much better known than the great Jedediah Smith.

friendship with South Carolina's Joel Poinsett,* secretary of war under Martin Van Buren, he was commissioned as a second lieutenant in the newly formed United States Corps of Topological Engineers and was assigned to a reconnaissance party that took him through the territory between the upper Mississippi and Missouri Rivers. The party was headed by the French scientist Joseph N. Nicollet, who trained Frémont in surveying and mapmaking. On October 19, 1841, Frémont eloped with seventeen-year-old Jessie Benton, a lively, intelligent, and headstrong young woman, who was the daughter of the powerful senator from Missouri, Thomas Hart Benton. Benton was an ardent advocate of western expansion, and once his opposition to the marriage faded, he aggressively supported his new son-in-law's expeditions. Frémont, in turn, became an instrument of his father-in-law's expansionist policies.

Frémont led five western expeditions. The first, primarily a survey of the Platte River, which was becoming one of the main thoroughfares to the West, eventually took him over South Pass to the Green River but stopped short of the Great Basin.† His second expedition, which took him around the Great Basin, left Kaw Landing (Kansas City) on May 29, 1843, and headed up the northern fork of the Kansas River to the Sweetwater and on to South Pass. Ostensibly his mission was to complete his survey of the Oregon Trail "so as to give a connected survey of the interior of our continent." Frémont took along a cart loaded with scientific equipment, and he was again accompanied by his cartographer, Charles Preuss. But his party had a military look to it; his thirty-nine men were armed with carbines and two mules were

---

* Poinsett was also known, in Frémont's words, "by the Scarlett Poinsettia which he contributed to botany."

† Once in the Rockies, Frémont climbed what he wrongly claimed was the highest peak in the range. His ascent of Frémont Peak with a sword in one hand and a flag in the other—"I sprang upon the summit and another step would have precipitated me into an immense snowfield five hundred feet below"—is an illustration of how Frémont could dramatize a fairly routine event.

needed to pull a twelve-pound howitzer. Historians suspect that Senator Benton secretly encouraged him to make a military reconnaissance of the West, particularly California.

Frémont's second expedition reached South Pass—"already traversed by several different roads"—on August 13, 1843. A barometric reading put the elevation of the pass at 7,490 feet. The pass's "importance," Frémont wrote, "as the great gate through which commerce and travelling may hereafter pass between the valley of the Mississippi and the north Pacific, justifies a precise notice of its locality and distance from leading points,* in addition to this statement of its elevation."

From South Pass, the expedition moved to the Green River and on to the Great Basin. In the Bear River Valley, they came upon an encampment of emigrants, resting on the road, where the sight of women cooking and children playing "had an air of quiet security and civilized comfort that made a rare sight to the traveller in such a remote wilderness." As they approached the Great Salt Lake, Frémont began to look forward to seeing this "salient point among the remarkable geographic features of the country, and around which the vague and superstitious accounts of the trappers had thrown a delightful obscurity, which we anticipated pleasure in dispelling." While the lake was known to have "no visible outlet," many of his trappers believed, Frémont wrote with obvious delight, "that somewhere on its surface was a terrible whirlpool, through which its waters found their way to the ocean by some subterranean communication."

"Truly a Bucolic Region"

Frémont and his men caught their first view of the Great Salt Lake from a distant mountain on September 6. The sight moved Frémont to eloquence:

---

* Frémont calculated that "[South Pass] may be assumed to be about half way between the Mississippi and the Pacific ocean, on the common travelling route."

This time we reached the butte without any difficulty, and, ascending to the summit, immediately at our feet beheld the object of our anxious search—the waters of the Inland Sea stretching in still and solitary grandeur far beyond the limit of our vision. It was one of the great points of the exploration; and as we looked eagerly over the lake in the first emotions of excited pleasure, I am doubtful if the followers of Balboa felt more enthusiasm when, from the heights of the Andes, they saw for the first time the great Western Ocean. It was certainly a magnificent object, and a noble terminus to this part of our expedition; and to travellers so long shut up among mountain ranges a sudden view over the expanse of silent waters had in it something sublime.

The passage is vintage Frémont—expansive, dramatic, brimming with enthusiasm, and self-serving; trappers had been visiting the Great Salt Lake for nearly twenty years, but Fremont conveys the impression that he, Balboa-like, made the discovery himself. Two days later, Frémont and four others floated down to the lake in the inflatable rubber boat they carried with them. Frémont had earlier referred to "the idea of undefined danger with which the lake was generally associated," and early on September 9, the day they launched the boat on the lake, he noted that his men "looked very gloomy this morning." The gloom might have been related to the worrisome discovery that their boat was poorly made and that one man had to work the bellows constantly to keep it filled with air. As they set off, there was little danger: the lake was so shallow the men could touch the bottom with their paddles. But, Frémont noted, "gradually, as the water deepened, we became more still in our frail batteau of gum cloth distended with air, and with pasted seams."

After surviving some rough water, the party reached an island of salt-encrusted cliffs and rocks. Climbing to the highest point, a peak eight hundred feet above the water, the men "searched for some indications of a communication with other bodies of water, or the entrance of other rivers; but the distance was so great that we could make out nothing with certainty." They slept that night in shelters made of driftwood to the sound of "the roar of an ocean surf; and the strangeness of our situation, and the excitement we felt in the associated interests of the place, made this one of the most interesting nights I remember during our long expedition." Still, Frémont was disappointed in the aridity and lack of life on the island, and so he named it Disappointment Island.*

Back safely on shore, Frémont, on September 11, boiled down five gallons of lake water, which "yielded fourteen pints of a very fine-grained and very white salt, of which the whole lake may be regarded as a saturated solution." With their food in short supply, they dined on roots they had learned about from the local Indians, but, said Frémont, "a cup of good coffee still distinguished us from our *Digger* acquaintances." The expedition left the Great Basin headed for Fort Hall by way of the Bear River.

Frémont's visit to a valley that many had been to before him was nothing extraordinary; his description of it, however, had an impact that was truly historic. Like Hastings's *Emigrants' Guide*, published in 1845, Frémont's *Report* on his second expedition of 1843–1844 went out to a country that was eager for any information about the Far West. Among those who read the report with great interest were the Mormon leader Brigham Young and other ranking members of the Church of Jesus Christ of Latter-day Saints. The Mormons, then beleaguered in Nauvoo, Illinois, were looking for an isolated place to settle, where they would be safe away from their enemies, and Frémont's *Report* helped steer them to the Great Basin.† As Frémont described it, a would-be settler could hardly hope for more:

---

* The government surveyor of the Salt Lake Valley, Howard Stansbury, renamed it Frémont Island in 1850 "in honor of him who first set foot upon its shore."

† Brigham Young later accused Frémont of misrepresenting the region as a fertile valley. F. S. Dellenbaugh in his 1913 biography, *Frémont and '49*, considered the charge: "The answer to this is the aspect of Salt Lake Valley today: a rich garden in the midst of the mountains."

The bottoms are extensive; water excellent; timber sufficient; the soil good, and well adapted to the grains and grasses suited to such an elevated region. A military post, and a civilized settlement, would be of great value here; and cattle and horses would do well where grass and salt so much abound. The lake will furnish exhaustless supplies of salt. All the mountain sides here are covered with a valuable nutritious grass, called bunch grass, from the form in which it grows, which has a second growth in the fall. The beasts of the Indians were fat upon it; our own found it a good subsistence; and its quality will sustain any amount of cattle, and make this truly a bucolic region.

At Fort Hall, where he arrived on September 18, Frémont sent back "all who were not ready to face the rigors of steady midwinter exploration . . ." and, with the remaining men, set off down the Snake River Valley. Four days out of Fort Hall, they took a wrong turn down a wagon road before they realized it was not the Oregon Trail but the route taken by Joseph Walker, when he guided the party formed by Chiles toward the Humboldt. As Frémont proceeded on to Fort Boise, he described "a melancholy and strange-looking country—one of fracture, and violence, and fire." By November 5, the party was at The Dalles, the narrow gorge on the Columbia River, and from there, Frémont proceeded on with three others to Fort Vancouver, where he filled the letter of his mission by completing his survey of the Oregon Trail.* Two weeks later, Frémont was back at the The Dalles, ready to proceed south and reenter the Great Basin.

---

* Frémont's orders from the War Department instructed him to connect his reconnaissance "with the surveys of Commander Wilkes on the coast of the Pacific Ocean, so as to give a connected survey of the interior of our continent." Lieutenant Charles Wilkes had explored the Columbia River and much of the west coast of the continent during the last leg of his 1838–1842 worldwide naval exploring expedition.

INTRODUCING THE GREAT BASIN

It was on the stretch between Fort Boise and The Dalles that Frémont, in his journal entry for October 13, introduced the Great Basin, "a term which I apply to the intermediate region between the Rocky mountains and the next range, containing many lakes, with their own system of rivers and creeks, (of which the Great Salt is the principal,) and which have no connexion with the ocean, or the great rivers which flow into it."* The term appears again on November 18, as Frémont, now back in the The Dalles, explained, instead of simply following the Oregon Trail home, "our homeward journey, which, though homeward, contemplated a new route, a great circuit to the south and southeast, the exploration of the Great Basin between the Rocky mountains and the *Sierra Nevada*."

In the same entry, November 18, Frémont wrote that an objective of his swing through the Great Basin was the discovery of "the reputed *Buenaventura* river, which has had a place on so many maps, and countenanced the belief of the existence of a great river flowing from the Rocky mountains to the bay of San Francisco." Frémont was being inconsistent here: If the rivers of the Great Basin had "no connexion with the ocean," there could not be a river flowing through it from the Rockies to the Pacific. Frémont probably understood the discrepancy in his report but chose to ignore it; several historians have suggested that Frémont never really believed that the Buenaventura existed—none of the earlier explorations in the Great Basin had come across it, and several recent maps, including the one Bonneville published, omitted it entirely. Introducing the Buenaventura into his narrative, however, added a touch of mystery and drama to his report, and, in the end, he could take credit for proving once and for all that the fabled river did not exist.†

* Frémont wrote his *Report* after his return to Washington, so it is unlikely he understood the nature of the Great Basin at this time (October 13).

† In their four-volume *Expeditions of John Charles Frémont*, editors Donald Jackson and Mary Lee Spence recorded their "suspicion that Jessie Benton Fré-

Frémont was not obliged to go on to the Great Basin; in fact, his orders instructed him "to return by the Oregon road"—in other words backtrack along the way he came. Backtracking, however, was not in Frémont's nature, and we do not know what father-in-law Benton expected of him after he had completed the Oregon Trail survey. With twenty-five men, several Indian guides, and more than one hundred mules and horses, Frémont began the push south from The Dalles on November 25 and for the next three weeks moved up the Deschutes River and along the eastern base of the Cascade Range. Frémont had explained to his men that they were heading into uncharted territory but, in his report at least, managed to portray the detour into the Great Basin as the beginning of the homeward journey. As it turned out, the journey was far from half over, and the worst part, an unprecedented winter crossing of the treacherous Sierra Nevada, lay ahead. Still, Frémont was able to write, in the entry dated November 25: "We were all up early, in the excitement of turning towards home."

On December 11, in the vicinity of Klamath Marsh in southern Oregon, Frémont again mentioned the Buenaventura: "Forming agreeably to the best maps in my possession, a connected water line from the Rocky mountains to the Pacific ocean, I felt no other anxiety than to pass safely across the intervening desert to the banks of the Buenaventura, where, in the softer climate of a more southern latitude, our horses might find grass to sustain them, and ourselves be sheltered from the rigors of winter and from the inhospitable desert." After crossing the Klamath watershed, the party, on December 16, was passing through a pine forest in a snowstorm, uncertain of what lay ahead, when, about noon, the men saw clear sky ahead.

> Riding rapidly ahead to this spot we found ourselves on the verge of a vertical and rocky wall of the mountain. At our

---

mont's flair for the dramatic is somehow involved" with the frequent references to the Buenaventura. Frémont's wife, an accomplished writer, collaborated with him on all his reports and memoirs.

feet—more than a thousand feet below—we looked into a green prairie country, in which a beautiful lake, some twenty miles in length, was spread along the foot of the mountains, its shores bordered with green grass. Just then the sun broke out among the clouds, and illuminated the country below, while around us the storm raged fiercely. Not a particle of ice was to be seen on the lake, or snow on its borders, and all was like summer or spring. The glow of the sun in the valley below brightened up our heart with sudden pleasure; and we made the woods ring with joyful shouts to those behind; and gradually, as each came up, he stopped to enjoy the unexpected scene. Shivering on snow three feet deep, and stiffening in a cold north wind, we exclaimed at once that the names of Summer Lake and Winter Ridge should be applied to these two proximate places of such sudden and violent contrast.

"Rock upon Rock"

Never before—or perhaps since—had the sight of the Great Basin been greeted with such enthusiasm. Once they had made the difficult descent into the valley, reality set in, and Frémont acknowledged, "We were now in a country where the scarcity of water and of grass makes travelling dangerous, and great caution was necessary." Following Indian paths, the expedition camped on Christmas Eve on the shore of a lake. They greeted the dawn of the next day by firing the howitzer and named the site Christmas Lake. The following night, "a partial observation" of the stars showed them to be camped "directly on the 42d parallel," the present Oregon-Nevada line, ten miles east of the California border. On January 10, they came upon "a sheet of green water, some twenty miles broad. It broke upon our eyes like the ocean." Frémont named it Pyramid Lake, for a rock rising, they estimated, some six hundred feet above the surface of the lake, which, "from the point we viewed it, presented a pretty exact outline of the great pyramid of Cheops."

On January 18, Frémont, citing the poor condition of his animals—"their feet so much cut up by the rocks, and so many of them lame"—decided "to cross the Sierra Nevada into the valley of the Sacramento, wherever a practical pass could be found." Why Frémont decided to cross the mountains to California, without direct orders to do so, is a historical question not answered by the state of his animals' feet. Historians have pointed out that Frémont could have passed an easy winter, with plenty of game for food and grass for his animals, on one of the rivers flowing out of the Sierra Nevada into the Great Basin. Perhaps Frémont wanted to be the first white man to cross the Sierra Nevada in the dead of winter; maybe he had verbal orders from Benton to make a political and military reconnaissance of California. Or perhaps Frémont and his men just wanted to pass the winter in California's salubrious clime.

But things would get much worse before the group saw sunny California. The snow deepened as the party moved up the Carson River. On January 25, when their Indian guides wore out their moccasins, they put one on a horse and "enjoyed the unusual sight of an Indian who could not ride." The exact route Frémont followed across the mountains is still a matter of speculation; he wrote that a faulty chronometer "will account for the absence of longitudes along this interval of our journey." On January 25, the party abandoned the howitzer amid rocks and snow, but whether this occurred on East Walker River, Mill Creek, or, less likely, Lost Cannon Creek, is uncertain.* By February 2, they had reached the base of peaks they could see looming six or seven thousand feet above them. As they followed a streambed up the mountains, Frémont wrote, "The people were unusually silent; for every man knew that our enterprise was hazardous, and the issue doubtful." Their provisions were now perilously low; the day before they had killed and eaten the dog that had grown fat in their care since they found it in the Bear River Valley.

* In the same entry, Frémont wrote that the howitzer was "of the kind invented by the French for the mountain part of their war in Algiers; and the distance it had come with us proved how well it was adapted to its purpose."

By now the snow was so deep that progress was possible only by breaking a path through it with the horses, and the way was strewn with packs, gear, and equipment that the men abandoned to lighten their load. The Indians who guided them and those they met along the way all agreed that it was impossible to cross the mountains in winter. On February 4, two Indians came into their camp. One of them, an old man, began a loud dirgelike oration to which "there was a singular repetition of phrases and arrangement of words, which rendered his speech striking, and not unmusical":

We had now begun to understand some words, and, with the aid of signs, easily comprehended the old man's simple ideas. "Rock upon rock—rock upon rock—snow upon snow—snow upon snow," said he; "even if you get over the snow, you will not be able to get down from the mountains." He made us a sign of precipices, and showed us how the feet of the horses would slip, and throw them off from the narrow trails which led along their sides. Our Chinook, who comprehended even more readily than ourselves, and believed our situation hopeless, covered his head with his blanket, and began to weep and lament. . . .

Seated around the tree, the fire illuminating the rocks and the tall bolls of the pines round about, and the old Indian haranguing, we presented a group of very serious faces.

"Victorious over the Mountain"

On February 6, Frémont struck out ahead with a small party on snowshoes, and, from a peak, beheld a welcome sight—a snowless valley and, some one hundred miles away, a small mountain, Mt. Diablo, which Carson recognized from an earlier California trip. "It is fifteen years ago since I saw it," Frémont recorded him as saying, "but I am just as sure as if I had seen it yesterday." Even better, the men could see bare ground and grass beckoning thirty miles away, but there were still rugged mountains and snowfields to cross. Four days passed and Frémont noted with discouragement: "We are now 1,000 feet above the level of the South Pass in the Rocky mountains; and still we are not done ascending." The glare of the snow and fatigue was causing snow blindness, and the men had to wear black silk handkerchiefs as veils to save their eyes.

Eight hard days later, Frémont and party reached what he called "the dividing ridge of the Sierra," and, with Preuss, he climbed a peak and had a view of Lake Tahoe. On February 16 they had a sure sign that they had left the Great Basin—"the head water of a little creek, where at last the water found its way to the Pacific." Further reconnoitering satisfied Frémont that "we had struck the stream on which Mr. Sutter lived," a hopeful sign since Sutter's Fort at the confluence of the American and Sacramento Rivers was their destination. By timing how long it took for water to boil, a daily ritual, Frémont determined their elevation at 9,333 feet. Again, he paused in his narrative to reflect on the Great Basin.

This was 2,000 feet higher than the South Pass in the Rocky mountains, and several peaks in view rose several thousand feet still higher. Thus, at the extremity of the continent, and near the coast, the phenomenon was seen of a range of mountains still higher than the great Rocky mountains themselves. This extraordinary fact accounts for the Great Basin, and shows that there must be a system of small lakes and rivers here scattered over a flat country, and which the extended and lofty range of the Sierra Nevada prevents from escaping into the Pacific ocean.*

The next day, Frémont declared the expedition "victorious over the mountain; having only the descent before us." But he added that "this was a case in which the descent was *not* facile." Indeed, February 23 was the most taxing day yet, and soon afterward

---

* Here Frémont got it wrong. The Great Basin, hardly "flat country" as he surmised, is laced with mountain ranges.

two men became delirious "from an extremity of suffering." Riding ahead with a small party, Frémont reached Sutter's Fort on March 6. John Augustus Sutter, the Swiss emigrant with a dubious background who had established a colony of his own in California, received Frémont graciously and the ordeal was over.

Frémont didn't linger in California, where his sudden appearance on Mexican soil made the authorities suspicious of his intentions.* On March 22, Frémont and his men—minus five who opted to stay in California—started south well stocked with provisions and driving a herd of animals "consisting of 130 horses and mules, and about thirty head of cattle." The party probably didn't differ much from other early expeditions, but the picture Frémont included in his report was unusually vivid:

> a civilized Indian, attended by two wild ones from the Sierra; a Chinook from the Columbia; and our own mixture of American, French, German—all armed; four or five languages heard at once; above a hundred horses and mules, half wild; American, Spanish, and Indian dresses and equipments intermingled—such was our composition. . . . In this form we journeyed; looking more like we belonged to Asia than to the United States of America.

It took them three weeks to travel the distance to the pass over the Sierra Nevada.† As they were crossing the mountains, a Spanish-speaking Indian dissuaded Frémont from traveling directly across the Great Basin to the Great Salt Lake over "an

---

* Sutter later wrote the American consul at Monterey that he believed self-preservation—not political or military aims—had driven Frémont and his men to California and that the "starvation and fatigue they had endured rendered them truly deplorable objects."

† Frémont thought he was at Walker Pass, the opening in the mountains that Joseph Walker had pioneered. Certain historians have him crossing at Tehachapi Pass, but editors Jackson and Spence report it was Oak Creek Pass, "five or six air-miles farther south."

arid and barren desert, that had repulsed by its sterility all the attempts of Indians to penetrate it." Instead, Frémont went back to his original plan, which was, once he had crossed the Sierras, to follow the eastern base of the Sierras south to the Old Spanish Trail.

Coming through the pass, Frémont was struck by the contrast between the verdant San Joaquin Valley they left behind and, "within a few miles ride," the seemingly endless desert of the Great Basin "from which the boldest traveller turned away in despair." His route to Utah Lake and out of the Great Basin brought him first south to the Old Spanish Trail a few miles north of El Cajon Pass, then in a northwesterly direction along the Mojave River, which he had difficulty following as it made its erratic way, disappearing and reappearing in the desert. The party passed out of the Great Basin just west of Las Vegas and continued on to the Muddy and Virgin Rivers. On May 12, they reached the summit of a ridge, "which forms here the dividing chain between the waters of the *Rio Virgen*, which goes south to the Colorado, and those of the Sevier river, flowing northwardly, and belonging to the Great Basin."*

Frémont found the grassy meadows a perfect place to recuperate from "the fatigue and exhaustion of a month's suffering in the hot and sterile desert." The desert crossing had not been uneventful. On May 4, the men and animals had to endure "intolerable thirst" for fifty or sixty miles as they plodded along a desert trail strewn with the skeletons of horses; finally near midnight the mules scented water and stampeded on ahead to the banks of the Muddy River.

Indians were also a constant and menacing presence. As they neared Mountain Meadows, a trapper, Baptiste Tabeau, who had gone back alone to retrieve a lame mule, was killed by southern Paiutes. Earlier, while still in the Mojave Desert, they had encountered two survivors—a Mexican man and boy—of an

* The ridge is the site now known as Mountain Meadows in southern Utah, scene of the 1857 massacre described in chapter 11.

Indian attack on the Old Spanish Trail. The Indians had killed the rest of the men, abducted the women, and stolen the large herd of horses the Mexicans were taking to Santa Fe. Carson and Alexis Godey tracked the thieves some fifty miles and, after sneaking up on them, killed two and scattered the rest in a surprise attack. As the two whites were taking scalps, one fallen Indian jumped screaming to his feet, whereupon, Frémont wrote, his men "did what humanity required, and quickly terminated the agonies of the gory savage." Any qualms Frémont might have had about the scalping vanished four days later when they came upon the mutilated bodies of the Mexican horse traders. He wrote: "We rejoiced that Carson and Godey had been able to give so useful a lesson to these American Arabs, who lie in wait to murder and plunder the innocent traveller."

While the Frémont expedition was resting near Mountain Meadows, it was joined by Joseph Walker, the famous guide and mountain man, who had been taking a herd of horse east over the Old Spanish Trail. Because he knew the territory better than any other white man, Walker took over as guide and led the party to the northeast, away from Old Spanish Trail, into "a region of great pastoral promise, abounding with fine streams, the rich bunch grass, soil that could produce wheat, and indigenous flax growing as if it had been sown." Along the way, they met the predatory Ute Indian chief Walker (or Walkara) and his men, whom Frémont described as "robbers of a higher order than those of the desert," and with whom Joseph Walker was personally acquainted. On May 23, the party reached the Sevier River, one of the principal streams of the Great Basin, and, a few days later, arrived at Utah Lake, having "completed an immense circuit of twelve degrees diameter north and south, and ten degrees east and west; and found ourselves, in May, 1844, on the same sheet of water which we had left in September, 1843. The Utah is the southern limb of the Great Salt lake. . . ."*

* Utah Lake, of course, is not "a limb" of Great Salt Lake but a freshwater lake connected to it by thirty miles of the Jordan River. How Frémont came to the

Earlier in the narrative, as he passed over the Sierra Nevada, Frémont destroyed once and for all the myth of the Rio Buenaventura: "No river from the interior does, or can, cross the Sierra Nevada—itself more lofty than the Rocky mountains. . . ." Now, with the expedition at Lake Utah, he paused again "to look back upon our footsteps, and take some brief view of the leading features and general structure of the country we have traversed." Once again he asserted that the Columbia is "the only river which traverses the whole breadth of the country, breaking through all the ranges, and entering the sea, . . . its three forks lead to passes in the mountains; it is therefore the only line of communication between the Pacific and the interior of North America."

Next he turned his attention to "the Great interior Basin, of which I have so often spoken, and the whole form and character of which I was so anxious to ascertain." He wrote that, on this expedition, he had seen the rim of the Great Basin, successively east, north, west, and south. He had listened to American traders and hunters—as well as "Mr. Joseph Walker, who is so well acquainted in those parts"—and their reports added to the certainty that the Great Basin existed. In addition, he wrote, "the structure of the Sierra Nevada range of mountains requires it to be there; and my own observations, confirm it." Frémont's next words made the Great Basin official:

> The existence of the Basin is therefore an established fact in my mind; its extent and contents are yet to be better ascertained. It cannot be less than four or five hundred miles each way, and must lie principally in the Alta California; the demarcation latitude of 42° probably cutting a segment from the north part of the rim.* Of its interior, but

conclusion that the two lakes were one is hard to understand; he did recognize, however, that the difference in water—one salt, the other fresh—presented "a problem which requires to be solved."

* At the time, Alta—or Upper—California included the entire area, belonging to Mexico, between the Colorado River, the forty-second parallel, and the Pacific.

little is known. It is called a *desert*, and from what I saw of it, sterility may be its prominent characteristic; but where there is so much water, there must be some oasis . . . where there is so much snow, there must be streams; and where there is no outlet, there must be lakes to hold the accumulated waters, or sands to swallow them up.

In the next paragraph of the report, Frémont described the people of the Great Basin, "humanity . . . in its most elementary state," especially the despised Indians known as Diggers who lived on roots, seeds, and insects, and dressed in rabbit skins. Frémont concluded:

The whole idea of such a desert, and such a people, is a novelty in our country, and excites Asiatic, not American ideas. Interior basins, with their own systems of lakes and rivers, and often sterile, are common enough in Asia; people still in the elementary state of families, living in deserts, with no other occupation than the mere animal search for food, may still be seen in that ancient quarter of the globe; but in America such things are new and strange, unknown and unsuspected, and discredited when related. But I flatter myself that what is discovered, though not enough to satisfy curiosity, is sufficient to excite it, and that subsequent explorations will complete what has been commenced.

CONTINGENCIES ANTICIPATED AND WEIGHED

Frémont would conduct "subsequent explorations" of the Great Basin; his third expedition, in fact, left Bent's Fort on August 26, 1845, just over a year after the previous one ended. (The second expedition reached St. Louis on August 6, 1844.) But the geopolitical situation had changed drastically in the interim. On March 1, 1845, the same day that Frémont submitted his second expedition report, Congress voted to admit Texas to the Union, thereby making war with Mexico inevitable. In such an atmosphere, the party that Frémont put together, although officially a topographical party, had a warlike cast to it. The men, sixty of them, were well armed and well equipped; Frémont even purchased twelve carbines to be offered as prizes to his men for marksmanship. Military reconnaissance rather than topography or scientific exploration seemed to be the order of the day.

The expedition had among its official goals the completion of "the examination of the Great Salt Lake and its interesting region" as well as a survey of the Sierra Nevada and Cascade Mountains. "All this," Nevin wrote in his biography, "pointed straight toward California," and, as Frémont later explained in his *Memoirs*, the importance of holding California for the United States "was talked over fully during the time of preparation for the third expedition and the contingencies anticipated and weighed." The third expedition included some familiar faces: Joseph Walker as chief guide; Kit Carson, who responded to Frémont's summons in a fashion that the leader characterized as "prompt, self-sacrificing, and true," and Alexis Godey, Carson's fellow Indian scalper in the Mojave Desert incident.

The party followed the White River to the Green, then moved westward over the mountains to the site of present-day Provo on Utah Lake, and from there to the Great Salt Lake. The desert west of the lake was an imposing challenge. "It had never before been crossed by white men," Carson wrote in his autobiography.* "I was often here. Old trappers would speak of the impossibility of crossing, that water could not be found, grass for the animals, there was none. Frémont was bound to cross. Nothing was impossible for him to perform if required in his explorations."

About sixty miles across the desert, Frémont could see a mountain that looked as if it might be the source of water and in two days managed to cross his entire party to Pilot Peak, which turned out to be a veritable oasis for the emigrant parties that followed.

* Apparently Carson and the rest of the party were unaware that Jedediah Smith had crossed the Great Basin, west to east, in 1827.

When he reached the Ogden River, he renamed it after the great German scientist Alexander von Humboldt, an act for which his detractors have never forgiven him. At the Humboldt, Frémont divided his party. He sent most of the men with Walker to keep moving west along the Humboldt. He and Carson took ten men and struck out to the southwest across central Nevada. In this instance, Frémont was a true pathfinder: The route he blazed across Utah became the most direct route from Salt Lake to northern California, and his exploration in Nevada filled in a large blank spot on the map of the Great Basin. "Where much had been white, save for the arching legend 'Unknown,' now much was etched with physical symbols and place names," wrote Edwin L. Sabin in his 1935 work, *Kit Carson Days, 1809–1868*. At a lake on the far side of the Great Basin, Frémont and Walker joined up as planned, and Frémont named it Walker Lake after his guide.

With winter approaching, Frémont sent Walker and his group south to cross by the pass that the guide had discovered in 1833, while he took his men north up the Salmon Trout River, which feeds Pyramid Lake, and, in early December, over a pass—Truckee or Donner—and into California before the first heavy snowfall. Frémont beat the snow and this time had a relatively easy and uneventful crossing of the Sierra Nevada. He arrived at Sutter's Fort on December 10, 1845.

The year and a half that Frémont stayed in California was a vital period for the territory and a busy time for the young brevet captain, who participated in many of the events that brought California under the control of the United States. Briefly (because the events took place outside the Great Basin), they included Frémont's armed defiance of the Mexican authorities, his participation in the Bear Flag Revolt, his leadership of the California Battalion, his brief reign as governor of California, and his unfortunate power struggle with a vindictive U.S. general, Stephen Watts Kearny. In opposing Kearny, Frémont miscalculated; as a result, in mid-June 1847, Frémont was forced to accompany the general back east, where he faced a court-martial on charges of mutiny, disobedience, and conduct prejudicial to military discipline. In crossing the Sierra, they passed the site of the Donner party, where Frémont paused to destroy the wagons and equipment that the unfortunate party had left behind. Frémont was afraid these relics would demoralize other emigrants attempting to cross that rugged pass.

The court-martial, which lasted nearly three months, was front-page news all over the country; on November 9, 1847, a week after it started, the *New York Herald* devoted nearly the entire front page to the trial. On January 31, 1848, Frémont was convicted on all counts and sentenced to be dismissed from the Army. President Polk upheld the conviction but overruled the sentence and ordered Frémont "to resume his sword, and report for duty." Frémont, however, refused to accept the verdict of the court and resigned from the Army. At age thirty-four, Frémont, again a civilian, was both a national hero and a martyr.

On balance, Allan Nevins concluded, the trial redounded to Frémont's favor by etching "indelibly into the public mind the fact that he had played an early, daring, and important part in the events which gave California to the nation." And honors continued to come his way. California, for its part, presented him with a gold sword "in high appreciation of the gallantry and science he has displayed in his services in Oregon and California." The Royal Geographic Society decorated him with a medal, and he was praised on the floor of the U.S. Senate as the man who had "kept California out of the hands of British subjects."*

Frémont, resilient as always, bounced back after the court-martial. He went on to make a fortune in gold in California and became one of that new state's first U.S. senators. Frémont also led two more expeditions west, both privately financed, to scout a central route for the transcontinental railroad. His fourth expedition of 1848–1849 came to disaster in the San Juan Mountains, although Frémont managed to make his way to California by a southern route

* The names Frémont and Kearny "have been strangely linked in our geography," Nevins wrote. For example, "in more than one city, like San Francisco, Frémont Street and Kearny Street lie close together."

that largely skirted the Great Basin. On his fifth expedition he almost perished crossing the Rockies in midwinter, but he managed to lead his party to the tiny settlement of Parowan, Utah, on February 8, 1854, where Mormons welcomed the starving men into their homes. From Parowan he crossed unexplored territory in Utah and Nevada, finally crossing the Sierras in the vicinity of Walker's Pass.

Frémont never wrote a report on his fifth expedition; he was distracted from it by his run for president in 1856. His last written word on the Great Basin remains a relatively brief *Geographical Memoir* with maps based on information and surveys that Frémont passed on to Preuss.*

By the time the *Memoir* was published in June 1848, gold had been discovered in California, and, in the Great Basin, the Mormons had founded Salt Lake City and were beginning to move out into the surrounding territory. In this, the map was remarkably up-to-date. Preuss was able to include both the location of the earliest gold strikes in California and the sites of the first Mormon settlements along the Great Salt Lake. The *Memoir* praised the Great Basin as being "very fit for the residence of a civilized people; and of these parts, the Mormons have lately established themselves in one of the largest and best. . . ."† Frémont also repeated his observation that the Great Basin was "shut in all around by mountains, with its own system of lakes and rivers, and having no connexion whatever with the sea," adding that what "was advanced as a theory after the second expedition . . . is now established as a geographical fact." He concluded:

* Preuss, Frémont's cartographer, did not accompany Frémont's third expedition; he was replaced by Philadelphia artist Edward Kern. Frémont asked Preuss to join his fifth expedition, but the melancholy German immigrant, who by now resented the explorer, refused. In September 1854 he hanged himself in a woods near Washington, D.C.

† This is a lukewarm endorsement of the Great Basin compared with the praise Frémont lavished on California: "Geographically, the position of this California is one of the best in the world; lying on the coast of the Pacific, fronting Asia, on the line of an American road to Asia, and possessed of advantages to give full effect to its grand geographical position."

Such is the Great Basin, heretofore characterized as a desert, and in some respects meriting that appellation; but already demanding the qualification of great exceptions, and deserving the full examination of a thorough exploration.

The publication of Frémont's *Geographical Memoir* marks the end of the first period of the Great Basin's recorded history. In the seventy years or so between the first penetration by a white man and the last expedition by Frémont, the Great Basin had been traveled, trapped, mapped, and, thanks to the Pathfinder, defined and at least partially understood. The second period would see the "thorough exploration" that Frémont called for and the arrival there of many different peoples. Some would just be passing through, but others, like the Mormons who followed Brigham Young to the Great Basin in 1847, stayed to establish settlements that have flourished to this day.

Part Two

LAND OF THE LATTER-DAY SAINT

Chapter Seven

SAINTS TO THE

GREAT BASIN

With the exception of a mountain man or two, members of the Church of Jesus Christ of Latter-day Saints were the first white people to settle in the Great Basin. They arrived there in July 1847, led by Brigham Young to the Great Salt Lake Valley. There they hoped to find refuge from persecution that had driven them from settlements they had established in Ohio, then Missouri, and finally Illinois. The myth of the Mormons' westward trek holds that God led them to the Great Basin, but, be that as it may, before they departed, they did as much research into the West as any other pioneer or traveler. Probably they did more. Like others, they turned to what were effectively the only two sources of printed information about the West: John Charles Frémont's *Report* and Lansford Hastings's *Emigrants' Guide*. The opportunistic Hastings even lectured on the Far West to Mormons in Illinois and most certainly tried to lure them to California, where he hoped to make his fortune by attracting settlers.

Joseph Smith had founded the Church of Jesus Christ of Latterday Saints in Fayette, New York, in 1830. A heavenly messenger named Moroni had visited Smith seven years earlier and instructed him where to find and how to translate golden plates that told the story, compiled by the prophet Mormon, of ancient peoples who came to the American continent about 600 B.C. and who were visited by Jesus Christ after His resurrection. Smith's translation became the Book of Mormon, which is, with the Bible, the foundation of the Mormon faith. As Joseph Smith envisioned it, the Mormon Church is the restoration of the Christian church that Jesus founded on earth and the only true embodiment of its doctrine.

The Book of Mormon also provided an answer to a question that was perplexing white Americans in the early nineteenth century: Who were the American Indians and where had they come from? As the text explained it, the six tribes of Israelites who came to this continent in 600 B.C. eventually split into two warring factions, one good (the Nephites), the other bad (the Lamanites). Evil eventually triumphed over good, but before they were wiped out, the Nephites recorded their story on the golden tablets that Joseph Smith was called upon to translate. The surviving Lamanites, whom God had cursed by darkening their skin, were, in the Mormon view, the ancestors of the present-day Indians, who, in turn, were the fallen brothers of the Mormons. Furthermore, the Book of Mormon promised, the Lamanites would become "a pure and delightsome people" once they accepted the gospel of Jesus Christ. This promise deeply influenced the Mormon attitude toward the Indians. The Mormon Church had no sooner been founded than Joseph Smith sent missionaries "into the wilderness among the Lamanites," as he was commanded to do by a revelation from God.* Thereby began a long Mormon tradition of ministering

* The revelations received by Smith and other Mormon leaders appear in a work known as the Doctrine and Covenants, which is usually bound together with the Book of Mormon. The first collection of revelations was printed in 1833. The

to the Indians that non-Mormons often feared was the Saints' attempt to turn the natives against all non-Mormon settlers and the U.S. government.

The church, originally and briefly called the Church of Christ, only had six members to start, but it had a brilliant and charismatic leader in Joseph Smith, whom Yale scholar Harold Bloom called "an authentic religious genius, unique in our national history" in his 1992 *American Religion*. Furthermore, it was established in a time of religious turmoil that was particularly intense in upstate New York, where the emphasis on the restoration of the true gospel had wide appeal. Less than a year after he founded it, Smith moved the church to Kirtland, Ohio, where hundreds of new Saints, as Mormons call themselves, were already established.*

In Ohio, as in Missouri and Illinois, the Mormons were soon successful as settlers. This caused their neighbors to envy and resent them and finally, with persecution leading to violence, to drive them away. Exacerbating the situation were the Mormons' peculiar and clannish ways, or what the Mormon-born historian Bernard DeVoto called "the complete smugness of a people on whom a monopoly of truth and virtue was conferred by Almighty God."

The Gentiles (the Mormon term for those not of their faith) in Missouri were particularly hostile.† By then rumors that the Saints practiced polygamy were adding to the general hostility.

---

revelation cited here concerning the Lamanites appears in section 32; Smith received it in October 1830.

* To Mormons the word *Saints* simply denotes church members or, according to the *Encyclopedia of Mormonism*, "a community of believers set apart from non-believers." Unlike the Catholic Church and others, the Mormon Church has no saints or people worthy of veneration.

† In *Inside U.S.A.* (1947), John Gunther wrote: "Jews in Utah, being non-Mormon, are theoretically subject to classification as Gentiles, which gave rise to the well-known remark that 'Utah is the only place in the world where Jews are Gentiles.' "

On October 27, 1838, Missouri Governor Lilburn W. Boggs issued a military order, known in Mormon history as the Extermination Order, directing that "the Mormons must be treated as enemies, and must be exterminated or driven from the state if necessary for the public peace—their outrages are beyond all description."* After some armed conflict and the jailing of their leader, Joseph Smith, they moved again, this time to Illinois. Here they stopped and founded a city on a great bend in the Mississippi River. Barely escaping with his life from Missouri after being imprisoned, Joseph Smith stood on the high bank above the river and declared, "It is a beautiful site, and it shall be called Nauvoo, which means in Hebrew a beautiful plantation."†

"Where the Devil Cannot Dig Us Out . . ."

To the Mormons, it seemed that they had at last found the Promised Land. The officials of the State of Illinois and the Mormons' neighbors on the Mississippi at first welcomed the industrious new settlers. In the first year the Saints built 250 homes, laid out on a strict grid with wide streets and sidewalks as dictated by Smith, who also possessed a knack for city planning. By 1845, there were almost twelve thousand residents in the city, making it, next to Chicago, the fastest-growing city in the state. In a gesture of goodwill, the Illinois legislature granted the city the Nauvoo Charter, which gave it semi-independent status, and allowed it to recruit and field its own militia, a volunteer force known as the Nauvoo Legion. As the city grew and prospered, the citizens rushed to complete their new temple, where the most sacred rituals of their faith would be held. Some of these rituals, such as bap-

* Mormons today are still aware that they are the only group in America against which an extermination order has been issued (although certain Indian tribes might make a similar claim). In 1976, Missouri rescinded the order and apologized to them.

† Other accounts have Smith translating Nauvoo as "a beautiful location, a place of rest." Either way, there is no such word in Hebrew.

tism and marriage, are similar to those practiced by other Christian denominations; others, such as "sealings," or the bonding of families in eternal relationships and endowments, a process of testing and instruction that includes ceremonial washing and anointing, are unique to Mormonism.

Whether Smith ever thought of Nauvoo as the sect's final destination is a question that history has never settled. A letter written just one year after Smith arrived in Nauvoo quotes his reference to "a place of safety preparing for [the Saints] away towards the Rocky Mountains." Smith was also thinking about Texas and Oregon as possible destinations; in early 1844 he sent his trusted lieutenants Orson Hyde and Parley Pratt to Washington to petition Congress for permission to settle in the Northwest.* He instructed his governing body, the Quorum of the Twelve Apostles, to send out an exploring party to "investigate the locations of California and Oregon, and hunt out a good location, where we can remove to after the temple is completed, and where we can build a city in a day, and have a government of our own, get up into the mountains, where the devil cannot dig us out, and live in a healthful climate, where we can live as old as we have a mind to."

It soon became obvious that time was running out for the Mormons at Nauvoo. Violence against the sect was on the increase; in February 1844, a newspaper editor in nearby Warsaw printed this warning to Smith: "We claim not to be a prophet nor the son of a prophet. Yet we tell you that your career of infamy cannot continue but a little longer! Your days are numbered!" The situation only worsened when Smith announced in 1844 that he was running for president of the United States; his exaggerated claims of up to two hundred thousand supporters made his enemies fear that the Mormons could influence the outcome of the election. And then there was polygamy, an issue that would rankle the nation for the next fifty years. In 1844 it was only rumored that

---

* While they were in Washington, Pratt and Hyde obtained a copy of Frémont's report on his 1843–1844 expedition through the Great Basin, which they brought back with them to Nauvoo.

Smith and others high in the Mormon hierarchy had more than one wife, but these reports shocked the country. They also caused problems with the rank-and-file members of the church, for the practice of polygamy among them was a closely guarded secret known only to the Mormon leadership. At that point in Mormon history, the average Saint was just as monogamous as the average Gentile.*

The mounting pressure against the Mormons early in 1844 meant there would not be time to send out an expedition to Oregon and California to scout out a new homeland. Nor would Joseph Smith live to see a place where he and his people could "live as old as we have a mind to." On June 24, 1844, Joseph and his brother Hyrum, who had fled into Iowa to avoid arrest, surrendered to authorities and were jailed in Carthage, Illinois. Three days later, a mob broke into the jail and murdered the two men. Smith's martyrdom, Wilford Woodruff wrote in his journal, left the Saints feeling "like sheep without a shepherd, as being without a father, as their head had been taken away." But one thing was certain: Staying in Nauvoo was no longer an option for the Saints. The only questions remaining were when and where would they go and who would lead them?

As empty and unsettled as the trans-Mississippi West was in the antebellum era, the Mormons were limited in their choices of destinations. Much of the land west of the river was Indian territory and not open to settlement. Besides, the Saints wanted to get as far away as possible from Gentiles who had driven them out of Ohio and Missouri and who were about to do the same in Illinois. Far-off places like Oregon and Texas were losing their appeal for the Mormons. Oregon was filling up fast with Americans, many of them from the hated state of Missouri, and the thought of once again having hostile neighbors was hardly appealing to

* Fawn Brodie, in her 1945 biography of Joseph Smith, *No Man Knows My History*, estimates that Smith, who began his first polygamous relationship in 1836, might have had as many as fifty wives. He received his first divine revelation approving the practice in 1843, a year before his death.

the Saints. For the same reasons, Texas was even less attractive. With the Mexican War looming, a move there, historian Fawn Brodie wrote, would have made the Mormon Church "a buffer state in the most explosive section of the continent" and ensured its destruction.

WEST FROM NAUVOO

After Smith's death, Brigham Young, a Mormon since 1832 assumed leadership of the church. Like Joseph Smith, Young was born in Vermont and moved as a child to New York State, where as a youth he became a carpenter and glazier. Young was introduced to Mormonism when he saw an early copy of the Book of Mormon in 1830; he was not baptized for two more years, however. Typically, he advised his family to "wait a little while . . . I [want] to see whether good common sense [is] manifest." Young caught up with Joseph Smith in Kirtland, Ohio, and in 1834 followed him to Missouri, and on to Nauvoo, Illinois, where, after a successful stint as a Mormon missionary in England, whence so many of the new converts came, he oversaw the building of the "beautiful city" on the Mississippi.

On August 8, 1844, less than two months after Smith was killed, Young was elected President of the Quorum of the Twelve Apostles. This office made him only first among equals—he was not yet president of the church, as Smith had been—but he still took charge of Mormon affairs. Brigham Young was a practical man, as exceptional in his sphere as Joseph Smith was in his, and, for the thirty-three years remaining in his life, his presence dominated Mormon history. The following April the Quorum of the Twelve issued a proclamation that affirmed the Saints' determination to establish a homeland of their own. Addressed with typical bravado to "ALL THE KINGS OF THE WORLD, TO THE PRESIDENT OF THE UNITED STATES OF AMERICA; TO THE GOVERNORS OF THE SEVERAL STATES, AND TO THE RULERS AND PEOPLE OF ALL NATIONS," it read in part:

The city of Zion, with its sanctuary and priesthood, and the glorious fulness of the gospel, will constitute a *standard* which will put an end to jarring creeds and political wranglings, by uniting the republics, states, provinces, territories, nations, tribes, kindred tongues, people, and sects of North and South America in one great and common bond of brotherhood; while truth and knowledge shall make them free, and love cement their union.

The winter of 1845–1846 was, in the words of Brigham Young biographer Eugene England (*Brother Brigham*, 1980), a time of "intense preparation," with Young totally occupied with "the process of determining where to go and by what timetable." In January 1845, the Illinois legislature revoked Nauvoo's charter, and in September, to appease the mobs and forestall further attacks on Nauvoo, Brigham Young and the Twelve Apostles promised that the Saints would leave Illinois "as soon as grass grows and water runs." By this time, Young was seriously considering taking his people to the Great Basin. On December 20 Young and a few of the Twelve Apostles listened to a reading of Frémont's journal of his trip through the Great Basin and into California. A week later Parley P. Pratt, one of the original members of the Quorum of the Twelve Apostles, read from Hastings's guidebook at a meeting at which immigration to California was discussed. On the last day of 1845, according to records kept by his clerk, Young and the prominent leader Heber C. Kimball pored over maps of the Great Basin and discussed locations where the beleaguered Saints might settle.

As it turned out, the Mormons could not even wait for the grass to grow before they had to start evacuating Nauvoo. With violence against them increasing, the first group of Mormons left the city on February 4, 1846, and crossed the Mississippi, heading west toward destinations that were, at least to most of them, unknown.

There was a certain drama to the evacuation, but it is not true, as legend has it, that the Mississippi froze over that night so the Saints could walk across. The Saints crossed the river by boat, their ferries, wrote DeVoto, "jammed with men, women, children, horses, oxen, cows, swine, chickens, feather beds, Boston rockers, a miscellany of families and goods hastily brought together in the fear of death." But DeVoto's words notwithstanding, the Saints did not abandon Nauvoo in a rush or panic. Only the advance party left on February 4. Brigham Young did not leave for another eleven days, and the city was not completely emptied of Mormons until after a mob attack in mid-September, a bloody clash called the Battle of Nauvoo. And while the evacuations were proceeding, work on the Nauvoo temple continued, so that the remaining Saints could complete as many rituals as possible before departing. The temple was dedicated on April 30, 1845, with prayers, Woodruff wrote in his diary, "for the Camp of Israel, for good weather, [and] that we might not be disturbed by any mob until the dedication was over."

WINTER ON THE MISSOURI

The Mormon trek westward from Nauvoo to the Salt Lake Valley is one of the great migrations in American history.* Some fifteen thousand people had to be moved in stages from Nauvoo to an unspecified destination. If Brigham Young knew where they were going when the Mormons left Nauvoo, he had good reasons for keeping it a secret: There were reports abroad that the federal government might try to stop or obstruct the Mormon exodus or that the Saints' enemies might waylay them as they proceeded west. In Washington, President James Polk and the federal government were not at all sure what the Saints were up to; there were always questions about the Mormons' loyalty to the United States, and, at this particular time, there was concern that the

* The saga is told in a most readable form by the novelist and historian Wallace Stegner in his nonfiction work *The Gathering of Zion: The Story of the Mormon Trail* (1964).

Mormons might ally themselves with the British in the Northwest. So, when a U.S. Army captain, James Allen, rode into their camp on the Missouri River in the summer of 1846, the Mormons suspected a plot to delay or detain them.

Allen was seeking five hundred volunteers to join an overland expedition to California as part of the war effort against Mexico. Most of the Mormons at the Missouri were suspicious, but Brigham Young was savvy enough to see that the call for troops could prove to be what he later called the Mormon's "temporal salvation." By the time Captain Allen caught up with them on the Missouri, 265 miles from Nauvoo, it was clear that the Saints would not reach their final destination before winter set in. So Young struck a bargain: In return for the Mormons' providing the five hundred men, the government would permit the Mormons to establish a winter camp on Indian land on the west bank of the Missouri. The agreement with the government also provided the Mormons with needed cash: The church would be allowed to keep each recruit's clothing allowance of forty-two dollars—a total of twenty-one thousand dollars—and could count on a portion of future pay and allowances. And, as another bonus, the recruitment would give the Mormons an opportunity to demonstrate their loyalty to the United States, or as President Polk wrote in his diary, "attach them to our country, & prevent them from taking part against us."*

Young had trouble convincing his followers to honor his pledge, although Wilford Woodruff later wrote that the five hundred volunteers "stepped forth instantly at the call of the President . . . and went away with cheerful hearts . . . preparing the way for the building of Zion." The Mormons did not trust the federal government, and there was consternation over the report that the rest of the battalion would be made up of volunteers from the hated state of Missouri. Even the loyal Hosea Stout, a brigadier general in the Nauvoo Legion, expressed misgivings that the

---

* In *Mormons at the Missouri* (1987), Richard E. Bennett pointed out that the delay caused by the call for troops for the Mormon Battalion "provided Young with the ideal excuse for not reaching the mountains, as predicted, in 1846."

government would "have 500 of our men in their power to be destroyed as they had done our leaders at Carthage." In a speech at a mass meeting Brigham Young laid down the law; in doing so he expressed a belief that the Constitution of the United States was divinely inspired, a position that he would consistently hold even when he was at odds with the government responsible for upholding that document.

After we get through talking, we will call out the companies; and if there are not young men enough we will take the old men, and if they are not enough we will take the women. I want to say to every man, the Constitution of the United States, as formed by our fathers, was dictated, was revealed, was put into their hearts by the Almighty, who sits enthroned in the midst of the heavens; although unknown to them, it was dictated by the revelations of Jesus Christ, and I tell you, in the name of Jesus Christ, it is as good as ever I could ask for. I say unto you, magnify the laws. There is no law in the United States, or in the Constitution but I am ready to make honorable.

The Mormon Battalion, some 497 strong (plus some 80 women and children) undertook one of the great marches of history, two thousand–odd miles from the Missouri to Santa Fe to California. The Mormons did no fighting, but they built a wagon road from the Rio Grande to the Gila River in southern California; this rude thoroughfare—plus the fact that they were an American presence in California—helped secure that territory for the United States. Battalion members also contributed in a crucial way to the development of the Great Basin. When they were discharged in California, the men were told they could either return to Salt Lake City or seek work in California. Some of those who stayed were among the men at Sutter's Mill who discovered gold in 1848, and the bullion they brought back to Salt Lake City fed the cash-starved economy of the early Mormon settlement.

"A Thousand Questions" about the Great Basin

After the departure of the Mormon Battalion on July 21, 1846, the Mormons settled in for an arduous winter at Winter Quarters, as the camp was called. By December, nearly four thousand Mormons had gathered there. Still, the question remained of where they were headed, and the Saints continued to question everyone they met with knowledge about the land beyond the Rockies On the Missouri, they discussed with a fur trader and ferry operator named Peter Sarpy "the road, country, and climate to and about the Rocky Mountains," in particular the Bear River Valley.* In November of 1846, the Jesuit explorer and missionary Father Pierre Jean de Smet arrived at Winter Quarters, and, although it is not clear that De Smet's travels had ever taken him to the Salt Lake Valley, he told the Mormons what he knew of the region. "They asked me a thousand questions about the regions I had explored," the Jesuit later wrote, "and the spot I have just described to you [the Great Basin] pleased them greatly from the account I gave them of it."

Other snippets of reports and recollections confirm the direction in which the Mormons were headed. At Winter Quarters, the prominent Mormon pioneer John D. Lee recorded that the Saints "intend settling the greater part of our people in the great Basin between the Mountains near the Bear River Valley." And early in February 1847, Willard Richards, the camp historian, wrote: "We have not changed our views relative to a location. . . . It must be somewhere in the Great Basin, we have no doubt."

On April 7, the pioneer company of 143 men, 2 women, and 3 children left Winter Quarters to establish an advance camp in the eventual Mormon homeland. The party followed the Platte River—the north bank so as to avoid hostile Missourians and other Gentiles traveling west on the other side—crossing the river

---

* There is also a Bear River in Wyoming (in addition to the one that runs through the Cache Valley in northern Utah), and at least one historian has suggested that the Mormons were considering it as a destination.

at Fort Laramie and following the North Platte to the Sweet-water. Along the way, William Clayton, to measure the distance they traveled each day, devised an odometer based on the calculation of 360 revolutions of a wagon wheel to a mile. At South Pass, where the Mormons crossed over the Continental Divide, wrote Brigham Young biographer Stanley P. Hirshon, "with childlike fascination they searched for the point at which the waters running into the Atlantic and Pacific Oceans separated." And as they neared the Great Basin, Wilford Woodruff tried out a fly rod he had acquired while on a mission in England and was "highly gratifyed when I saw the nimble trout dart my fly hook himself & run away with the line . . ."

As they moved along, the Saints continued to meet and closely question men with firsthand knowledge of the Great Basin. On June 26, the pioneer party met a fur trapper named Moses "Black" Harris, whose outlook, Orson Pratt wrote, "is rather unfavorable to the formation of a colony in this basin, principally on account of the scarcity of timber." The same day, another veteran of the fur trade, Thomas "Peg-Leg" Smith, showed up and tried to steer the Saints to the Bear River's Cache Valley, north of Salt Lake Valley. Smith offered to guide the Mormons to this destination, but when he failed to show up for a rendezvous, the pioneers took it, in Erastus Snow's words, as "a providence of an all-wise God" that the Salt Lake Valley—and not the Cache Valley to the north—was indeed where the Saints should go.

Two days later, the Saints encountered another familiar figure in the Great Basin story, the legendary Jim Bridger, by some accounts the first white man to see the Great Salt Lake. Bridger furnished the Saints with glowing descriptions of the Salt Lake Valley, but his proprietary attitude toward the territory—he called it "my paradise"—might have irked Brigham Young. Bridger's motive for wanting the Saints to settle there was obvious: emigrants heading for the valley would have to pass through Fort Bridger, his supply post on the Oregon Trail. (Otherwise, they might detour around his establishment via the more northerly

Hudspeth Cutoff.) Bridger also warned that it might not be possible to grow corn in the Valley and advised the Mormons (sensibly, as it turned out) to wait before bringing large numbers of people to the region. Before Young and Bridger parted, the mountain man offered the Mormon leader one thousand dollars for a bushel of corn raised in the Great Basin, a story that has come down to us in several versions.

The Mormons were impressed with Bridger's worldliness and knowledge of the Great Basin but suspected, as one of them put it, that he might not be "a man of truth." They were similarly suspicious when, on the last leg of their journey between Fort Bridger and the Salt Lake Valley, they were visited by Miles Goodyear, another mountain man who had put down roots in the Great Basin's Bear River Valley. Goodyear praised the region and assured the Mormons that he had actually raised and harvested crops in the arid soil. He also pointed out to them the easiest route to the Salt Lake Valley. The Mormons realized that Goodyear, like Bridger, had much to gain from their presence and suspected, as one Saint recorded in his diary, that he was exaggerating "on account of his anxiety that we should travel through there, thereby making a road, and ensuring the passage of other emigrants in that direction."

The Mormons had one other significant encounter on their way to the Great Basin. On June 30, they met three fellow Saints: an interesting character named Samuel Brannan and his two companions. Brannan had been in charge of a group of 235 Mormons who had sailed from New York harbor to San Francisco aboard the *Brooklyn*—hence their name, the Brooklyn Saints—with orders to scout out a possible homeland for the Mormons on the California coast.* The Brooklyn Saints landed at San Francisco Bay, then called Yerba Buena, on July 29, 1846, and quickly established a colony called New Hope.

* After several delays, the Brooklyn Saints embarked from New York on February 4, 1846, the same day that the first contingent of Mormons left Nauvoo, Illinois. Two babies were born on the voyage, one on each ocean, and were named Atlantic and Pacific.

Brannan soon became a California enthusiast, and on April 4, 1847, left to meet Brigham Young and the pioneer party in hopes of persuading the Mormon leader to settle in California. By this time, however, Brigham Young had set his sights on the Salt Lake Valley, so Brannan's words failed to move him. Young could foresee that California would become so populous that the Mormons eventually would be forced to move on again, just as they had in Ohio, Missouri, and Illinois. Ten years later Young recalled his choice of the Great Basin with considerable satisfaction: "I remarked, 'Let us go to California, and we cannot stay there over five years; but let us stay in the mountains, and we can raise our own potatoes, and eat them; and I calculate to stay here.' We are still on the backbone of the animal, and we intend to stay here, and all hell cannot help themselves."*

On July 10, the same day that they met Miles Goodyear, Brigham Young fell ill with mountain fever, and for the first time the pioneer company split up, with Brigham Young remaining in the rear. As the advance party prepared to leave him, Young sent them on their way with these nearly prophetic words: "My impressions are that when you emerge from the mountains into the open country, you bear to the northward and stop at the first convenient place for putting in your seed."

"This Is the Right Place"

For the advance party, the next thirty-six miles were the worst of all. "It was as if sanctuary withheld itself," Wallace Stegner wrote, "as if safety could be had only by intensifying ordeal." The route

---

* Brannan returned to California and new ventures. To him goes credit for setting off the California gold rush by shouting, "Gold! Gold from the American River" on the streets of San Francisco. Brannan also became California's first millionaire by cornering the market on mining supplies during the gold rush. He was expelled from the church for diverting funds to his own use. When Brigham Young later asked him to return the "Lord's money," Brannan asked for a receipt signed by the Lord. Brannan acquired large tracts of land in California but eventually took to drink and died in poverty in 1889.

they followed was the one originally cut through the Wasatch
Mountains by the Donner party. On July 22, Orson Pratt and
Erastus Snow climbed to the top of Donner Hill and caught the
first full view of the Salt Lake Valley: the dark, azure Great Salt
Lake; the curving arm of the Wasatch defining the valley to the
north; and the Oquirrh Mountains (from a Goshute Indian word
meaning "wooded mountain") twenty-five miles across the valley.
"We could not refrain from a shout of joy," Orson Hyde wrote,
and after three Hosannahs the men made a quick tour of the valley
and joyfully reported back that they had found good soil and clear
streams running out of the mountains. Only the lack of timber
appeared a serious drawback.

There is a traditional belief that the Great Salt Lake Valley was,
in 1847, an arid desert that the Mormons, by dint of hard work,
righteous living, and the grace of God, made bloom. It is true that
some of the Mormons found the timberless expanse of the valley
disorienting and depressing; Harriet Young, the pregnant wife of
Brigham's brother Lorenzo, "felt heartsick" when she caught her
first view of the desert extending west of the Wasatch Mountains.
Still, most of the pioneers were encouraged by what they saw, particularly the potential of the land for agriculture. To Woodruff,
the land, "clothed with the Heaviest garb of green vegetation,"
looked fertile. William Clayton, the English convert who served
as historian for the pioneer camp, wrote enthusiastically of the
land he found on July 22:

> There is but little timber in sight anywhere, . . . which is
> about the only objection which could be raised in my estima-
> tion to this being one of the most beautiful valleys and pleas-
> ant places for a home for the Saints which could be found. . . .
> For my own part I am happily disappointed in the appearance
> of the valley of the Salt lake, but if the land be as rich as it has
> the appearance of being, I have no fears but the Saints can live
> here and do well while we will do right. When I commune
> with my own heart and ask myself whether I would choose to

live here in this wild looking country amongst the Saints surrounded by friends. . . ; or dwell amongst the gentiles with all their wealth and good things of the earth, to be eternally mobbed, harassed, hunted, our best men murdered and every good man's life continually in danger, the soft whisper echoes loud and reverberates back in tones of stern determination; give me the quiet wilderness and my family to associate with, surrounded by the Saints and adieu to the gentile world till God says return and avenge you of your enemies.

The Saints moved fast to put their mark on the land. On July 23, the advance company moved three miles north of their previous night's camp, plowed three acres of land, and dammed the waters of City Creek and diverted the flow to the garden, the first instance of the communal irrigation that the Saints would soon be practicing on a large scale. Seed and potatoes were already in the ground when, the next day, July 24, Brigham Young, riding in a carriage driven by Wilford Woodruff, arrived at the mouth of Emigration Canyon. Woodruff paused at this vantage point to allow the leader his first unobstructed view of the valley. Woodruff's journal recorded only that Brigham Young "expressed his full satisfaction in the Appearance of the valley as A resting place for the Saints & was Amply repaid for his journey." Thirty-three years later, on the fiftieth anniversary of the church, Woodruff recalled in more detail that Young took in the sight, paused as if in a reverie, and then said: "It is enough. This is the right place, drive on."*

---

* On the question of whether Brigham Young ever uttered those memorable words, Stegner wrote: "If Brother Brigham didn't make that reverberating phrase, he should have. . . ." The mouth of Emigration Canyon is now marked by the This Is the Place Monument, designed by Brigham Young's grandson, the sculptor Mahroni Young, and dedicated in 1947 on the centennial of the Mormon arrival in the valley. Sixty feet tall, the granite monument is topped by bronze statues of Brigham Young flanked by Heber C. Kimball and Wilford Woodruff. Orson Pratt and Erastus Snow, the first to enter the valley, appear at the base. Other representations depict leading figures in the history of the Great Basin: the Escalante party of 1776, Etienne Provost, Peter Skene Ogden, William Ashley, Captain Bonneville, Father De Smet, and John C. Frémont.

Chapter Eight

BRIGHAM YOUNG
AND EARLY GREAT
BASIN DAYS

It rained the first night that Brigham Young spent in the Great Salt Lake Valley. The Saints must have taken that as a good omen, for others had convinced them that it never rained there during the summer. In the first few days, the Mormons sent out exploring parties in all directions, perhaps with the thought that they might find a better spot in which to settle. The men, who explored the foothills of the Wasatch Range and went out into the desert as far as the Oquirrh Mountains, encountered large numbers of rattlesnakes and "loathsome" black crickets and discovered a substantial stand of timber only seven miles away in a canyon. The members of an expedition to the Great Salt Lake, who agreed that the body of salty water "ought to be added as the eighth wonder of the world," tried swimming but managed only to bob around, corklike, on the briny surface. "It is almost equal to vinegar to make you smart in the eyes and nose," remarked

Brigham Young, who recommended a swim in the briny water as a tonic to all.*

But most of the terrain beyond them was parched desert, nothing to tempt the Saints to move elsewhere. They had already decided against Utah Valley farther to the south because of the menace from Indians. And they had vetoed Cache Valley to the north, today one of the most productive agricultural areas in the state, because Lansford Hastings, that notoriously unreliable "expert" on the Great Basin, had assured them that the area was unfit for farming and settlement.

The day after Young's arrival, July 25, a Sunday, the pioneers gathered to worship and give thanks for their safe arrival in the valley. The preacher that first Sunday was Orson Pratt, one of the Twelve Apostles, who took as his text: "How beautiful upon the mountains are the feet of him that bringeth good tidings." Then Brigham Young, still weak from his illness, rose to speak. His words, uncharacteristically brief, provided a direction for the new city: "No man can buy land here, for no one has any land to sell. But every man shall have his land measured out to him, which he must cultivate in order to keep it. Besides, there shall be no private ownership of the streams that come out of the canyons, nor the timber that grows on the hills. These belong to the people: all the people."†

LION OF THE LORD

For the next thirty years, from the Saints' arrival in the Great Basin to his death in 1877, Brigham Young dominated every aspect of Mormon life as the undisputed leader who directed the

---

* Young saw another use for the lake when he warned: "A man may live here with us and worship what God he pleases or none at all, but he must not blaspheme the God of Israel or damn old Jo Smith or his religion, for we will salt him down in the lake."

† Private ownership was not really an option. The Great Basin in 1847 belonged to Mexico, and after it was ceded to the United States in 1848, it was designated as Indian land, technically not open to white settlement. Mormons could not have legal title to Utah land until 1868, when a treaty ended the Indian claim.

affairs of both church and state. He exercised power over the fate of individuals. He sent out missions to settle the Great Basin, often handpicking those involved. He assigned tasks and trades, and he founded businesses and named people to man them. He was able to make the Saints see that the sacrifices they made not only were for the common good, but were God's will as well. When, in 1861, Brigham Young sent a successful merchant on a three-year mission to collect rags for a paper mill, "the humiliating prospect almost stunned me," the individual wrote, "but a few moments' reflection reminded me that I came to these valleys of the mountains from my native country, England, for the purpose of doing the will of my Heavenly Father, my time and means must be at His disposal. I therefore answered President Young in the affirmative. . . ."

Young was a great sermonizer, and his pronouncements carried such weight that a few words from him smoothed over a troublesome situation or set a wrong right. From the pulpit he lectured his people on a variety of subjects—care and feeding of children, adultery, education, dress. He exhorted them to pay their tithes, which was usually surplus property in the Mormons' cash-short economy, and, in his earthy style, complained when farmers tried to fill this obligation with worthless livestock, such as "an old three-titted cow—one that would kick the tobacco out of the mouth of a man who went to milk her." In 1849, Young inveighed against cattle owners who refused to accept the paper currency that the church had issued, and two days later the Mormon diarist Hosea Stout noted, "There is again beef in the market to be had for paper money so salutary was the sermon of the president on Sunday on that subject."

Young's lack of formal education was not unusual in early Mormons. "In my youthful days," he once said, "instead of going to school, I had to chop logs, to sow and plant, to plow in the midst of roots barefooted, and if I had on a pair of pants that would cover me I did pretty well." Richard Burton, a world traveler passing through Salt Lake City, noted that Brigham Young's "mind was uncorrupted by books." Young took considerable pride in his humble beginnings. When a writer visiting from England addressed him as Governor of Utah, Indian Agent for the Territory, and President of the Church of Jesus Christ of Latter-day Saints, Young informed him that he had forgotten a title and that next time "you put it in by itself without the others. It will read then right sprucely, 'For his Excellency, Brigham Young, Painter and Glazier.' "

Unlike Joseph Smith, Brigham Young was not of a theological bent. From the pulpit he demanded rigorous adherence to the faith but rarely added anything new. One of Young's contributions, the arcane idea that God and Adam were one and the same, ran counter to Mormon belief, and, when he met resistance to the idea, Young sensibly suggested "to lay it aside and not to teach it until the Saints were more fully prepared." Young, in fact, disliked and mistrusted the musing and postulating of intellectuals. He once said: "When I read some of the writings of such philosophers, they make me think, 'O dear, granny, what a long tail our puss has got!' "

Young's critics claimed that he was ruthless and ruled by fear; but whether it was fear or persuasion or a combination thereof, his hold over his people was extraordinary. Not that the Kingdom always benefited from having its affairs so completely in the hands of one man. Young often insisted on persevering with projects that were dubious from the start. In the early years in the Salt Lake Valley, he spent the church's resources lavishly in an attempt to manufacture sugar from beets that might have had a chance of succeeding had he listened to the experts in the business. In his drive for self-sufficiency, he pushed the Mormons into an iron-producing enterprise that resulted in one disaster after another, and, in the southern part of the territory, Utah's Dixie, he zealously forced the Saints into the production of cotton that was unable, once the Civil War ended, to compete on the free market.

Young was also criticized for profiting personally from the growth of the Mormon homeland. Certainly he looked out for his own interests, and, as time went on, he became involved in a bewildering array of businesses. He was, to name only a few titles, president of the Bank of Deseret, trustee of the Brigham Young Express and Carrying Company, and part owner of a distillery; his considerable real estate holdings resulted partly from his practice of buying out any dissatisfied Mormon who left the territory. Later, starting in the 1860s, Congress began passing anti-Mormon legislation that made it difficult for the Mormon Church to own anything, so much of the church's property was transferred to Brigham Young. But Young always denied profiting personally from his ecclesiastical office; in an 1859 interview with Horace Greeley, editor of the *New York Herald*, Brigham Young put his worth at $250,000 but added "no dollar of it was ever paid me by the church nor for any service as a minister." It is true that Young drew no salary from the church, but even church historian Leonard Arrington conceded that, in the area of finance, there is "no clear-cut way to distinguish Brigham the Family Provider from Brigham the President of the Church."

Young was extremely sensitive about his business dealings and did not take kindly to criticism. In the 1850s, he launched a particularly virulent attack on all "grunters, grumblers, whiners, hypocrites and sycophants" who dared to question why he had an adobe wall built around the city. As Young explained it, it was a make-work project "to provide ways and means for sustaining and preserving the destitute." And, he added, irritably:

> I am not to be called in question as to what I do with my funds, whether I build high walls or low walls, garden walls or city walls, and if I please, it is my right to pull down my walls tomorrow. If any one wishes to apostatize upon such grounds, the quicker he does so the better; and if he wishes to leave the territory, but is too poor to do so, I will assist him to go. We are much better off without such characters.

As an innovator, Young confidently ventured into areas in which he had no expertise. He designed a dress and hat combination that was so dowdy that Mormon women, hardly paragons of fashion in any era, refused to wear it. He also designed the so-called Deseret Alphabet, with thirty-eight Greek-like symbols representing the sounds of English, in hopes that the alphabet would help foreign immigrants to Utah learn English and also that it would contribute to the Mormons' isolation from the Gentile world. Although the alphabet never caught on—Mormon immigrants from non-English-speaking countries found it harder to master than English letters—it died hard; in 1868, thirteen years after he first came up with the alphabet, the legislature appropriated twenty thousand dollars to print the Book of Mormon in the odd-looking characters.*

Brigham Young is undeniably one of the great men of American history. He led the Mormons to the Great Basin and he set the course they followed for the first three decades. Young ruled as a monarch—benevolent, ruthless, dictatorial, and capricious. He treated his subjects as children, lecturing them, encouraging, cajoling, and praising them, punishing their transgressions. There were those who complained about his iron hand but no serious opposition ever gained a foothold. Young's critics would say that his opponents never survived long enough to challenge him, for reports of Brigham Young's ruthlessness when opposed have never gone away. In particular, his enemies accused him of directing the activities, among them murder, of a band of vigilantes, the so-called Danites, against outsiders who had incurred the wrath of the Mormon prophet.

The task that Young took on in the settlement of the Great Basin was incredibly complex. In the thirty years of his reign, he

---

* In a sermon, Brigham Young expressed his hopes for other advancements in the art of communication: "I long for the time that a point of the finger, or a motion of the hand, will express every idea without utterance. When a man is full of the light of eternity, then the eye is not the only medium through which he sees, his ear is not the only medium by which he hears, nor the brain the only means by which he understands. . . . I shall yet see the time that I can converse with this people, and not speak to them, but the expression of my countenance will tell the congregation what I wish to convey, without opening my mouth."

brought in thousands of emigrants to the Great Basin and then directed their dispersal throughout the Mormon empire. By 1870, twenty-three years after the Mormon pioneers had first arrived in the Salt Lake Valley, the mostly Mormon population of Utah was 86,786, over one-third of whom were foreign-born. Young preached isolation and self-sufficiency for the Mormon people, and he struggled to keep the dream alive. But he was also wise enough to realize that total self-sufficiency was an unrealistic goal in a fast moving world and flexible enough to change with the changing times. When the transcontinental telegraph reached Utah in 1861, Young decreed that the Saints would build their own line through their territory, which they soon did. And so it was with the railroad. Just days after the transcontinental rails were joined in 1869, the Mormons broke ground for their own railroad to connect with it.

Above all, Young believed in agriculture, and the way he persuaded the Saints to stay on their farms and resist the lure of gold in California is among his great achievements. As President of the Church of Jesus Christ of Latter-day Saints—as well as its Revelator, Seer, and Prophet—it was his duty to defend, propagate, and, on occasion, interpret the complex Mormon faith. As a polygamist, Brigham Young had the largest immediate family in America. No other Mormon institution aroused such curiosity or hostility among non-Mormons, some of whom believed that, as an evil, it equaled or surpassed slavery.

In the political realm, he had to establish a territory and invent a government. As leader, he had to work with a federal government whose attitude toward the Saints of the Great Basin kept changing throughout the thirty years he was in control. He had to deal with federal officials, some of them hardly fit for their jobs and hostile to the Mormon people, and, in 1857, he had to defend the realm from an invasion of federal troops in the so-called Utah War.

Brigham Young did not work this miracle alone; there were other forces contributing to the Mormons' success in the Great

Basin. And luck certainly played its part. But it is impossible to see how the Mormons could have survived, let alone thrived, in the Great Basin without Brigham Young at their head.

THE FIRST DAYS

Three days after Brigham Young arrived, 200 more Mormons came to the settlement. They were led by Samuel Brannan, who had gone from his meeting with Brigham Young on the trail to Colorado, where this group had wintered, to guide them to the Great Salt Lake. About 140 of them were members of the Mormon Battalion, who had been left behind because of illness; the rest were Saints from Mississippi. With their coming, the population of Salt Lake burgeoned—to about 350 persons.

The following week, the city began to take rough form. From the beginning it was a cooperative effort, each individual assigned to a cadre or committee, each with its assigned task. One block of the settlement was selected for a fort where the settlers would live until their homes were built, and in less than a month there were twenty-nine log houses in the walled fort. In short order the Mormons had established a blacksmith shop, built a storehouse, and set aside a public yard for the production of bricks, for, to save scarce lumber, it had been decreed that all permanent buildings in Great Salt Lake City would be of adobe construction.

On July 28, Brigham Young, accompanied by the Twelve, walked to a point between two creeks and announced: "Here is the forty acres [later reduced to ten] for the Temple. The city can be laid out perfectly square, north and south, east and west." For the Saints' spiritual needs, a "Bowery" of brush and branches was erected on Temple Square where services could be held, and a pool was dug out of a creek so they could be rebaptized. This symbolic gesture was called for, Erastus Snow wrote, "because we had, as it were, entered a new world, and wished to renew our covenants and commence a newness of life."

Young's layout of the city was a variation of the City of Zion plan that Joseph Smith had devised in 1833, a plan that would set the standard for most future Mormon settlements. Young's original layout called for a city of 135 ten-acre blocks. Every block contained eight individual lots of one and a quarter acres each. Each house was to be in the middle of the lot, set back twenty feet from the sidewalk, so that, Young said, "if they took fire they would not burn up their neighbors." The lots were large enough for gardens, fruit trees, and barns. All streets were to be eight rods (132 feet) wide, enough room for a team of oxen to turn around in comfortably.

For his own home, he chose the block east of Temple Square, allowing other Apostles to select their own choice lots.* From this beginning, his compound expanded rapidly, with Young adding buildings and land to house his growing family and provide working space for himself. In the compound were barns and corrals, a gristmill, granaries, a store, a school, and even a cemetery. The gate to the compound also controlled the entrance to City Creek Canyon, one of the main sources of firewood and lumber, and residents using the road, which cost thirty thousand dollars to build, had to pay Young a toll amounting to a third of the timber they took out of the canyon.

Considerable effort was devoted to naming things: The stream through the city was designated City Creek, the river from Lake Utah became the Western Jordan, and the settlement itself was named Great Salt Lake City, Great Basin, North America. On Monday, July 26, Woodruff and others took Young on an "exploring expedition," and "we all went onto the top of A high Peak in the edge of the Mountain which we considered A good place to raise An ensign upon which we named ensign Peak or Hill."

This expedition took them from Ensign Peak to the Great Salt

---

* On August 7, Woodruff noted: "In the afternoon the Twelve went onto the Temple Block & picked out there inheritances. President Young took a block east of the temple & running S.E. to settle his friends around him. Br H.C. Kimball took A Block North of the Temple. Will settle his friends on the north . . ." "Friends" is obviously a euphemism for plural wives.

Lake, across the Jordan River, south along the eastern front of the Oquirrh Mountains, and back across the Jordan to their new home. It also produced an early encounter with the Indians of the Great Basin. Riding alone one day, Wilford Woodruff came across a band of Utes, a tribe about whom the Mormons had been warned. Since they seemed friendly, Woodruff tried sign language to indicate the Mormons' willingness to trade. One of the Utes returned with Woodruff to the Mormon camp, and, after swapping some goods, Brigham Young expressed his opinion that the Indians should be taught "to labour and cultivate the earth." This became Mormon policy. Soon they were sending missionaries to teach the Indians how to farm and eventually established a string of Indian farms along the Wasatch Front.

At the time, experts guess, there were about twenty thousand Indians in the Great Basin, including the warlike Utes to the south and the potentially troublesome Shoshone to the north. Brigham Young's policy went beyond peaceful coexistence. In an early message in the Great Basin, he said that the Mormons should establish ties "with every tribe of Indians throughout America" and teach them the civilizing art of agriculture. It was a self-serving but benevolent policy that was based on his oft-repeated reasoning that it was cheaper to feed the Indians than to fight them.

Young recognized that the Indians had a rightful claim to the Great Basin: "This is the land that they and their fathers have walked over and called their own; and they have just as good a right to call it theirs today as any people have to call any land their own." But this right did not have more validity or take precedence over the Mormons' claim. Responding in 1849 to a series of Indian raids, the Mormons reactivated the Nauvoo Legion and pursued the Indians vigorously until Brigham Young concluded that punishing the Indians was more trouble than it was worth and would only make relations between the two peoples worse. In 1850, Young became so discouraged by the continuing violence and the Indians' unwillingness to take up the plow that he concluded, temporarily, that it would be better to remove them to reservations where they would not interfere with Mormon expansion. "We would have taught them to plow and sow, and reap and thresh, but they prefer idleness and theft," he wrote the Mormon representative in Washington.

WATERING AND PLANTING ZION

As the future city was being planned, other cadres were breaking ground, planting, cultivating, and irrigating a thirty-five-acre garden, which was planted with corn, oats, buckwheat, potatoes, beans, and garden seeds. To the pioneers' delight, the soil, when watered, proved to be wonderfully fertile. In a week, one settler noted, "about two acres of corn was up two inches above the ground, and beans and potatoes were up and looking well."

City Creek had, in fact, been dammed up and its water diverted to the first plantings before Brigham Young even arrived in the valley. This diversion was the first step in what turned out to be among the Mormons' most successful communal projects—irrigation. Although the Saints had studied irrigation before they left Nauvoo, there were few precedents for them to go by. The East was too wet and humid to require irrigation. The Indians in the Southwest, including some in southern Utah, and the Spanish along the Rio Grande had practiced irrigation, but the Mormons were the first in North America to try it on a large scale and make it succeed.

For the first five years, the local bishops were in charge of the local irrigation projects. Farmers built the dams, ditches, and canals, and the amount of water that was doled out depended on both their need and the labor they put into the project. This way of distributing water was something new in the land; in the East, where most of the Mormons came from, landowners owned the water on their property. In Mormon Utah, by contrast, the water belonged to no one, and the flow of streams out of the mountains was parceled out to benefit the greatest number of people.

The first Mormon irrigation projects were crude affairs—dams built of rock and earth and logs and any other available material and ditches dug by horses or oxen pulling crude implements such as go-devils, which were made by bolting two logs or planks together to form a wedge. Proper incline was determined with makeshift levels improvised out of bottles or pans filled with water. Achieving the correct rate of flow was a knack that took time to acquire: if the water moved too fast, it would wash the banks away; too slowly and the ditches would fill up with mud. By putting its bishops in charge of irrigation, the church maintained firm control over the supply and distribution of water. In 1852, to keep the federal government's hands off the irrigation system, the territorial legislature gave control to the county courts and, in 1865, permitted the creation of self-governing water districts. That year eastern newspaper editor Samuel Bowles, on a visit to Utah, was impressed by the Mormon way with irrigation, noting that the gardens in Utah were "tropical in their rich greenness and luxuriance."

As farmers broke ground, hunters and fishermen were sent out to augment the food supply with, it turned out, discouraging results. Leonard Arrington noted that, in eight days, "the fishing expedition had netted 'only four fish,' " but that a committee assigned to tap the Great Salt Lake had come back with 125 bushels of coarse salt and a barrel of table salt.*

Parties were sent out of the city—on what the Mormons called "missions"—to make contact with the Brooklyn Saints and members of the Mormon Battalion in California and to purchase provisions such as beef and flour from Fort Hall on the Oregon Trail. On August 9, Samuel Brannan left for California. On the trail he met some Salt Lake City–bound members of the Mormon Battalion and, as one recorded his words, told them that

---

* Many important details about the all-important first month in the Great Basin are included in Leonard Arrington's classic work, *Great Basin Kingdom: An Economic History of the Latter-day Saints, 1830–1900* (1966).

The saints could not possibly subsist in the Great Salt Lake Valley, as according to the testimony of the mountaineers, it froze there every month in the year, and the ground was too dry to sprout seeds without irrigation, and irrigated with the cold mountain streams the seeds planted would be chilled and prevented from growing. . . . He [Brannan] considered it no place for an agricultural people. . . . On being asked if he had given his views to President Brigham Young he answered that he had [and that] the president had laughed and made some rather insignificant remark, "but," said Brannan, "when he has fairly tried it, he will find that I was right and he was wrong, and will come to California."

Some land outside the city was temporarily distributed the first August in the Great Basin, but it would be a full year before the Mormons doled out more than eleven thousand acres that had been set aside for farming. "It is our intention," Brigham Young said, "to have the five acre lots next to the city to accommodate the mechanics and artisans, the ten acres next, then the twenty acres, followed by the forty and eighty acre lots, where farmers can build and reside." There was so much demand for the land, Arrington noted, almost nine hundred applicants, that only five- and ten-acre lots in the Big Field, as it was called, were distributed.

Brigham Young regained his health quickly and soon was speaking to the Saints in his usual vigorous style. On the evening of July 28, he roundly cursed the murderers of Joseph Smith as well as "all the governors and presidents of the U.S.A." and voiced his opinion that President Polk had forced Mormons into the Mormon Battalion and that Polk and the government's men "should be damned for these things & if they ever sent any men to interfere with us here they shall have there throats cut & sent to Hell." And before he left the valley to return to Winter Quarters he declared the Mormons economically independent of the Gentile world, a policy he would practice at times—and pay lip service to at others—for the next twenty years:

MORMONS BEFORE THE GREAT BASIN:
JOSEPH SMITH AND NAUVOO, ILLINOIS

Joseph Smith (a contemporary engraving, from *Brigham Young* by Werner)

Joseph Smith haranguing the Nauvoo Legion (from *Brigham Young* by Werner)

Death of Joseph Smith
(from *Life in Utah* by Beadle)

Mormon Temple at
Nauvoo (from *Life in
Utah* by Beadle)

Portraits of leading Mormons (from *Life in Utah* by Beadle)

Brigham Young preaching in the wilderness (from *Life in Utah* by Beadle)

Fort Bridger (etching by Frederick Piercy, courtesy Church of Jesus Christ of Latter-day Saints, Museum of Church History and Art)

Mormon Tabernacle camp on the Mormon's arrival in Utah (from *Life in Utah* by Beadle)

Brigham Young in middle age (from *Brigham Young* by Werner)

Bowery, mint, and president's
house, Great Salt Lake City
(from *An Expedition to the Valley
of the Great Salt Lake* by Stansbury)

Great Salt Lake City (etching
by Frederick Piercy, courtesy
Church of Jesus Christ of
Latter-day Saints, Museum of
Church History and Art)

Fort Utah on the Timpanogas—valley of the Great Salt Lake (from *An Expedition to the Valley of the Great Salt Lake* by Stansbury)

Devil's Gate (etching by Frederick Piercy, courtesy Church of Jesus Christ of Latter-day Saints, Museum of Church History and Art)

Great Salt Lake (etching by Frederick Piercy, courtesy Church of Jesus Christ of Latter-day Saints, Museum of Church History and Art)

Mormon leaders: Parley P. Pratt, Heber Kimball, Jedediah M. Grant, Orson Pratt
(from *Brigham Young* by Werner)

Brigham Young's proposed Mormon Temple, Salt Lake City
(from *Our New West* by Bowles)

Mormon baptism (from *Life in Utah* by Beadle)

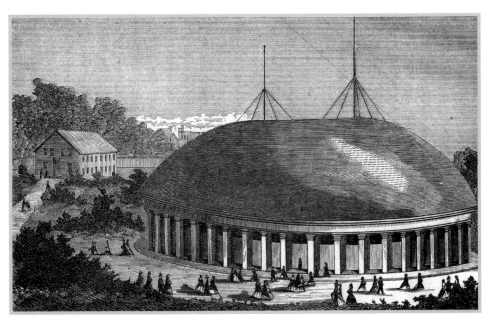

Mormon Tabernacle; Endowment House in the distance (from *Life in Utah* by Beadle)

Mormon Temple being built in Salt Lake City (from *Life in Utah* by Beadle)

Mountain Meadows Massacre (from *Life in Utah* by Beadle)

Visitor's outlook, present-day Mountain Meadows, Utah

In Memoriam: The Monument at Mountain Meadows.

Massacre of the Morrisites, 1862 (from *Life in Utah* by Beadle)

A view of polygamy—a Mormon and his family (from *Our New West* by Bowles)

In a contemporary cartoon titled "The Mormon Problem Solved," the following exchange between Brigham Young and President U.S. Grant takes place. YOUNG: "I must submit to your laws—but what shall I do with all these?" GRANT: "Do as I do—give them offices." (from *Brigham Young* by Werner)

Some of Brigham Young's wives (from *Brigham Young* by Werner)

We do not intend to have any trade or commerce with the gentile world, for so long as we buy of them we are in a degree dependent upon them. The Kingdom of God cannot rise independent of the gentile nations until we produce, manufacture, and make every article of use, convenience, or necessity among our own people. We shall have Elders abroad among all nations, and until we can obtain and collect the raw material for our manufactures it will be their business to gather in such things as are, or may be, needed. So we shall need no commerce with the nations. I am determined to cut every thread of this kind and live free and independent, untrammeled by any of their detestable customs and practices.

BACK TO WINTER QUARTERS . . .

All through August the pioneers were leaving the Great Salt Lake and retracing their steps to Winter Quarters, where they would spend the winter and, in the spring, lead the Saints who had congregated there back to the Great Basin. On August 8, Ezra Taft Benson and Porter Rockwell, the latter a reputed leader of the Danites known widely as "The Destroying Angel," were among the first to depart.* Some left a week later, and, soon after that, William Clayton with a new roadometer and seventy-one men took their leave.

Before Brigham Young left Great Salt Lake City to return to Winter Quarters in late August, he and Heber Kimball appointed John Smith, uncle of Joseph Smith, to be president of the fledgling colony of Great Salt Lake City. To be Smith's counselors,

---

* Benson, an apostle and pioneer, was the great-grandfather of his namesake, the thirteenth president of the Mormon Church and secretary of agriculture under President Eisenhower. Rockwell, who had been Joseph Smith's bodyguard, had been jailed in Missouri for the attempted murder of Governor Lilburn Boggs, who had issued the Extermination Order against the Mormons. Rockwell wore his hair long, claiming that Smith had promised no harm would come to him if he did not cut it.

146 • *Land of the Latter-day Saint*

they chose John Young, Brigham's brother, and Charles C. Rich, a commander of the Nauvoo Legion, the militia that continued to function in Great Salt Lake City. The other arm of the government was a high council of twelve men, a reflection of the Quorum of the Twelve Apostles that oversaw the affairs of the church. Like all governmental endeavors in the early days of the Mormon state, it was firmly in the control of Brigham Young and evinced no distinction between church and state.

Brigham Young and Heber Kimball and 108 men left Great Salt Lake City on August 26. They had been in the Great Basin barely a month, but already a city was on the rise. On the evening before he left with Young for Winter Quarters, Wilford Woodruff looked back on what the Mormons had accomplished in just one month and penned this summary:

We as A pioneer company have accomplished more this season then can be found on record concerning any set of men since the days of Adam. Having travled with heavy load waggons over one thousand miles having made our road more than one half of the way over & through the rough mountains & canions & searched out a glorious land as a resting place for the Saints & in one month after our arival laid out a city two miles square & built A fort & fortification of hewn timber drawn 7 miles from the mountains & and of unburnt brick surrounding 10 acres of ground 40 rods of which was coverd with Block Houses, Besides planting about 100 Acres of corn, potatoes, Buckwheat turnip gardens &c. The pioneers did not exceed 150 men during the time. 140 of the Battalion arived. I think there was not over 100 men labouring on the work at a time, besides much exploring was done. And after accomplishing this work the company returned to winter Quarters the place of Begining making nearly 2,500 miles traveling during one summer besides all the labour.

En route back to Winter Quarters, Young encountered ten separate companies of Mormons, or a total of 1,553 people, headed for Great Salt Lake. The large numbers alarmed him; he had left instructions that no more than 400 people should migrate to the Great Basin that first year. He gave one party a letter advising his comrades back in the valley to plant seed "as soon as the snow is gone in the spring, so that we might know by experiments whether it is possible to ripen grain in the valley before the summer drouth shall demand the labor of irrigation." He also wrote lovingly to Clara Decker (the only one of his wives to accompany the pioneer party to the Great Basin), who had stayed in Great Salt Lake City: "I due feel to bless and pray for you. You have been a grate comfort to me this sumer. . . . O that I had my famely here."*

On September 4, near South Pass, Young and his contingent met a Salt Lake City–bound party that included two more wives: Eliza R. Snow, the poet and leader of Mormon women, who had been married to Joseph Smith, and Margaret Pierce, whom he married in 1846 before leaving Nauvoo. On this same occasion, Brigham Young treated the two leaders of the emigrant party, Parley Pratt and John Taylor, to a display of his fearsome temper. The men, who were members of the Quorum of the Twelve, had arrived at Winter Quarters from an overseas mission while Young was with the pioneer company in the Salt Lake Valley. As Young saw it, Pratt and Taylor had violated his orders when, by virtue of their rank, they had taken over command of the company from the two men Young had appointed as leaders. Young also excoriated Pratt for taking two wives in his absence, making it clear that no plural marriages were to be performed without his permission. The tongue-lashing was followed by a feast and dancing, and, while these festivities were in progress, Indians stole fifty of their horses, including Young's. His response

---

* By then Brigham Young had twelve wives with whom he had or would have children and several more "caretaker" wives for whose support he was responsible. His first wife, Miriam Works, died in 1832.

to this misfortune was typical: They would walk to Winter Quarters, he announced.

Young arrived at Winter Quarters on the last day of October. On December 5, the Quorum of the Twelve Apostles voted to revive the first presidency with Young as President and Heber Kimball and Willard Richards as his counselors. Four days later, a public conference confirmed Young as President with the titles, previously held by Joseph Smith, of Prophet, Seer, and Revelator. Thomas F. O'Dea in his scholarly 1957 work, *The Mormons*, wrote that Brigham Young's "position was now completely established, and a new era in the history of his people had begun."

Back in the Valley of the Saints . . .

To accommodate the newcomers arriving in the fall of 1847, the colonists built two more forts and put more land under cultivation: The original thirty-five-acre garden was enlarged until some two thousand acres had been seeded with winter wheat. Still the harvest from the planting in late July 1847 was disappointing; crickets had eaten the stubby corn and the potatoes had been stunted by an early frost. The winter of 1847–1848 was fairly mild, but with three thousand people in a community that was barely three months old, food was in short supply. The council that Brigham Young had put in place to run the community in his absence passed laws regulating the use of timber and water and outlawed, with punishment not to exceed thirty-nine lashes, various crimes and misdemeanors, including the very un-Mormon-like vice of indolence.

That first fall the Mormons had their first unpleasant encounter with Indians. A small band of Utes came to the settlement with two Indian prisoners, a boy and a girl, they had taken in a skirmish with a rival band and announced that they would be killed unless the Mormons purchased them. The Saints thought they were bluffing and were horrified when the Indians killed the boy. They traded a rifle for the young woman, who was given to one of

Brigham Young's plural wives, Lucy Decker, older sister of the aforementioned Clara, to raise.*

The first winter was hard, particularly for a people who believed they had arrived in the Promised Land. The poor harvest that year was made even more meager when livestock got loose in the field and raised havoc with the planted crops. Then Indians and wolves made off with cattle and horses that surely would have been eaten as the winter progressed. To stretch out their stores, the Mormons resorted to rationing and price controls and added to their diets unfamiliar prey such as wolf and crow and indigenous plants such as thistle tops, tree bark, and the bulb of the lovely sego lily, now the state flower. The edibility of the sego lily bulb was the discovery of John Taylor, who had ministered to the ailing son of a Goshute Indian chief by the laying on of hands. When the boy recovered, the grateful Indians showed Taylor how to dig for sego bulbs and lily roots. They also demonstrated how to round up crickets by setting fire to a field. Once the crickets were in hand, they ground the bodies into a coarse meal, which, when mixed with honey, made a tasty cake. Taylor, who, after Brigham Young's death in 1877, would succeed him as president of the Mormon Church, took some of the meal home to his family, which included two pregnant wives.† They found the mixture delicious, although Taylor never told them about the unusual ingredients.

With the onset of winter came the snow, something the settlers had not counted on—this being the semiarid desert—in building their makeshift cabins with flat roofs inside the fort. As the snow

* This purchase of an Indian child was the first example of the Mormon practice, encouraged by Brigham Young, of purchasing Indian children and raising them in their homes. While their critics claimed this was a form of involuntary servitude, the Mormons contended that these children would otherwise be sold as slaves in Mexico.

† Until the church admitted in 1853 to the practice of polygamy (see chapter 10), additional wives who were pregnant usually claimed they were married to men who had since been sent away on missions, a deception that could not have fooled many people, Gentile or Mormon.

piled up, the roofs, mostly made of willows and mud, began to leak and sag. Eliza Snow vividly described one wet night: ". . . I spread my umbrella over my head and shoulders as I ensconced myself in bed, the lower part of which, not shielded by the umbrella, was wet enough before morning. The earth overhead was thoroughly saturated, and after it commenced to drip the storm was much worse indoors than out."

The settlers continued to plant the following spring: some three to four thousand more acres of wheat, corn, and garden vegetables. The early results were promising. By late May wheat was sprouting, vegetables were on the way, and there were buds on the young fruit trees planted the year before. In late May, however, disaster struck: Hoards of voracious black crickets appeared and began attacking the crops. These insects were as large as a man's thumb or the size of a mouse; Thomas L. Kane, an influential supporter of the Mormons, described them as "wingless, dumpy, black, swollen-headed, with bulging eyes in case like goggles, mounted upon legs of steel wire and clock-spring . . ." in a speech he gave before the Philadelphia Historical Society in 1850.

To combat the hordes, the Mormons did what they did in all difficult situations: They prayed and they took action. Action did no good at all; the Saints beat the crickets with boards and wet rags and even tried to drown them by opening the irrigation ditches, but succeeded only in clogging the channels with the insect bodies.

Mormon prayers might have been more efficacious. When it seemed certain that the harvest would be lost that year, the sky suddenly filled with seagulls from the islands in the Great Salt Lake. At first the Mormons were afraid that the birds were also after their crops; as it turned out, the gulls gorged themselves on crickets. When they could eat no more, they drank water, regurgitated the insects, and started the feast over again. Although the story of the Miracle of the Seagulls is now as much legend as fact, the gulls certainly contributed to saving the Mormon harvest. In a letter to Brigham Young, a thankful settler observed: "The sea gulls have come in large flocks from the lake and sweep the crickets as they go; it seems the hand of the Lord is in our favor."*

THE RETURN OF BRIGHAM YOUNG

The fall harvest was well under way when Brigham Young arrived back in Great Salt Lake City on September 20, 1848, after the 1,031-mile trip from Winter Quarters. It took four days for the entire caravan of 2,417 men, women, and children to straggle into the settlement. During the year Young had been away, over four hundred houses had been built and ten other settlements had sprung up throughout the valley. Young was now free to devote himself to the building of God's Kingdom in the Salt Lake Valley. He would live twenty-nine more years. In that time he traveled all over the Great Basin, but he never again left Mormon territory.

The next winter was worse. The fall harvest in 1848 was poor: Crops barely survived bad weather and the return of the hungry crickets. Rationing was reinstituted and some Saints simply gave up and moved on to California. When extortion among the Saints became a problem, Brigham Young dealt with it in his no-nonsense manner: "If those that have do not sell to those that have not, we will just take it & distribute among the Poor, & those that have & will not divide willingly may be thankful that their Heads are not found wallowing in the Snow. . . ."†

Brigham Young tried hard to reassure the hungry and worried colonists. If the climate of the Great Basin was not suited to settlement, he promised, then the Lord would change the climate: "[God] will temper the elements for the good of His Saints; He

---

* Called the California gull, the bird is protected as an insectivore and is now the state bird. In 1913, a monument, sculpted by Mahroni Young, a grandson of Brigham Young, to the seagulls was erected on Temple Square in Salt Lake City.

† Young's words often had a violent tinge: "If you want to know what to do with a thief, . . . I say kill him on the spot," he said once, "and never suffer him to commit another iniquity." At the same time he admitted, "I have never hurt any person any other way except with this unruly member, my tongue."

will rebuke the frost and the sterility of the soil, and the land shall become fruitful." Then early in 1849, just as things in Great Salt Lake City were at their bleakest, First Counselor Heber C. Kimball, a man noted for his foresight and prophetic powers, made an extraordinary prediction: "In less than one year there will be plenty of clothes and everything that we shall want sold at less than St. Louis prices."*

In less than a year, this prophecy was fulfilled—prices were not only less but often less than half what they were in St. Louis. And it was all due to the gold rush of 1849. In the two years, 1849 to 1850, some one hundred thousand people crossed the continent in a hurry to get to California; an estimated one-quarter of these chose to travel via the Hastings Cutoff, a route that brought them through Salt Lake City.

The gold rush—or the "Harvest of '49," as Arrington called it—was the Mormons' salvation. The outsiders brought in those items that the Saints needed most—food, clothing, currency, tools, and equipment. The Mormons made the most of this economic opportunity, which overnight transformed the settlement. In July 1849, a forty-niner wrote back to his wife in Ohio: "The Mormons have had a pretty hard time since they came here, but at this time they have got things pretty comfortable around them." Arrington considered the gold rush a turning point in Mormon history, writing that "the Mormon colonists would most likely have had to give up—or at least postpone—their dream of a Great Basin empire had not the Argonauts passed through, strewing their many and varied benefits."

---

* Kimball's prophecies were legendary. In *Desert Saints*, scholar Nels Anderson wrote of Kimball's promise to a destitute neighbor that "next year this time you will have a team and wagon of your own." When the neighbor came back in a year with only one horse, Kimball told him: "Go out in my stable and pick a horse to match yours.... If the Lord will not fulfill my prophecies, I will myself."

"Go and Be Damned"

Gold fever made the forty-niners poor bargainers. By the time they reached Salt Lake City, they were in such a hurry to reach the gold fields that they willingly shed their worldly goods to be able to move faster. In this overheated market, a thirty-dollar horse could be sold for two hundred dollars or a couple of horses swapped for an ox team and wagon worth many times more. Prices of coffee and sugar, scarce commodities in Great Salt Lake City in pre-gold-rush days, dropped to one-fifth their previous level. Mormons knew how to drive a hard bargain. Leonard Arrington quoted the diary of Mormon Priddy Meeks, a kindhearted but needy man, who traded an Indian pony to an emigrant in this manner:

> "What is your price?" says the man. I said, "I have no price but I want clothing for my family," which was five in number. I believe his heart was softened for he handed out goods, some readymade, and some not, until we all had two suits each from top to toe, both shoes and stockings and everything that was needed. He said, "How much more?" I said, "Hand out and I will tell you when to stop." He handed out factory and calico until I was almost ashamed; even my conscience reminded me of stopping. I said, "Here is a great coat and a high pair of boots for winter," and he handed them out without a word. . . .

Some of the gold-seekers thought well of the Mormons, and their letters home reporting their hosts' kindnesses were often reprinted in their local papers. "I find the Mormons very accomodating, and willing to extend to the emigrants all the hospitality they possibly can," wrote John B. Hazlip in the *Missouri Whig*. Others were not so taken with the Saints and complained bitterly in their letters about Mormon price gouging. Brigham Young had no scruples about charging the transients whatever the market would bear. "What!" he exclaimed. "Sell bread to the man who is going to earn one hundred and fifty dollars a day, at the same price as you do to the poor laborer, who works hard here for one dollar a day? I say, you men who are going to get gold to make golden images . . . pay for your flour!"

Goods and equipment that forty-niners abandoned along the way added to the new prosperity; these were often salvaged by parties of Mormon emigrants heading west or by special gleaning details sent out from Salt Lake City. On his way to the Great Basin, Howard Stansbury, a government surveyor, described a "road literally strewn with articles that have been thrown away: Bar-iron and steel, large blacksmiths' anvils and bellows, crowbars, drills, augers, gold-washers, chisels, axes, lead, trunks, spades, ploughs, large grindstones, baking-ovens, cooking-stoves without number, kegs, barrels, harness, clothing, bacon, and beans . . ."

In the midst of this frenzy, Brigham Young did his utmost to persuade the Saints to stay calm and stay put, for the Mormons were not immune to gold fever, and a number abandoned Salt Lake City to go prospecting.* Young combined theological and economic arguments with appeals to the mystical ties that bound the Mormons to the land. The Great Basin, he argued, "is the place that the Lord has appointed, and we shall stay here, until He tells us to go somewhere else." Or: "Gold is good for nothing, only as men value it. It is no better than a piece of iron, a piece of limestone, or a piece of sandstone, and it is not half so good as the soil from which we raise our wheat, and other necessaries of life." Young stopped just short of forbidding the Saints to go to the gold fields. "If you Elders of Israel want to go to the gold mines, go and be damned," he said on one occasion. At other times, he

---

* Had the Mormons moved on to join the "strong nucleus of church members already in California, . . . the Saints could have acquired a giant share of the precious metal," Arrington wrote. How that would have changed the Mormon story is certainly one of the more intriguing questions in the history of the American West.

tempered his language with prophecy: "Go to California, if you will; we will not curse you—we will not injure or destroy you, but we will pity you. If you must go for gold, and this is your god, go, and I will promise you one thing: Every man that stays here and pays attention to his business will be able, within ten years, to buy out four of those who leave for the gold-mines."

Given Brigham Young's aversion to gold prospecting, it is irony indeed that Mormons—members of the Mormon Battalion who were left in California—were among the men who made the first discovery of the gold rush near Sutter's Mill on January 24, 1848. One of them, a battalion veteran named Henry W. Bigler, has gone down in history as California's first gold prospector. He also provided the first written record of the first strike: "This day some kind of mettle was found in the tail race that looks like goald." Within a few months, he was joined by other California Mormons, who uncovered gold on a sandbar in the South Fork of the American River, a location that became known as Mormon Island. And it was Mormon dissenter Brannan, back in California after failing to persuade Young to bring the Saints there, who set off the rush by shouting "Gold!" on the streets of San Francisco in early May 1848.

The gold dust or gold coin that the California Mormons contributed to the church "probably amounted to more than $60,000 during the period 1848–1851," Arrington wrote. Young needed gold to mint coins to stimulate the economy, so he quietly put aside his opposition to gold seeking and recruited two companies of Mormon miners to go to California. The expedition was known as the Gold Mission, and one of the missionaries was none other than original prospector Henry Bigler, who had turned his back on the California lodes and joined his fellow Mormons in the Salt Lake Valley in the summer of 1848. Bigler was not happy about being sent back to California. "I was not looking for any such mission," he wrote in his diary. He was also well aware of the irony of being called to a task that was officially disapproved: "Indeed, it had been the Presidents counsil not to go to the gold mines and those who went after such counsil had been given was looked upon as 'jack Mormons' as they were called."

The two companies of gold missionaries, over fifty men in all, left Salt Lake City in the fall of 1849. As miners, they were not successful. Simply reaching California was more arduous and time-consuming than they had anticipated. By the time they reached the gold field, the hills were crowded with prospectors, and the claims that the Mormons managed to stake soon gave out. After prospecting for seven hard months, Bigler complained that "it fairly makes the hair on my head stand erect when I think how little I have. . . . I am tired of mineing and long to be at home in the vallies of the mountains among the Saints." That is exactly what Brigham Young would hope a loyal Saint would say. The gold mission had been his idea, but its failure only proved his point: that the Saints who stayed home and helped build Zion would prosper more and better than those who pursued dreams of riches in far-off gold fields.

Chapter Nine

GETTING SETTLED

IN THE

GREAT BASIN

When Brigham Young returned from Winter Quarters in 1848, the new Mormon homeland was now part of the United States, having been ceded to this country by Mexico with the signing of the Treaty of Guadalupe Hidalgo. How the Mormon leader reacted to the news was not recorded. At the time the Mormons' enemies suspected that they wanted to set up a separate country or establish a homeland on the territory of a foreign power. If this were the case—and there is no evidence that it was—the Mormon leaders must have been disappointed to find themselves once again on U.S. soil. A more plausible goal for the Mormons was statehood, which was now, thanks to the treaty, a possibility. As a state, the Saints could hold their own elections, elect other Mormons to office, and live as they wanted, legally part of the United States but separated from it by the natural barriers that form the Great Basin. "All we care about," Young wrote

Utah's territorial representative in Washington in 1856, "is for them [the federal government] to let us alone, to keep away their trash and officers so far as possible, to give us our admission into the Union just as we are . . ."

THE STATE OF DESERET

In anticipation of statehood, Young staked out a claim to a sweep of territory, nearly a half million square miles, which he hoped would enter the Union as a state under the name of Deseret.* The border of Deseret (see map page 161) extended far beyond the Great Basin. It encompassed all of present-day Utah, nearly all of Nevada, and most of Arizona—or that part of it north of the Gila River. Deseret reached up into central Oregon and took in the thin slice of eastern California that falls within the Great Basin. It cut a swath across southern California to San Diego, which the Mormons wanted as an outlet to the sea and an entry point for emigrants. Eastern Deseret took in western New Mexico, western Colorado, and the southwestern corner of present-day Wyoming. The Mormons, perhaps naively, claimed the vast territory as their due. In a petition, they pointed to the service of the Mormon Battalion in the Mexican War and argued that "we have done more by our arms and influence than any other equal number of citizens to obtain and secure this country to the government of the United States."

In March 1849, Young called a convention to draft a constitution for the provisional State of Deseret that would govern the new Mormon homeland until it became part of the Union. The constitution provided for the usual array of governmental branches and offices—a bicameral legislature consisting of a House and a Senate; a supreme court; governor, lieutenant governor, sec-

---

* *Deseret* is a term from the Book of Mormon (Ether 2:3): "And they did also carry with them deseret, which, by interpretation, is a honey bee." As a symbol of industriousness, the beehive appears in the State Seal of Utah. Brigham Young's house in Salt Lake City is called the Beehive House. Mormons often include cooperativeness among the virtues symbolized by the beehive.

retary of state; and a bill of rights. Consistent with the times, only white males over twenty-one were allowed to vote.

On March 12, there was an election and, not surprisingly since there was only one candidate for each office, Young was elected governor and Heber C. Kimball chief justice. The election bestowed civil titles on ecclesiastical leaders and little else, but the Mormons now had a government, or at least the appearance of one. All other officers of the State of Deseret were members of the church governing body known as the Council of Fifty. The arrangement reflected the Mormon belief that the only duty of government is to prepare the earth for the millennium, the second coming of Christ, after which there would be no further need for civil authority. This unusual melding of church and state was obvious to early visitors, such as Howard Stansbury, the government surveyor, who wrote in 1852:

> While there are all the external evidences of a government strictly temporal, it cannot be concealed that it is so intimately blended with the Church that it would be impossible to separate one from the other. This intimate connection of the church and state seems to pervade everything that is done. The supreme power in both being lodged in the hands of the same individuals, it is difficult to separate their two official characters and to determine whether in any one instance they act as spiritual or merely temporal officers.

There also was uncertainty among the Mormon leadership whether to apply for territorial status—and risk having the federal government send outsiders to govern them—or apply at once for statehood.* In November 1849, John M. Bernhisel, who was on

---

* In his diary, John D. Lee, Young's private secretary, reported that the Mormons wanted territorial status but on their own terms; at a meeting in December 1848, the Council of Fifty "took into consideration the propriety of petitioning Congress for a Territorial Government, giving them to understand at the same time that we wanted officers of our own nomination."

his way to Washington with a petition for territorial status for Utah, and Wilford Woodruff met Thomas Kane, a Gentile and a well-connected friend of the Mormons, in Philadelphia. Kane dissuaded them from presenting the petition to Congress, telling the Mormons: "You are better off without any government from the hands of Congress than with a Territorial government. . . . You can govern yourselves better than they can govern you. . . . You do not want corrupt political men from Washington strutting around you, with military epaulettes and dress, who will speculate out of you all they can."

Congress, however, not only refused to consider the petition, but also voted not to seat Almon Babbitt, Deseret's chosen delegate to the legislative body. In debate some words were said in favor of the Mormons. "I know nothing of them," a legislator said, "but the extraordinary fact that they have a power of organization which can collect the idle, vicious and unproductive and make in a short time a prosperous community." President Zachary Taylor, however, said publicly that he was opposed to any official status for the Mormons, "that they were a pack of outlaws, and had been driven out of two states and were not fit for self-government."

The State of Deseret existed officially for two years. In that time, it founded a university, set boundaries, made it against the law to sell liquor or ammunition to the Indians, regulated the use of the all-important water and timber, and granted charters to Great Salt Lake City and to newer municipalities created as they expanded outward—Ogden, Manti, Provo, and Parowan. It also incorporated the Church of Jesus Christ of Latter-day Saints. "Deseret is not three years old," Brigham Young said with evident satisfaction while addressing the legislature in December 1850, " . . . and yet such has been the rapidity of her growth, the extent of her improvements, and the development of her resources, as to command the admiration, and the respect of all those whose lot has been cast within her bounds. . . ."

To become a state, Brigham Young considered becoming part of California, but the question became moot when Congress, as

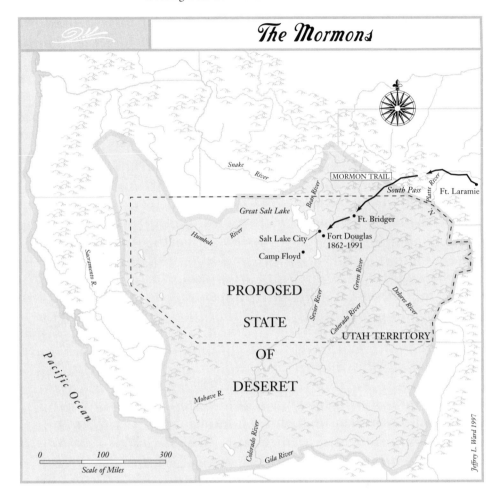

The Mormons

part of the Compromise of 1850,* created the Territory of Utah in September 1850.† The territory, although pared down from

* As every schoolchild knows, the Compromise of 1850 dealt with slavery in the territory gained from the Mexican War. California was admitted as a free state. Utah and New Mexico were created as territories, with slavery to be decided by popular vote, and the slave trade was ended in Washington, D.C.

† The Mormons did not get the name they wanted either: "Congress did not like the name 'Deseret'—too much like 'Desert,' they reasoned—so the territory was named after the Yutas or the Utah Indians," Leonard Arrington wrote in his 1985 biography, *Brigham Young: American Moses*.

the State of Deseret, still was vast, encompassing all of Nevada and Utah and a small piece of both present-day Colorado and Wyoming. There was some question about who President Fillmore would name as governor, but on September 20, 1850, he appointed Brigham Young as both Territorial Governor and Superintendent of Indian Affairs. Then, in what was ostensibly its last official act, the Deseret legislature dissolved itself and the provisional state. In reality, however, the State of Deseret did not disappear for another twenty years at least, a fact, wrote historian James Clark, that "is generally known to students of Utah history . . . Some have called this the 'ghost' government of the 'Ghost State of Deseret.' "

As governor, Young had to deal with federal appointees sent to Utah as territorial officials. Most of these individuals were, wrote Ray B. West in *Kingdom of the Saints*, "inferior men of lofty ambition" and certainly no match for Brigham Young. Exercising his flair for invective, Young described the men as "white livered, blackhearted, sycophantic demagogues." One of them, the odious W. W. Drummond, offended the Mormons by arriving in Utah accompanied by his mistress; Young characterized him as "vain as a peacock and ignorant as a jack-ass," while Heber Kimball termed Drummond "full of pox from the crown of his head to the point of its beginning." Earlier, Associate Justice Perry E. Brocchus had to leave the territory after he made the serious mistake of lecturing the Mormons on morality; in return Young called the judge "an illiterate ranter."* Before he left on October 1, 1851, Brocchus wrote that "most gladly will I go, for I am sick and tired of this place—of the fanaticism of itspeople, followed by the violence of feeling towards the *'Gentiles,'* as they style all persons not belonging to their Church."

Young also had trouble with Indian agents appointed by Washington. Several of these men were outspokenly anti-Mormon, and one, in a report to the commissioner of Indian affairs in Washing-

---

* To contribute a block of Utah marble for the Washington Monument, Brocchus said, "you must become virtuous and teach your daughters to become virtuous, or your offering had better remain in the bosom of your native mountains."

ton, D.C., accurately observed, "[Young's] power and influence is so great, that no officer either of the Territory or the Government, who is a Mormon, will dare to disobey his will."

A few federal appointees came to admire the Mormon leader: Judge Lazarus H. Reed, whom Young described as "very gentlemanly thus far," wrote with considerable insight that Brigham Young "is a man who will reciprocate kindness and good intentions as heartily as any one, but if abused, or crowded hard, I think he may be found exceedingly hard to handle." An Army officer, Colonel Edward J. Steptoe, who wintered his California-bound troops in Salt Lake City in 1854–1855, was offered the governorship of Utah when Young's term expired; he not only declined but recommended that Young be reappointed. He reasoned that the citizens of Utah would accept no one else as their leader. And, when President Buchanan replaced Young as governor in 1857 with a Gentile, Alfred Cumming of Georgia—and sent an army to install him—the Mormon president surprised everyone by cooperating with his successor.*

Young's thirty years in Utah spanned the terms of eight presidents. The attitudes of these men toward the Mormon people varied considerably. Zachary Taylor was outspokenly anti-Mormon. Fillmore was sympathetic enough to appoint Young governor of the new territory, and his successor, Franklin Pierce, took Steptoe's advice and let him stay in office. Buchanan removed Young from the governorship and sent federal troops to Utah, and his successor, Abraham Lincoln, with a war of his own to pursue, diminished Utah Territory by creating Nevada out of it and signed the first piece of anti-polygamy legislation. Still, in a famous statement to T. B. H. Stenhouse, a well-known Mormon newspaperman and writer, Lincoln claimed he wanted to take a hands-off approach to the Mormons:

Stenhouse, when I was a boy on the farm in Illinois there was a great deal of timber on the farms we had to clear away.

* See chapter 11, "The Utah War."

Occasionally we would come to a log which had fallen down. It was too hard to split, too wet to burn and too heavy to move, so we plowed around it. That's what I intend to do with the Mormons. You go back and tell Brigham Young that if he will let me alone I will let him alone.

Brigham Young never ceased his quest for statehood: after the initial attempt in 1849, the Mormons applied three more times in his lifetime. Even when he was removed from office, Young continued to regard himself as the governor of Utah (even though he was never reappointed), and he acted accordingly. In 1853 he stirred up a storm by stating publicly that only the Lord Almighty had the power to remove him from office. Young later tried to soften the statement, but other words he spoke in 1862 made it clear that he was beholden to only one authority:

When Mr. Fillmore appointed me Governor of Utah, I proclaimed that my Priesthood should govern and control that office. I am of the same mind today. . . . should I be elected Governor of the State of Deseret, that office shall be sustained and controlled by the power of the eternal Priesthood of the Son of God, or I will walk the office under my feet. Hear it, both Saint and sinner, and send it to the uttermost parts of the earth, that whatever office I hold from any Government on this earth shall honor the Government of heaven, or I will not hold it.

"Every Hole and Corner"

The impulse to explore and to settle the Great Basin was evident from the beginning: Within days of arriving in Great Salt Lake City, Brigham Young vowed to make "every hole and corner from the Bay of San Francisco to the Hudson Bay known to us," and the Mormons had sent out exploring parties to bring back information about nearby terrain. One of these explorers was Perrigrine Sessions, who, in September 1847, drove three hundred head of cattle into the South Davis Valley just north of Salt Lake City and began building a fort and laying out a town, the second community established by Mormons in the Great Basin. By 1850, fifty-three other families had established farms outside Sessions's Settlement, which, after several name changes, came to be called Bountiful.

The next tentative move outside Salt Lake City came in early November 1848. Captain James Brown of the Mormon Battalion had arrived in the Salt Lake Valley with the accumulated back pay of his men, and he was sent north to buy out the mountain man Miles Goodyear. The purchase made it clear how unwilling the Mormons were to tolerate an outside presence, no matter how small, in the Great Basin. Goodyear's Fort Buenaventura was fifty miles north of Salt Lake City, and it covered only a half acre of ground, but its owner was a Gentile and he had to go. Brown paid $1,950 for the fort, some cattle, goats, sheep, six horses, and a cat and named the settlement Brownsville after himself.*

With the colonizing efforts being directed by Brigham Young, the Mormons wasted no time in settling the Great Basin; within three years of their arrival they had established five major communities, of which Great Salt Lake City was one, and some forty smaller ones surrounding them. By 1851, there were five thousand Saints in Salt Lake City and twenty-five thousand more settled in outlying communities. Within ten years, there were one hundred communities, and by the time Brigham Young died in 1877, thirty years after his arrival in the Great Basin, settlements in and around the region numbered over three hundred.

New communities were needed just to absorb the thousands of emigrants who were answering the call to gather in the new Zion. Colonies were also established for missionary work with the

---

*The town would later be named Ogden after the Hudson's Bay Company trapper Peter Skene Ogden, one of the early explorers of the Great Basin. Because Goodyear established his fort in 1845, Ogden claims to be the oldest settlement in Utah.

Indians, to found industries such as iron or cotton, and, at strategic entrances to the Great Basin such as Nevada's Carson Valley or Fort Supply in Wyoming, to supervise the flow of emigrants into the Great Basin. At first the colonizing effort was focused on the fertile stretch of land between the mountains and the desert known as the Wasatch Front, particularly the land in Utah Valley to the east of the freshwater Utah Lake. But Young wanted to claim the best area in the entire Great Basin, such as the oasis on the Old Spanish Trail known as Las Vegas in present-day Nevada. Gentiles had been bad neighbors for the Mormons ever since the church was founded. Settling the best areas, Brigham Young figured, would be the most effective way of keeping Gentiles at bay.

The Latter-day Saints were experienced settlers by the time they arrived in the Great Basin. The church was not yet twenty years old, but the Mormons had already put down roots in Ohio, Missouri, and Illinois, only to be forced to move on again. By the time they reached the Salt Lake Valley, they knew what they were about, but this time they intended to settle for keeps. As mentioned in chapter 7, Joseph Smith had dreamed of a place "where the devil cannot dig us out . . ."

"Up to the Mountains of the Lord's House"

After founding Great Salt Lake City, Great Basin, U.S.A., the next task at hand was to populate the city and region with Mormons. Bringing all the Saints to one place—"the Gathering," as it was called—had always been a goal of the church. Soon after he organized the church in 1830, Joseph Smith revealed that God desired that the Mormons "be gathered in unto one place upon the face of this land, to prepare their hearts and be prepared in all things against the day when tribulation and desolation are sent forth upon the wicked." In Smith's lifetime, the place of the gathering kept changing—from Kirtland, Ohio, to Missouri, to Nauvoo, Illinois, but wherever it was, the first thing the Saints did was start work on a temple.

In his first churchwide communication after he was named President of the Church in December 1847, Brigham Young repeated a call for Mormons to come to the Salt Lake Valley, where they would build a nation dedicated to the Lord, prepare the earth for the Second Coming of Christ, and, like the Hebrews of the Bible, fulfill their destiny as a chosen people. Young's epistle of December 23, 1847, read in part:

> Let all Saints who love God more than their own dear selves—and none else are Saints—gather without delay to the place appointed, bringing their gold, their silver, their copper, their zinc, their tin, and brass, and iron, and choice steel, and ivory, and precious stones; their curiosities of science, of art, of nature, and every thing in their possession or within their reach, to build in strength and stability, to beautify, to adorn, to embellish, to delight, and to cast a fragrance over the House of the Lord. . . . Come then, walking in righteousness before God, and your labour shall be accepted . . . for the time has come for the Saints to go up to the mountains of the Lord's House, and help to establish it upon the tops of the mountains.

Brigham Young's rhetoric must have been either metaphorical or ironic; most Mormon converts in the 1840s were dirt poor and few had anything in the way of gold or silver or "curiosities of science." Poverty, however, is a powerful reason to emigrate, and the Mormons, who were indefatigable missionaries, had no trouble finding converts willing to make the trip. In the first decade of the English mission, founded in 1837, nearly five thousand new Saints traveled to the United States to end up in Nauvoo. And while the Mormons were spending their first winter in Winter Quarters, English converts petitioned Queen Victoria for permission to emigrate, a document that was 168 feet long and contained nearly thirteen thousand signatures. By the time the Saints reached Salt Lake City, the tradition and practice of "the Gathering" was an integral part of the Mormon faith.

The first priority in the emigration process was the relocation of the fifteen thousand or so Saints still in Winter Quarters. The U.S. government had given the Mormons permission to spend the winter of 1846–1847 on Indian land on the west bank of the Missouri River, but now its agents were afraid that the Saints were settling in for good and were pressuring them to move on. Brigham Young had similar worries. A number had already left the church to settle in the Missouri Valley, and the longer the Mormons were left there, the more likely it was that others would join them.

In September 1850, a committee of five was appointed to oversee the transportation of the Saints from the Missouri River camps. Some six thousand dollars was donated, mostly by former Mormon Battalion members, to buy, on the Missouri River, livestock, wagons, and provisions, which, after being used to transport Saints, could be resold for higher prices in the Salt Lake Valley. In this way twenty five hundred persons were brought each summer from the Missouri River to Salt Lake City in 1850 and 1851, and a major push to bring the rest of them, some ten thousand more, in 1852 was preceded by a call from Brigham Young "to come by the tens of thousands . . . to the place of gathering, even, in flocks, as doves fly to their windows before a storm."

Profits from the gold rush trade made it possible for the Saints to finance the large-scale emigration into the Great Basin. In the fall of 1849 a revolving fund, the Perpetual Emigrating Fund, was established "for the purpose of helping the poor Saints to emigrate to this place." The fund was established by donations, mostly produce, equipment, and the like, which the church converted into cash. The money was loaned to those who needed it to emigrate; and the fund was perpetuated, in theory at least, by repayments made by the fund's beneficiaries, the emigrants themselves. In this way, wrote Brigham Young for the first presidency, "these funds are designed to increase until Israel is gathered from all nations, and the poor can sit under their own vine, and inhabit their own house, and worship God in Zion." On September 11,

1850, the legislature of the State of Deseret incorporated the Perpetual Emigrating Fund Company (or PEF, as it was known) to administer the monies.

The PEF more than served its purpose. In 1855, some 4,225 people emigrated from England and Scandinavia. Not all of the newcomers took advantage of the fund; a few paid their own way or had their passage paid by relatives or friends already in Utah but used the ships and wagon trains organized by the company. Others came as part of what was called the ten-pound plan, ten pounds sterling being the amount emigrants paid for passage. Others borrowed the entire amount for their journey from the PEF.

There were a few who converted to Mormonism simply to gain passage to America. Some others apostatized as they crossed the continent, particularly if they had to spend any time in way stations. Otherwise, the migrations were models of efficiency, particularly when compared with the haphazard way most Gentile pioneers made their way across the country. In his *Uncommercial Traveler*, Charles Dickens described the "perfect order and propriety" of a Mormon-chartered ship before it left England. "They had not been a couple of hours on board," he wrote, "when they established their own police, made their own regulations, and set their own watches at all the hatchways. Before nine o'clock the ship was as orderly and as quiet as a man of war."

After arriving in Salt Lake City, the immigrants were assigned to church wards and their welfare made the responsibility of the local bishops. For the first winter the men were usually assigned jobs on a public works project. In the spring, the immigrants might be sent as individuals or groups to colonize a new area or join an already established community. Once they were settled they were expected to begin paying back their loans from the emigrating fund.

Repayments to the PEF, however, were never what the church had hoped; Mormons in the early years did not have wealth to spare, and they were as slow to pay back the emigrating company as they were to pay their tithes. Adding to the cash shortage, the harvests in both 1855 and 1856 were exceptionally bad. Faced with the reality that "we cannot afford to purchase wagons and teams as in times past," Brigham Young came up with an ingenious plan to provide the immigrants with handcarts and let them "foot it," pulling the carts across the country. The plan was based on Young's observation that a "great majority of them walk now even with the teams which are provided, and have a great deal more care and perplexity than they would have if they came without them."

Pulling a handcart loaded with four to five hundred pounds of food and belongings a thousand miles and more from Iowa City or Florence, Nebraska, to Salt Lake City was a grueling ordeal, but the newcomers had the grit to do it. Between 1856 and 1860, more than three thousand people hauling 650 carts successfully made the trip. In the first year, many died when two companies ran into blizzards, but the cause of the tragedy lay in their getting a late start in the season and not in the handcarts themselves.*

Emigration ceased entirely in 1858, the year that federal troops entered Utah, but the influx resumed in full force in 1859. Over the next decade the population of Utah doubled from forty thousand to eighty thousand. After 1869, emigrants were able to cross the plains and mountains in relative safety and comfort aboard the transcontinental railroad.

In his second General Epistle of 1849, Brigham Young wrote that immigrants were needed "until we can say, enough—the valleys of Ephraim are full." By 1887, the year that the Edmunds-Tucker Act disbanded the Perpetual Emigrating Fund Company, that time had come; the Saints were running out of places to send the new arrivals.† In its thirty-eight-year history, the Perpetual

---

* About two hundred members of the Willie and Martin handcart companies died in late 1856. It was the worst tragedy in the history of overland travel. Still, five more handcart companies made the trip successfully in 1857–1860.

† The Edmunds-Tucker Act, the so-called Anti-Polygamy Act, dissolved the Corporation of the Church of Jesus Christ of Latter-day Saints. Arrington called it "a direct bid to destroy the temporal power of the Mormon Church." It also abolished women's suffrage in Utah; the territorial legislature had given women the vote in 1870.

Emigrating Fund had helped some one hundred thousand people emigrate at a cost of over twelve million dollars. This was population enough to make Utah eligible for statehood. The fund and company it supported also "furnished people to settle the territory," Arrington wrote, "and pre-empt its valuable lands before the Gentiles could come in."

"Called" to the Hinterlands

For the Mormons a "call" to settle a remote part of the Great Basin was both an obligation and a test of faith. In the eyes of the church, colonizers were missionaries, just like those who went abroad to spread the faith and gather converts. Brigham Young put together colonizing parties with great care and forethought, making sure that their members were versed in the basic skills needed to succeed in the hinterlands. Often their names were announced from the pulpit or at a church conference. At one such reading a correspondent for the *New York Times* found it "amusing" to watch the anxious faces of the congregation. " 'Is it I?' 'Is it I?' could be plainly read on many a one."

Occasionally men just recently settled in and around Great Salt Lake resisted being uprooted. The prominent Mormon pioneer John D. Lee protested when Young informed him that he was going south to help establish an iron industry. Lee told the Mormon leader that he found the prospect "repugnant," and that he would willingly pay "two thousand dollars in money or goods, if I could furnish and fit out a family to take my place . . ." But Lee went. So did the father of Elijah Averett, who, when he learned that he had been called to southern Utah, reacted angrily: "I'll be damned if I'll go." Then, his son recalled, after sitting with his face in his hands, he looked up and said, "Well, if we are going, we had better start to get ready."

For Young, sending a man on a mission to colonize a remote area was an effective way to get someone he did not like or trust away from the seat of power. This was apparently the reason why

Orson Hyde, an Apostle whose intellectualism Young found distasteful, was assigned to so many colonizing missions. A mission was also a good way to put the idle to work, which is what happened to a group of loiterers that Brigham Young noticed one day. Young sent his secretary to get their names, and the men were soon "called" to settle a remote part of Utah.

The first major move south of Salt Lake City came in March 1848, when a company of 150 people was formed to go to the valley surrounding Utah Lake, the large body of fresh water covering about 150 square miles that was first visited by Europeans in 1776 when the Escalante party made its way over the Wasatch Mountains to its shores. Under its leader, John S. Higbee, the company arrived at the Provo River about April 1, built a fort on its south bank, and began its appointed tasks of "fishing, farming and instructing the Indians in cultivating the earth and teaching them civilization." In September, Brigham Young visited the fort and ordered it moved to higher ground to the east.* This settlement eventually became the city of Provo, named for the trapper Etienne Provost, that early white visitor to the lake. Provo had some trouble with Indians, but it soon took on the trappings of a permanent community with a tannery, sawmill, gristmill, two major canals, and, by 1855, a two-story adobe school.

Another major thrust out of the Salt Lake and Utah Lake Valleys came in November 1849, when the famous Indian chief Wakara invited the Mormons to settle in the Sanpete Valley, about one hundred miles southeast of Salt Lake City. Isaac Morley and the 224 people sent there to minister to the Indians spent a rugged winter in dugouts on the hillside before beginning to build a town the following spring. An epistle from the presidency issued the next year praised the pioneers for persevering "through the deep snows and severe frosts" and for laying "the foundation

---

* Young did the same in Ogden; on a visit there in late 1849 he personally picked a new location for the town. After Salt Lake City, Provo and Ogden were the first major settlements in the Great Basin, and they became the second- and third-largest cities in Utah, with Ogden surpassing Provo after it became a railroad center in 1869.

for a great and glorious work." Brigham Young, on a visit there, named the settlement Manti, from a town in the Book of Mormon, and, a few months before he died, he dedicated the site of the Mormon Temple that took eleven years to build.

While Morley was suffering through the tough winter in Manti, Parley P. Pratt led an exploring expedition to the southern regions of the Great Basin to scout out new areas for settlement. Pratt eventually crossed out of the Great Basin and followed the Colorado River drainage basin to the Virgin River before making his way back to Salt Lake City. He brought back information about natural resources such as iron and timber, the placement of rivers and streams, and the distances between various locations.

The church leadership was particularly impressed with Pratt's description of an area some 250 miles south of Salt Lake, where, on January 8, 1850, he raised a liberty pole and dedicated the spot as "Little Salt Lake City." Not only did the area appear fertile, but there were rich deposits of coal and iron nearby. Accordingly the call went out that fall for "50 or more good and effective men with teams and wagons, provisions and clothing . . ." The company that was formed under Apostle George Smith consisted of 119 men, 30 women, and 9 children. After a difficult winter trip, the group reached the site, which would be called Parowan after a local Indian chief, on January 13, 1851; its mission was to establish an agricultural community to support iron miners and workers who would be sent later to tap the deposits of ore that Pratt had discovered nearby.* As Nels Anderson pointed out in his *Desert Saints: The Mormon Frontier in Utah*, "Brother Brigham, for all his opposition to gold-mining, was of a different mind about iron-mining. He considered iron a civilizer."

* The settlement was first named Fort Louisa after Louisa Beaman, the "first woman of polygamy," who had died the previous May. She had married Joseph Smith on April 5 or 6, 1841, in what Richard S. Van Wagoner, in *Mormon Polygamy: A History*, called the "first distinctly polygamous marriage ceremony." Fawn Brodie, however, in her biography of Smith, listed Beaman as Smith's sixth polygamous wife after his original spouse, Emma Hale. When she died, Beaman was married to Brigham Young.

In November 1851, after the first harvest from Parowan was in, a group of 55 skilled men established the pioneer iron mission at Cedar City, twenty miles south of Parowan. In less than a year, the colony had a small blast furnace working and had produced a small but promising amount of iron. To further the enterprise, a stock company was formed, iron-producing equipment imported from Europe, nearby coal mined, several more furnaces built, money appropriated from the legislature, and 150 men with special skills sent to Cedar City. Brigham Young was sufficiently interested in the project to make several trips to Iron County, as the area was designated, where he advised moving the Cedar City settlement to higher ground. However, technical problems, poor luck, and bad weather plagued the enterprise. Moreover, the iron colony, which had to suspend operation during the Utah War, closed for good in late 1858.

THE WALKER WAR

As the Mormons moved out, north and south, from Salt Lake City, conflicts with Indians increased. There was more to the problem than disputes over land. The Indians were also actively engaged in selling slaves—usually children they captured in raids on other tribes but occasionally white children—to Mexican slave traders, a practice that the Mormons found abhorrent and tried to stop. In 1852, the Utah legislature passed a law outlawing the slave trade within the territory. This outraged Ute chief Wakara (or Walker), a friend and trading partner of the mountain men, who had originally invited the Mormons to settle on Ute land and who, in 1850, had allowed himself to be baptized in the Mormon faith. In parleys with the Mormons over the slavery issue, Walker argued that to stop the trade with the Mexicans, the Mormons must buy the children. Although that solution was not acceptable to the Mormons, Brigham Young had earlier thought along similar lines. In reporting on an address he gave in Parowan in 1851, he said: "I advised them to buy up the Lamanite children as fast as they could, and educate them, and teach them in the Gospel, so that not many generations would pass ere they would become a white and delightsome people."*

Walker's growing distrust of the Mormons came to a head in July 1853 when a Mormon settler near Springville killed a Ute and wounded two others in a trading dispute. Walker, who was camped nearby, demanded that the Mormon killer be turned over to the Utes. When the Mormons refused, Walker began a series of raids on Mormon settlers and settlements that became known as the Walker War. The trouble lasted nine or ten months. In that time, between twelve and twenty Mormons were killed, but hundreds of families were uprooted and their homes destroyed. The Utes probably suffered more casualties; nine Indians were shot down when they came to a Mormon camp looking for food. Brigham Young blamed the Mormon casualties on the settlers' failure to take his advice to build forts and live together for mutual protection: "I told you six years ago to build a fort that the *Devil could not get into*, unless you were disposed to let him in, and that would keep the Indians out. . . ."

Young was instrumental in stopping the fighting. Soon after hostilities broke out, he sent a gift of tobacco to Chief Wakara with a promise of cattle and flour to come. In the accompanying letter, which he addressed to "Captain Walker," Young wrote: "You are a fool for fighting your best friends, for we are the best friends, and the only friends that you have in the world. Everybody else would kill you if they could get a chance. . . . When you get good natured again I would like to see you. Don't you think you should be ashamed? You know that I have always been your best friend." Further gifts and a face-to-face meeting between Young, Walker, and other chiefs at the Indians' camp secured the peace. Young continued to court Walker with gifts and letters, and just before the Indian leader died in January 1855 Young

---

* Brigham Young's phrase "white and delightsome" is a variation on a Book of Mormon prophecy that the Indians would become "a pure and a delightsome people."

wrote him that the Mormons were the Utes' best friends "because the Red Men have descended from the same fathers and are of the same family as the Mormons, and we love them, and shall continue to love them, and teach them things that may do them good."

In arranging a halt to the hostilities, Young was careful to distinguish between Mormons and other Americans ("Mormonee" and "Mericats," as the Indians called them). This distinction angered federal Indian agents and others in Washington who suspected that the Mormons were plotting to turn the Indians against all Gentiles. In reporting on the missionaries that the Mormons were sending out among the Indians, Indian Agent Garland Hurt speculated in a letter to his superiors in Washington: "And what sir may be expected of these missionaries? . . . I suspect their first object will be to teach these wretched savages that they are the rightful owners of the American soil and that it has been wrongfully taken from them by the whites and that the Great Spirit has sent the Mormons among them to help them recover their rights."

The Mormons were embroiled in this crisis, when, in October 1853, a band of Pahvant Utes attacked a U.S. surveying party, killing its leader, Captain John W. Gunnison, and six others. The failure of the Mormons to apprehend the culprits caused such an outcry in the East that Colonel E. J. Steptoe and a detachment of soldiers were sent to Utah for the purpose, among others, of apprehending the guilty Indians. To help defuse the situation, the Pahvant leader, the accommodating Chief Kanosh, turned over six members of his tribe, who may or may not have been directly involved in the massacre. In the 1855 trial, a Mormon jury convicted three of them of manslaughter and sentenced them to three-year terms. The light sentences and the unlikelihood that the defendants were truly guilty convinced many Gentiles that the Mormons were not interested in prosecuting Indian crimes against non-Mormons. To the Mormons' enemies, this perceived alliance with the Indians proved that the Mormons were in revolt against the U.S. government and contributed to the decision to send a federal army to Utah in 1857.

The Mormons were also worried that the Gentiles might turn the Indians against them. This was the excuse they gave for moving against their old acquaintance, Jim Bridger, whom they accused of selling arms to the natives. In 1853 they sent a large posse to Fort Bridger to arrest him. Bridger evaded them, but he was never again able to operate from his fort, and two years later he and his partner, Louis Vasquez, sold Fort Bridger to the Mormons for eight thousand dollars. After ousting Bridger, the Mormons built Fort Supply only a few miles away and took over Bridger's lucrative trade on the Oregon Trail and the ferries he operated on the Green River. The action against Bridger contributed to Brigham Young's reputation for ruthlessness and to the stories that he commanded a band of "Avenging Angels," or Danites, to send against his enemies.*

THE "OUTER CORDON"

Once they had gotten rid of Bridger, Fort Supply became part of the network of colonies and way stations that the Mormons established on the fringes of the Great Basin at some distance from Salt Lake City. The purpose of these far-flung settlements was to unite, protect, and lay claim to the immense territory contained within the boundaries of the State of Deseret. In 1855, Fort Lemhi was established on the Salmon River four hundred miles north of Salt Lake City and well outside the boundaries of the Great Basin. In 1855, Apostle Orson Hyde established a Mormon colony in Nevada's Carson Valley on the Great Basin's western edge, where a trading post known as Mormon Station on the

* In his colorful biography of Bridger, Stanley Vestal listed ten reasons why Brigham Young disliked the mountain man, most of which reflect poorly on the Mormon leader. Among them were the facts that Bridger was from the hated state of Missouri and that "Brigham had come to Utah to be the big buck of that lick, and here was Bridger before him—famous from Mexico to the British Possessions, from the Missouri to the Pacific."

route to San Francisco had been, by that time, in operation for five years. (Hyde renamed the site Genoa, because the mountains reminded him of Genoa, Italy, where he had been a missionary.) These far-flung colonies, often referred to as the Mormon "outer cordon," included San Bernardino in southern California and Moab in eastern Utah and stretched the Mormon presence out to the strategic entrances of its Great Basin empire.

In the colonization scheme, Mormon settlements often served more than one function. Las Vegas was an Indian mission and lead mining center. Parowan was for agriculture and iron production. Both settlements served as important way stations on the route from Salt Lake City to the Pacific Ocean known as the Mormon Corridor. As Brigham Young saw it, the corridor was the cord that held the Deseret empire together. Stretching from Salt Lake City to San Diego, the corridor gave the Mormons what every empire needed—an outlet to the sea. The Mormons also hoped it would become an easy land route for immigrants into the Great Basin. The plan, never realized, was for immigrants to come from Europe, by ship, around Cape Horn to California and on to Salt Lake City via the Mormon Corridor.

The westernmost settlement along the Mormon Corridor was San Bernardino, which began when Amasa M. Lyman and Charles Coulson Rich purchased a 35,500-acre ranch in 1851 for $77,500. Their charge, as recorded in Brigham Young's journal, was to select a site near the Cajon Pass; "to gather around them the Saints in California"; to scout out other locations for settlements between Parowan and the Pacific; to cultivate olives, grapes, sugar cane, cotton, "and any other desirable fruits and products"; and to collect information about a route across the Isthmus of Panama "or the passage around Cape Horn with a view to the gathering of the saints from Europe." In a grandiose flourish typical of Mormon proclamations, the journal entry ended by instructing the missionaries "to plant the standard of salvation in every county and kingdom, city and village, on the Pacific and the world over, as fast as God should give the ability."

The Mormons invested considerable time, money, and manpower in Las Vegas but the lead turned out to be impure. San Bernardino, by contrast, appeared to be a thriving proposition. Four years after the purchase of the ranch in 1851, there were fourteen hundred Saints in residence. Four thousand acres were under cultivation, timber was being felled, and the colony had become a way station for Mormon emigrants and missionaries heading in and out of the Great Basin. Still, Brigham Young never liked California, and he was not enthusiastic about a colony there. Besides, there was plenty of evidence that the San Bernardino colony was, as historian Eugene Campbell noted, "a costly failure," resulting from land disputes, conflicts with non-Mormon neighbors, and dissension among the Saints themselves. So, in 1857, when he learned that federal troops were on the way to Utah, Brigham Young called his missionary-colonizers in Las Vegas, San Bernardino, Carson Valley, and elsewhere to abandon their towns and settlements and come home to Salt Lake City, where they were needed to help protect the Kingdom from the godless hordes.

Chapter Ten

POLYGAMY:

"HOLY SEED

UNTO THE LORD"

n August 29, 1852, at a special church conference in Salt
Lake City, Apostle Orson Pratt announced from the pulpit that the Mormons practiced polygamy—or plural marriage, as
the Saints preferred to call it.* This was hardly news; there had
been reports, rumors, and accusations—all true but strenuously
denied—of polygamy among the Saints for nearly two decades.
What made Pratt's announcement important was the fact that the
years of lying and denying were over and that the Mormons now
felt secure enough and sufficiently isolated in the Great Basin to
admit to the world that they practiced a form of marriage that
most of their countrymen found morally repugnant (even though
there were no laws against polygamy at the time).

---

* Polygamy is what it was most often called, but the Mormon practice of it is
more accurately described as polygyny, "the condition or practice of having more
than one wife at a time." Polyandry, which the Saints did not practice, is "the

The institution had been part of Mormon theology almost from the beginning. Joseph Smith might have had his first revelation on polygamy as early as 1831, a year after the church began.* Rumors that Smith was practicing polygamy began to surface about 1835, the same year that, some believe, he was "sealed" to his first plural wife, a nineteen-year-old servant named Fanny Alger, "a varry nice & Comely young woman," according to a friend. In 1841, Smith, in confidence, told the Twelve about plural marriage with the admonition that they, too, were to "take extra wives or be damned."

Reports of polygamy followed the Saints from Ohio to Missouri to Illinois and contributed to the hostility they encountered wherever they settled. The dissent that polygamy caused within the church led directly to the arrest and murder of Joseph Smith in the Carthage (Illinois) jail on June 27, 1844, after he had ordered an anti-polygamist paper, the *Nauvoo Expositor*, destroyed. When Pratt's admission of polygamy reached England, droves of recent converts, who had been assured there was nothing to the rumors, deserted the church. But polygamy was also the glue that held the church together. Rarely did a man with more than one wife apostatize or even voice the mildest dissent from within the fold. The opposition that polygamy aroused made the Mormons defiant and molded them into a proud and truly peculiar people.

Apostle Pratt was an interesting choice to make the announcement: In Nauvoo he had been excommunicated for opposing polygamy, or, specifically, Joseph Smith's polygamous proposal to his wife, Sarah. Pratt was away on a mission in England when Smith asked Sarah Pratt to become one of his spiritual wives, telling her, "I have the blessing of Jacob granted me, as he granted

---

practice of having more than one husband at a time." Polygamy, strictly defined, covers both practices.

* In his later years Orson Pratt recalled Smith's telling him and a few others in early 1832 that the Lord had informed him "that the principle of taking more wives than one is a true principle, but the time had not yet come for it to be practiced."

holy men of old, and I have long looked upon you with favor." Sarah rebuffed him with a spirited reply: "I care not for the blessing of Jacob. I have one good husband, and that is enough for me." When Pratt confronted Smith on his return, the prophet tried but failed to convince him that he was only testing Sarah's faith and virtue, an explanation he had used successfully in several similar situations. The recalcitrant Pratt was excommunicated in August 1841, but he remained in Nauvoo and, after reconciling with Smith, was reinstated as both a church member and an Apostle a year and a half later. Pratt's selection to make the official announcement on polygamy in 1852 was a sign to Mormons and non-Mormons alike that the leadership of the Latter-day Saints stood together on plural marriage.

Pratt also had a theoretical bent, and he clearly laid out arguments in favor of polygamy that the Saints would use for years to come. Four-fifths of the people in the world practiced some form of polygamy, he told his audience. The proof that it was a righteous form of marriage was in the Bible: The Old Testament's Abraham, Isaac, and Jacob were all polygamists, and there was reason to believe that Jesus, too, had several wives.* Polygamy would give every woman the opportunity to be, as God intended, a wife and mother, and it would protect men, who were afflicted with stronger sex drives, from succumbing to the baser side of their own natures. The alternative to polygamy, Pratt explained, was "whoredom, adultery, and fornication." Finally, Pratt invoked the Constitution:

---

* Pratt and others argued that Jesus had three wives: Mary Magdalene, and Lazarus's two sisters, Mary and Martha. Orson Hyde went a step further and preached that "Jesus Christ was married at Cana of Galilee, that Mary, Martha, and others were his wives, and that he begat children." To those who accused him of blasphemy, Hyde responded that "they [his critics] worship a Saviour that is too pure and holy to fulfill the commands of his Father. I worship one that is just pure and holy enough 'to fulfill all righteousness'; not only the righteous law of baptism, but the still more righteous and important law to 'multiply and replenish the earth.' "

I think, if I am not mistaken, that the Constitution gives the privilege to all of the inhabitants of this country, of the free exercise of their religious notions, and the freedom of their faith and the practice of it. Then, if it can be proved to a demonstration that the Latter-day Saints have actually embraced, as a part and portion of their religion, the doctrine of a plurality of wives, it is constitutional. And should there ever be laws enacted by this government to restrict them from the free exercise of this part of their religion, such laws must be unconstitutional.

Pratt's description of polygamy as "part and portion" of the Mormon religion was particularly apt. For that is exactly what it was—not just an embellishment that Joseph Smith added on to Mormonism, but an integral part of a theology. This body of faith has been much altered since the nineteenth century, and it might seem as odd to Mormons of today as it does to Gentiles. Simplified—or, rather, oversimplified—it held that (1) God, before progressing to his exalted state in heaven, was once a man on earth; (2) before humans are born, they exist as spirits waiting for earthly bodies; (3) after death, men will gradually become godlike in heaven; and (4) produce more preexistent spirits in polygamous unions with the celestial wives who had been sealed to them for eternity on earth. Meanwhile (5) polygamous Mormons on earth are producing earthly bodies, sometimes called "tabernacles," for the preexisting spirits. And so it goes, in a cycle ending only at the millennium.

Theologically a major problem remained: Polygamy was expressly prohibited by the Book of Mormon, which read, "Wherefore, my brethren, hear me, and hearken to the word of the Lord: For there shall not any man among you have save it be one wife; and concubines he shall have none . . ." (Jacob 2:27).* Such an

---

* And, among other passages, Jacob 2:24: "Behold, David and Solomon truly had many wives and concubines, which thing was abominable before me, saith the Lord."

interdiction, however, was overlooked in deference to a greater need, stipulated by Mormon theology, to provide earthly bodies for waiting spirits, who would become Mormons on earth and progress to a godlike state in the hereafter. Since the Mormons believe the family continues after death, the larger the family, the more exalted would one be in Heaven. "I will tell you," Heber Kimball once preached, "that some of the most noble spirits are waiting with the Father to this day to come forth through the right channel and the right kind of men and women. That is what has to be yet; for there are thousands and millions of spirits waiting to obtain bodies upon this earth."

"All this," wrote the anti-Mormon J. H. Beadle in his 1870 book, *Life in Utah; or, the Mysteries and Crimes of Mormonism*, "points unerringly to polygamy," and, in *The American Religion*, a more balanced study published in 1992, Yale scholar Harold Bloom noted: "Marked by the glory and stigma of plural marriage, the Mormons of 1850 through 1890 indeed became a peculiar people, a nation apart. But . . . Joseph Smith did not wish merely to set his Saints apart. He wished them to become gods, and he decided that polygamy was necessary for that apotheosis." The Saints of the day regarded the institution in much the same light: A petition sent to Washington protesting proposed anti-polygamy legislation explained that Mormons were "believers in the principle of plural marriage or polygamy not simply as an elevating social relationship and a preventive of many terrible evils which afflict our race, but as a principle revealed by god, underlying our every hope of eternal salvation and happiness in heaven."

"All Good and More Good"

By 1852, the Mormon practice of plural marriage was a poorly kept secret. Three years earlier, during the winter he spent in Salt Lake City, the astute government surveyor Howard Stansbury wrote in his report that the practice of polygamy among the Mormons "cannot be concealed from any one of the most ordinary observation, who has spent even a short time in this community." Brigham Young had, in fact, publicly admitted his own multiplicity of wives more than a year before the 1852 announcement. "I have more wives than one," he told the territorial legislature on February 4, 1851. "I have many and I am not ashamed to have it known." (On the same occasion he asserted that it was the Mormons' saintly duty "to have more wives than one, to live holy and raise up holy seed unto the Lord.") A year later, on March 9, 1852, the Mormon polemicist, Jedediah M. Grant, wrote a letter to the *New York Herald* defending polygamy. This set off a debate in print between a Mormon writer, W. W. Phelps, and the *Herald*'s well-known editor, James Gordon Bennett, in which Phelps wrote: "Of two evils, a Mormon chooses neither but goes in for all good and more good; which, if, as Solomon said, a good wife is a good thing, then the more you have the more good you have." Phelps added words that would become a familiar refrain in the debate over polygamy: "The federal authorities have no power over morality—that belongs to the good old book, the word of the Lord."

Even after polygamy was publicly admitted, John Bernhisel, Utah's delegate to Congress in Washington, D.C., protested to Brigham Young that public exposure of the institution served only to confirm many Gentiles in their belief that Mormons were "among the most immoral and licentious beings on the face of the globe." The Mormons' perception was quite different: Polygamy, as Brigham Young preached and advocated it, was for the purpose of procreation in this life and salvation in the next. The Mormon leader railed continuously at the hypocrisy of those Gentiles who condoned prostitution and adultery but condemned polygamy. "Tell Christians that 'a Mormon' has two wives, they are shocked, and call it dreadful blasphemy," Young preached just weeks before Pratt's "Plurality of Wives" sermon; "if you whisper such a thing into the ears of a Gentile who takes a fresh woman every night, he is thunderstruck with the enormity of the crime."

While readers back east were continually treated to sensational and prurient reports of wantonness among the Mormons, more thoughtful visitors usually had to admit that Salt Lake City was an uncommonly orderly and law-abiding place, its streets virtually free of crime, disturbances, and women of the night. Nor did polygamy seem to them to be at all risqué. The English traveler Richard Burton stated the case dryly: "All sensuality in the married state is strictly forbidden beyond the requisite for ensuring progeny." Howard Stansbury admired how, among the Mormons of Salt Lake City, "Purity of life, in all the domestic relations, is strenuously inculcated." And Mark Twain, tongue firmly in cheek, passing through Salt Lake City in 1861, related how his own opposition to polygamy dissolved when he finally saw "the Mormon women":

> Then I was touched. My heart was wiser than my head. It warmed toward these poor, ungainly and pathetically "homely" creatures, and as I turned to hide the generous moisture in my eyes, I said, "No—the man that marries one of them has done an act of Christian charity which entitles him to the kindly applause of mankind, not their hard censure—and the man that marries sixty of them has done a deed of open-handed generosity so sublime that the nations should stand uncovered in his presence and worship in silence."*

"If Any Man Espouse a Virgin . . ."

Much of the literature on the early years of Mormonism may leave the reader with the impression that, sexually, Joseph Smith was a rogue. Smith's most distinguished biographer, the Mormon-born historian Fawn Brodie, was excommunicated after the publication of her *No Man Knows My History* (1945), acclaimed by non-Mormon critics, which portrayed Smith as something of a philanderer. The charge was certainly not new. In his 1870 anti-

---

* Not every visitor had this impression of Mormon women; Burton wrote of "the lofty, thoughtful brow, the clear transparent complexion, the long silky hair, and, greatest charm of all, the soft smile . . ."

Mormon book, *Life in Utah*, author J. H. Beadle claimed that a phrenologist, after measuring Joseph Smith's head, determined that his " 'amativeness,' or sexual passion," was almost off the chart—an eleven on a scale of one to twelve. In this "propensity," Beadle wrote, "was the real origin of polygamy." The few portraits we have of Smith—in elaborate tailcoat or the gaudy uniform of the Nauvoo Legion—add to his reputation as something of a dandy or roué.

When Smith told his Apostles to take extra wives, Brigham Young was shocked. It was, he recalled later, "the first time in my life that I had desired the grave . . . when I saw a funeral, I felt to envy the corpse in its situation and to regret that I was not in the coffin, the toil and labor that my body would have to undergo." Nor were the Apostles' wives pleased at the news. Phebe Woodruff, wife of Wilford Woodruff, thought the principle of plural marriage "was the most wicked thing I ever heard of; consequently I opposed it to the best of my ability, until I became sick and wretched." Joseph Smith's strong-willed wife, Emma, was another vociferous opponent of polygamy and, on that subject, a continual thorn in her husband's side.

Hyrum Smith, the prophet's brother, also had his doubts about taking another wife and asked his brother to seek assurances from God that polygamy was not a sin. The result was Joseph's famous revelation of July 12, 1843: "If any man espouse a virgin, and desire to espouse another, and the first give her consent, and if he espouse the second, and they are virgins, and have vowed to no other man, then he is justified: he cannot commit adultery."* The revelation also made clear that the purpose of plural marriage was to "multiply and replenish the earth," that a man's progress to godlike status in the hereafter depended on the number of wives he acquired in this world and the number of children he

---

* In *Mormon Polygamy: A History*, Richard S. Van Wagoner wrote that, since Smith was already an active polygamist, the church leaders "after his death concluded that the revelation was given as early as 1831 and merely written down on 12 July 1843." However, Van Wagoner pointed out, "Smith's journal for the day [July 12] pointedly says: 'Received a Revelation in the office in presence of Hyrum & Wm Clayton.' "

produced. As Richard S. Van Wagoner wrote in his history of Mormon polygamy, "Salvation became a family affair revolving around a husband whose plural wives and children were sealed to him for eternity under the 'new and everlasting covenant.' "

The most curious part of the July 12 revelation was the way it addressed itself directly "unto mine handmaid, Emma Smith, your wife," and ordered her to "receive all those that have been given unto my servant, Joseph, and who are virtuous and pure before me." It added that she was to "abide and cleave unto my servant Joseph" and to "forgive my servant Joseph his trespasses." Despite a warning that she would be destroyed if she didn't obey these commandments, Emma Smith was unmoved. Hyrum Smith, who volunteered to show the revelation to her, came back from the encounter shaken, saying he had never been so abused in his life. Emma later supposedly burned the revelation, but a copy wound up under lock and key in Brigham Young's office in Salt Lake City, so Young told the audience during the first public reading of the revelation following Orson Pratt's announcement in 1852.*

Despite any misgivings, Brigham Young soon became an active participant in the system of plural marriage. He took his first plural wife, twenty-year-old Lucy Ann Decker Seeley, in June of 1842 and two more—one forty-one years old, the other nineteen—in November of the following year. He married Lucy Ann's fifteen-year-old sister, Clarissa Decker, in May 1844—and, by marrying sisters, set a precedent that many other men would follow.† Over the next year he took fifteen more, including five wid-

---

* After the Saints left Nauvoo, Emma Smith, her son William, and other family members stayed in the Midwest and founded the Reorganized Church of Latter-day Saints, today the largest Mormon offshoot, headquartered in Independence, Missouri. The "Josephites," as they were sometimes called, maintained that Joseph Smith never practiced or preached polygamy.

† In his oddly titled study, *Isn't One Wife Enough?* (1954), Mormon sociologist Kimball Young estimated that 20 percent of polygamous Mormon men married sisters. Often her sister was the only additional wife that a first wife would accept.

ows of Joseph Smith, two of whom bore him children.* According to one count, by the year of the public announcement, 1852, Young had already sired thirty-two children. Denying that he or any other Mormon practiced polygamy when he was surrounded by wives and children must have been an ordeal for Brigham Young, so we can assume that he ordered the public announcement in 1852 with a sense of relief.

Now that polygamy was out in the open, Brigham Young had to endure his share of attacks; in the years immediately following the announcement, the apostate John Hyde described Young's wives as "companions of his passions, . . . panderers to his lusts," and Salt Lake City was decried as the "modern Gomorrah." Still, from today's perspective, it appears that history has been kinder to Brigham Young, the polygamist, than to his predecessor, Joseph Smith. This might stem from the fact that several of Young's marriages to older women were not connubial in a sexual sense, or the fact that Young's last wife, Ann Eliza Webb, a twenty-five-year-old divorcée whom he married in 1867, claimed after their divorce that their marriage was never consummated, although she was only twenty-five when she married him.† Or it might be the visual image we have of him: A widely published photograph taken later in his life shows him to be a dignified and patriarchal figure, and, unlike Joseph Smith, not at all sensual. Such a man could be believed when he said: "God never introduced the Patriarchal order of marriage with a view to please man in his carnal desires,

---

* Here is where the Mormon practice of plural marriage gets complicated. Since these widows were sealed to Joseph Smith for time and eternity, they remain married to Brigham Young only for his or their lifetime. In the next world, they will again be married to Joseph Smith. Similarly, the children they bore Brigham Young were his for "time" only. In eternity, they would become the children of Joseph Smith.

† In divorcing Young in 1876, Ann Eliza took him to court, and in 1877, the last year of his life, he was charged with contempt for failing to pay alimony. She later wrote an exposé, titled *The Nineteenth Wife*, which, when they were married, was her ranking among his living wives. Overall, she was the twenty-seventh.

nor to punish females for anything which they had done; but He introduced it for the express purpose of raising up to His name a royal Priesthood, a peculiar people."*

Brigham Young's marital situation was the subject of constant curiosity and speculation: One of many groundless reports had him, once he had decided which of his many wives he would spend the night with, making a chalk mark on her bedroom door to remind him when he returned later in the evening. For humorists his enormous family was a rich lode of material. Hence Josh Billings's quip: "All girls marry Young—in Utah" and Artemus Ward's vain attempt, on a visit to Salt Lake City, to estimate the size of Young's family: "I undertook to count the long stockings, on the clothes-line, in his back yard one day, and I used up the multiplication table in less than half an hour." For his part, Young seemed to enjoy the confusion his large family caused. Once, when speaking in public of his intention to take his family on an excursion around Salt Lake City, he added: "You know what they say about me in the east; should I take my ninety wives and their children, with carriages and waggons enough to convey them, it would make such a vacuum here . . . that there would be no Salt Lake City. I think I will take a few of them, but I dare not take the whole, for if I did they would then know how many wives I have got, and that would not do."

Some early visitors to Utah noticed that Mormon women appeared unnaturally quiet and withdrawn, a view that Horace Greeley shared when, in 1859, he wrote: "I have not observed a sign in the streets, and advertisement in the journals, of this Mormon metropolis, whereby a woman proposes to do anything whatever." It was a harsh judgment. Utah at that time was a frontier and pioneer society still struggling to survive, and we can be

---

* In his biography of Brigham Young, Leonard Arrington listed twenty-seven wives. Young had fifty-seven children by sixteen of these. In addition, Arrington wrote, there were "some thirty women who were 'sealed' to Brigham Young 'for eternity only,' with no intention that he would share earthly life with them or their children, if any, by earlier marriages."

sure that, behind the scenes, on farms and in households, women were doing plenty. In 1856 the Poetess of Zion, Eliza Snow, helped found the Polysophical Society with her brother Lorenzo, but otherwise there was little time or inclination for the cultural pastimes usually associated with women in the mid-nineteenth century. Author of the favorite Mormon hymn "O My Father" and ten volumes of poetry, Eliza Snow was an exception to any unfavorable generalization about Mormon women, but she also had impeccable credentials as a polygamous wife, having been married to both Joseph Smith and Brigham Young. In 1866, at Brigham Young's behest, she reorganized the Female Relief Society, a charitable and educational organization, and became, as its president and the wife of prophets, the first woman of Mormondom.

The enemies of Mormonism enjoyed depicting polygamy luridly as promiscuity run amok, but, when viewed statistically, the institution of plural marriage becomes considerably less titillating. Still, the numbers tell an interesting story. Recent studies indicate that only 10 to 15 percent of adult Mormon males had more than one wife. But when the plural wives are added into the figures, it becomes very possible that half of the adult Mormon population was in a polygamous relationship. These figures varied according to time and place. During the religious revival known as the Mormon Reformation, the rush into plural marriage was so great that Brigham Young was worn out conducting sealing ceremonies. As for location, polygamy was more prevalent in southern Utah, where there were also fewer monogamous Gentiles. In 1880, for example, 40 percent of the households in southern St. George were polygamous compared with a mere 5 percent in South Weber, north of Salt Lake City.

A frequently cited 1956 study by Stanley Ivins of six thousand families indicated that most men (66.3 percent) limited themselves to two wives, while 21.2 percent had three spouses. After that, the numbers fell off sharply: Only 6.7 percent of the men had four wives, and even fewer (5.8 percent) had families that included five

wives or more. From these figures, Ivins concluded, probably cor-
rectly, that the "typical polygamist, far from being the insatiable
male of popular fable, was a dispassionate fellow content to call a
halt after marrying one extra wife, required to assure him of his
chance to salvation."

Although polygamy was the ideal to which all Mormons were to
aspire, no man could take an additional wife without the permission of the church. In this way, Young managed to restrict the
practice to the prosperous and the devout. "Whose privilege is it
to have women sealed to him?" he asked in a sermon. "It is his
who has stood the test, whose integrity is unswerving, who loves
righteousness because it is right, and the truth because there is no
error therein. . . . It is such a man's privilege. . . . Who else? No
one. I tell you nobody else." As he pushed church leaders into
polygamy, Young made it clear that a plurality of wives was the
key to status in both church and heaven. On this as on most subjects, Brigham Young came right to the point: "Now if any of you
will deny the plurality of wives, and continue to do so, I promise
that you will be damned. . . ." Young also came up with the interesting idea that, in the afterlife, the wives of monogamists will be
taken away and given to other men, those worthies who, on earth,
had embraced polygamy.

Polygamy was practiced in the open for no more than two
decades before pressure from the federal government began to
drive it underground. That was hardly enough time for the Mormons to develop many rules governing its conduct, but there were
codes. Number one was contained in Joseph Smith's 1843 revelation: "If any man espouse a virgin, and desire to espouse another,
and the first give her consent . . ." In many marriages, the first wife
was involved in the process of choosing another wife for her husband, either by consent or by actively participating in the selection process. (A few women even pushed reluctant spouses into
polygamy in the belief that their own salvation and that of their
children depended on the men marrying again.) In the plural marriage ceremony, the first wife stood between the bride and groom,

and, after agreeing to the union, placed the new wife's right hand in her husband's. But not all wives were that agreeable, and the rule requiring their consent and/or participation in the ceremony was often flouted. The Mormon historian Juanita Brooks wrote that after her grandmother sabotaged one of her husband's courtships, he wooed and married his next wife in secret.

Polygamous husbands were supposed to provide each wife with her own residence, but, in fact, they often shared the same house. Brigham Young was no exception: He housed eighteen or twenty under the roof of the Beehive House in Salt Lake City. Men were also supposed to be impartial in their relationships with their wives. "I love my wives, respect them, and honor them," Young once said, "but to make a queen of one and peasants of the rest I have no such disposition, neither do I expect to do it." Then, in 1862, at age sixty-one, he met and fell in love with tall, beautiful, twenty-five-year-old Amelia Folsom, and impartiality was forgotten. After they were married in January the next year, she received a house of her own, occupied the place of honor by Brigham Young's side in his box at the theater, and was his sole wifely companion on his trips through the territory.* In her bitter recollection of marriage to Brigham Young, Ann Eliza wrote: "Polygamist, as he professes to be, he is under the influence of Amelia, rapidly becoming a monogamist, in all except the name."

How women fared in plural marriages is a subject of endless historical speculation. In an essay, "Plural Wives," Stephanie Smith Goodson observed, "Opinions about what it was like to live in polygamy range all the way from Fanny Stenhouse's and Ann Eliza Young's tirades against the indignities suffered by the women to the often saccharine 'never-a-cross-word-was-uttered' accounts of some of the descendants of polygamous families."

---

* In 1873, Young installed Amelia as hostess at his winter home in St. George, Utah, replacing the ailing Lucy Bigelow, who had filled that role in another house since 1870. Lucy's daughter wrote: "Mother's heart twisted with sorrow at the thought of her dear husband coming down to spend his winters in another woman's home. [After all] she was human—she was a woman."

Mormon men invariably took younger women as plural wives—usually they were in their late teens no matter how old the husband—and jealousy was the inevitable result. Sarah Pratt, whose husband Orson overcame his original aversion to polygamy, became an outspoken opponent of plural marriage when her husband announced, in 1868, that he would henceforth spend equal time with each of his six wives, in her words, "a week with one, a week with another and so on, and that I should have the sixth week." In another statement she characterized polygamy as the "direst curse with which a people or a nation could be afflicted . . . It completely demoralizes good men, and makes bad men correspondingly worse. As for the women—well, God help them!"

The Mormons permitted divorce, and, in polygamy, there were a significant number of marital breakups. Brigham Young, who publicly complained about "the everlasting whining of many of the women of this Territory," counseled women to stick with their husbands "until life became too burdensome, then leave and seek a divorce." Young also reminded women that the purpose of marriage was not romantic love but the production of more Mormons. Presumptuously putting himself in their place, he once said, "I would not care whether they [the husbands] loved a particle or not; but I would cry out, like one of old, in the joy of my heart, 'I have got a man from the Lord!' 'Hallelujah! I am a mother—I have borne an image of God!' "

"Saints, Live Your Religion!"

Polygamy was in the forefront in late 1856 when the Saints in Utah experienced a brief but intense religious revival, called the Mormon Reformation. The revival came at a low point in the Mormons' brief (nine-year) sojourn in the Great Basin. As winter approached, they were demoralized by a poor harvest, discouraged over the fate of the Willie and Martin handcart companies, and under increasing fire over polygamy. Then, on September 13, 1856, a firebrand named Jedediah Grant confronted a conference in Kaysville, Utah, with the challenge: "Saints, live your religion." Grant called for repentance, rebaptism, and spiritual renewal as well as a rededication to practical principles ranging from polygamy to tithing, and even personal cleanliness and orderliness.

Brigham Young had been previously urging the Mormons to shake off their lethargy and rededicate themselves to the task of establishing Zion in the Great Basin, but Grant just happened to strike the right chord, and Young let him take the lead in the Reformation. Within weeks, Mormons all over the territory were indulging themselves in a frenzy of speaking in tongues, rebaptisms, and personal confessions. All religious revivals breed excesses; this one produced Brigham Young's harsh dictum—the doctrine of blood atonement—that certain crimes are so serious that they must be atoned for with the transgressor's life. Historians have never agreed on how often blood was "spilt upon the ground" in observance of the doctrine, but there is evidence that certain Gentiles and apostates came to a violent end during this period.

A more benign instance of religious enthusiasm occurred when Young, at a church meeting, asked everyone who had committed adultery to stand up, and three-quarters of the all-male audience rose to its feet. Then the astonished prophet explained that he meant only adultery *after* they had become Mormons, but the men, in their determination to admit sin, remained standing. As Ray B. West, Jr., explained in *Kingdom of the Saints* (1957), the British-born Mormon writer T. B. H. Stenhouse, who observed the gathering, was astonished, "writing that during his twenty-five years of association with the Mormons, he 'never knew of more than two or three cases of this kind, and the transgressors were immediately excommunicated . . . There has always been a dreadful horror of the crime of adultery in the minds of the Mormons.' "

Much of the rhetoric of the Reformation was directed at wives and their complaints about polygamy. "We have women here who like everything but the Celestial Law of God," Grant said on September 21, "and if they could, would break asunder the cable of the Church of Christ; there is scarcely a mother in Israel but would do it this day." On the same occasion, Young made an unusual offer to women: If they decided within two weeks that they wanted to be free from their husbands, he would grant them a divorce. The offer applied to his own wives as well. "I will go to heaven alone rather than have scratching and fighting around me," he said.

The Saints responded not by divorcing, but by marrying more, a rush to matrimony sustained by a belief that the millennium was at hand and that God would look kindly on polygamists on Judgment Day. In short order, the Reformation became, in the words of a Salt Lake City woman, "the greatest time for marrying I ever knew." Brigham Young, Wilford Woodruff wrote, "hardly [had] time to eat, drink, or sleep, in consequence of marrying the people. . . ," adding that the supply of eligible females was quickly being depleted. "There is hardly a girl fourteen years old in Utah, but what is married, or just going to be."

The Reformation was short-lived but intense; Jedediah Grant died unexpectedly on December 1, 1856, and the revival died out about six months later. As the spirit waned, many men and women began to regret their hasty decisions to marry. In 1858, a year after the furor died down, Young was so overwhelmed by the number of divorces he had to grant that he threatened to stop performing marriages. The divorce rate might have caused him to think twice about polygamy; in his book, Van Wagoner speculated, "There is some evidence in the decade preceding his demise [in 1877] that Young may have been waning in his support for polygamy. . . ." In 1871 Young announced that a man did not have to take a second wife to "be justified before the Lord." Embracing the law of celestial marriage in his heart was enough.

A "Relic of Barbarism"

Once the doctrine of plural marriage was made public, most Saints supported the peculiar institution, although a few expressed doubt and dissent. In Washington, the Mormon representative to Congress, John Bernhisel, expressed apprehension that the cat was out of the bag concerning polygamy "to which," wrote M. R. Werner, author of a 1925 biography of Young, "Brigham Young and Heber Kimball remarked that the cat had many kittens, which would always be a source of antagonism, for 'Christ and Satan never can be friends; light and darkness will always remain opposites.'" In Utah, a group of anti-polygamists, called Gladdenites after their leader, Gladden Bishop, left the church over the issue, but their movement was short-lived after Brigham Young denounced Bishop from the pulpit as a "poor, dirty curse" and delivered one of his famous threats: "I say, rather than that apostates should flourish here, I will unsheath my bowie knife, and conquer or die. Now, you nasty apostates, clear out, or judgment will be put to the line—and righteousness to the plummet."

Outside Utah, it was a different story: The official announcement of polygamy stirred up a storm of anti-Mormon sentiment. Those Gentiles who had only vague reasons for disliking Mormons—their clannishness, perhaps—now had an issue they could focus on. For some Gentiles, polygamy, the "scarlet whore," was simply adultery under the guise of religion. A common argument held that polygamous unions produced defective offspring with undesirable characteristics: "The yellow, sunken, cadaverous visage; the greenish-colored eye; the thick, protuberant lips, the low forehead; the light, yellowish hair, and the lank, angular person, constitute an appearance so characteristic of the new race, the production of polygamy, as to distinguish them at a glance," a gathering of scientists at New Orleans was told in 1861.* The writer J. H. Beadle claimed that polygamy, an "Asiatic institution never meant to flourish on American soil," rather than increasing

---

* By contrast, the Mormons took the position that polygamy was good for you, at least for polygamous husbands. Said the lively Heber Kimball: "I have noticed that a man who has but one wife, and is inclined to that doctrine, soon begins to wither and dry up while a man who goes into plurality looks fresh, young, and sprightly. Why is this? Because God loves that man. . . ."

the Mormon population, resulted in an abnormally high infant mortality rate. ("A Mormon graveyard is the most melancholy sight on earth.") As for the surviving offspring of polygamous parents, Beadle wrote, "the effects of their social bias are seen in a strange dullness of moral perception, a general ignorance and apparently inherited tendency to vice."

Others saw polygamy in a political light. Not only did it brazenly defy the moral standards of the day, but it was just another sign to enemies of Mormonism that the Saints intended to defy federal authority and maybe even establish their own country west of the Rockies. A congressional report on polygamy deplored the "open and defiant license which, under the name of religion and latitudinous interpretation of our Constitution, has been given to this crime in one of our Territories." In its platform, the new Republican Party that nominated John C. Frémont as its first presidential candidate in 1856 denounced polygamy as one of the "twin relics of barbarism," the other twin, of course, being slavery. For the Democrats, Stephen Douglas called the Mormons "alien enemies and outlaws" and proposed "blotting the territorial government out of existence." Still, the Mormons preferred the Democratic presidential candidate, James Buchanan, but his election meant only that it was now up to him to do something about "the Mormon problem."

Not realizing that nothing strengthens the Mormons like adversity, Buchanan sent troops to Utah; the result was the Mormon—or Utah—War, a mostly bloodless conflict (covered in the next chapter) that ranks among the great blunders of American history. Other solutions were suggested. Mark Twain thought laughter was the best weapon against plural marriage, and, as cited earlier,* did his best to make a joke out of it. Others believed that polygamy would die out once the Mormons were exposed to the "civilizing" influences of the outside world. In Congress, legislators sought to legislate it out of existence. In 1862, Abraham Lin-

* See p. 186.

coln signed the ineffective Morrill Anti-Bigamy Act that outlawed plural marriage in the territories. It didn't work. Nothing worked.

The real struggle between the Mormons and the federal government did not begin until after 1869, when, with the completion of the transcontinental railroad, the pioneer era—and this account of the settlement of the Great Basin—ends. But if we briefly look past that date, Brigham Young was arrested two and a half years later and charged with "lascivious cohabitation," a fiasco that never came to trial. After Congress passed the Edmunds Act in 1882, which made "unlawful cohabitation" a punishable offense, the federal government began cracking down hard, arresting and imprisoning polygamist husbands, or "cohabs," as they were called.* Driving polygamy underground did not destroy the institution. The Mormons had to do that themselves: In 1890, Wilford Woodruff, by this time president of the church, issued a manifesto announcing the intention of the Latter-day Saints to adhere to the law of the United States regarding marriage. It was the will of God, he said. In 1896 came the payoff: Utah became a state in return for its capitulation on plural marriage.

Becoming monogamists was not easy for the Mormons. Men who had been taught that polygamy was the very foundation of their faith did not give up the institution willingly, and polygamy continued during the fourteen-year period between the Woodruff Manifesto and a similar decree (but one the church actually enforced) issued by Woodruff's successor, Joseph F. Smith, in 1904. There are those today who think that polygamy, had the government left it alone, would have diminished and eventually disappeared, and others who believe quite the opposite. Certainly polygamy served an important historical purpose. While it might not have produced that many Mormons (statistics show that

---

* The 1882 Edmunds Act amended and strengthened the weak 1862 Morrill Anti-Bigamy Act and was a precursor of the Edmunds-Tucker Act of 1887, which, among other measures, required plural wives to testify against their husbands and disbanded the Perpetual Emigrating Fund Company.

polygamous wives had somewhat fewer children than monogamous women), polygamy became the cause around which the Mormons could unite. From almost the day they arrived in the Great Basin, the Saints were under siege by all sorts—from forty-niners, government agents, federal officials, soldiers, railroaders, and an assortment of other Gentiles, who wanted to share, alter, take over, or destroy their Kingdom in the Great Basin. Could these elements and forces have destroyed Mormonism if the Saints did not have polygamy, the most peculiar feature of their peculiar religion, to rally around? No one can say for sure, but to speculate, as with all things Mormon, is always interesting.*

---

* Polygamy, in fact, survives today among fundamentalist groups in the mountain West; some estimates put the number of practicing polygamists at between 20,000 and 30,000. In *The American Religion*, Harold Bloom points out that, while the Mormon Church opposes these offshoots, it "never has repudiated plural marriage as a principle." He also asks: "What would the Mormons wish to do [regarding polygamy] if the United States ever has so large a Mormon population, and so wealthy a concentration of Mormon economic power, that governing our democracy became impossible without Mormon cooperation? What seems like science fiction now will not seem so in 2020, if the Mormons are then one American out of eight."

Chapter Eleven

THE UTAH WAR

Brigham Young arrived in the Great Basin in 1847 with one request of the world: "Give us ten years of peace, and we will ask no odds of Uncle Sam or the devil." On Pioneer Day, July 24, 1857, the ten years were up, and the Saints, of whom there were now thirty-five thousand in one hundred communities, were about to have an opportunity to test the odds. To celebrate the tenth anniversary, Brigham Young and several thousand followers took themselves to Big Cottonwood Canyon twenty-five miles from Salt Lake City for a Mormon-style wingding lasting several days.* There, with six brass bands for music, the Saints, in speeches and prayers, marveled at and gave thanks for their tri-

---

* In her *Mountain Meadows Massacre*, the Mormon historian Juanita Brooks wrote of the celebration in Big Cottonwood Canyon: "With characteristic Mormon attention to detail, the record shows that 2,587 people were present, that they had come in 464 carriages and wagons, with 1,028 horses and mules and 332

umph over adversity. Celebrating was something the Saints were good at; the persecution and suffering that they had endured in their twenty-seven-year history had not robbed them of their ability to have a good time.

As the celebration progressed, three travel-worn Mormons rode into the camp and reported directly to Brigham Young. Among them was the long-haired Porter Rockwell, the so-called Destroying Angel of Mormondom. Earlier in the month, Rockwell had been carrying the mail east to Missouri when he met Abraham O. Smoot, the mayor of Salt Lake City, and Judson Stoddard, who were driving cattle west to Salt Lake City. The two men informed Rockwell that federal troops were on their way to Utah to suppress a "rebellion" in the territory, replace Brigham Young as governor, and perhaps arrest him and other Mormon leaders. After turning the mail and the cattle over to others, the three men hurried back to Salt Lake City, covering the 513 miles from Fort Leavenworth to Salt Lake City in just five days. When they found the city nearly empty—for the Canyon procession had begun on July 22—they remounted and headed for Big Cottonwood Canyon, arriving there shortly before noon on July 24.

Brigham Young took the news calmly; even his rhetoric on the occasion seemed subdued. Leaving the tent, he gathered the celebrants and told them of the approach of the federal army. He also reminded them of his words a decade before: He had asked for and received ten years of peace; now "God is with us, and the devil has taken me at my word." Back in Salt Lake City, it was Heber Kimball who delivered the first rousing response to the threat of federal invasion of Utah: "Send 2,500 troops here, our brethren, to make a desolation of this people! God Almighty helping me, I will fight until there is not a drop of blood in my veins. Good God! I have wives enough to whip out the United States, for they will whip themselves. . . ."*

---

oxen and cows. The record lists also the songs and speeches, the music and prayers; but the loveliness of the setting, the couples romancing, cronies observing and gossiping, and children playing are left to the imagination."

* On the same occasion, Kimball delivered one of the truly great Mormon curses:

There had been talk of sending federal troops to Utah for some time, a threat that the Mormon firebrand Jedediah Grant attributed in March 1856 to a combination of Gentile "impudence and ignorance." The victor in the presidential election that year, proslavery Democrat James Buchanan, was anxious to show that he was not soft on polygamy and to demonstrate to the South, by taking a stand against Mormonism, that rebellion would not be tolerated. He was also under the impression that the Mormons were oppressed by their leaders and would welcome an invading army as liberators.

Charges of Mormon rebelliousness had been circulating since Utah became a territory. Prominent among the accusers were Perry Brocchus and his two fellow "runaway judges," who had deserted Utah in September 1851 in fear of their lives after Brocchus had publicly questioned the patriotism of all Mormons and the virtue of their women. In their report the men charged that the "lawless acts and the hostile and insidious feelings and sentiments of Brigham Young" had made their jobs impossible. The report also insinuated that Gentile lives were in danger in Utah and related how Mormon juries had set free two Saints who had murdered the Gentile lovers of their wives. The Mormons' alleged murderous ways were soon to become a familiar theme: In years to follow, anti-Mormons blamed the Saints for the deaths of Army explorer John W. Gunnison in 1853, Judge Leonidas Shaver in 1855, and Territorial Secretary Almon W. Babbitt,*

"Poor rotten curses! and the President of the United States, inasmuch as he has urned against us and will take a course to persist in pleasing the ungodly curses that are howling around him for the destruction of this people, he shall be cursed in the name of Israel's God, and he shall not rule over this Nation, because they are my brethren, but they have cast me out and will cast you out, and I curse him and all his coadjuters in his cursed deeds in the name of Jesus Christ and by the authority of the Holy Priesthood and all Israel shall say amen."

* Babbitt was a Mormon who was sent to Washington in 1849 to petition the government for statehood for Utah. He took his federal job of territorial secretary seriously, however, and, in doling out federal funds, annoyed Brigham Young with his pennypinching ways.

although it seemed clear that Gunnison, the leader of a government surveying party, and Babbitt were killed by Indians and that Shaver, a federal appointee who had actually won the respect of the Mormons, had died of natural causes. Soon after learning of the approach of the Utah expedition, Brigham Young denounced these charges: "What is now the news circulated throughout the United States? That Captain Gunnison was killed by Brigham Young, and that Babbitt was killed in the Plains by Brigham Young and his Danite band. What more? That Brigham Young has killed all the men who have died between the Missouri river and California. . . . Such reports are in the bellows, and editors and politicians are blowing them out. . . ."

Judge Drummond's Infamous Letter

There were other incidents leading to further accusations of Mormon involvement in wrongdoing. Back in Washington, federal agents reported that the Mormons were stirring up the Indians against the government; the feds were concerned about reports that the Mormons had taught the Indians to distinguish between friendly "Mormonee" and hostile "Mericats." President Buchanan, in fact, included the charges in his speech outlining the reasons for the Utah expedition. Other accusations were more specific: In 1855 a government surveyor, David H. Burr, was terrorized by suspicious Saints, who regarded all attempts to map the territory as a prelude to divesting them of their land. On the night of December 29, 1856, a mob broke into and wrecked the office of federal judge George P. Stiles and either destroyed or stole his records and papers.* The Stiles incident was included in a long list of charges that another federal judge, the odious W. W. Drummond, leveled

---

* Stiles, a Mormon apostate, was particularly offensive to the Latter-day Saints. In *The Mormon Conflict, 1850–1859*, Norman F. Furniss pointed out that in Nauvoo in 1844, Stiles advised Joseph Smith to destroy the press of the anti-polygamy newspaper, the *Expositor*, an act that led to Smith's arrest and murder in jail.

at the Mormons. Drummond, who left his family in the East, offended the Mormons when he arrived in Utah accompanied by his mistress, supposedly a Washington prostitute. And, in his official capacity, he outraged them when he tried to destroy the authority of the Mormon-controlled probate courts.

Drummond, Judge Shaver's replacement, was an appointee of the Pierce administration, but his complaints about the Mormons did not really get a hearing until he submitted his resignation to President Buchanan in late March 1857. Historians consider his widely published letter, a prime example of anti-Mormon ranting of the period, to be one of the main causes of the Utah War.* In it, Drummond held the Mormons responsible for the deaths of Gunnison, Shaver, and Babbitt; accused Brigham Young of despotism in that "the Mormons look to him, and to him alone, for the law by which they are to be governed"; attested to Drummond's personal knowledge of the existence of "a set of men, set apart by special order of the church, to take both the lives and property of persons who may question the authority of the Church"; and reported that "federal officers are daily compelled to hear the form of American government traduced, the chief executives of the nation, both living and dead, slandered and abused from the masses, as well as from all the leading members of the Church, in the most vulgar, loathsome, and wicked manner that the evil passions of men can possibly conceive." Drummond ended the letter with a recommendation: "I do believe that, if there was a man put in office as governor of that Territory, who is not a member of the church, (Mormon), and he supported with a sufficient military aid, much good would result from such a course."

* In his biography, *Orrin Porter Rockwell; Man of God, Son of Thunder*, Harold Schindler wrote that "I am persuaded that . . . the decision itself to send an army was predicated almost entirely on Drummond's vicious and unsubstantiated accusations." Furthermore, Buchanan appears to have ordered the troops to Utah without bothering to investigate the truth of the charges or the character of the man who was making them. Had he done so, Schindler wrote, "the Utah Expedition might never have been."

After resigning from office, Drummond hung around Washington in hopes that he would be appointed the next governor of Utah. But Buchanan was not that foolish. Instead, in May 1857, he appointed a portly Georgian, Alfred Cumming, a former mayor of Augusta and federal Indian superintendent, to the post and ordered troops to begin assembling at Fort Leavenworth. The first troops did not leave Fort Leavenworth until July 18, late in the season for such a long journey, a date that, for some, marks the start of the Utah War.* In mid September Cumming and his wife left Fort Leavenworth for Utah. He was escorted by Lieutenant Colonel Philip St. George Cooke, the respected officer who, eleven years earlier, had led the Mormon Battalion on its historic march to California. A War Department order issued to the commander of the Utah expedition, Albert Sidney Johnston, put the matter succinctly: "The community and, in part, the civil government of Utah Territory are in a state of substantial rebellion against the laws and authority of the United States."

It did not take the Mormons long to mobilize. A week after they received word that the army was on the way, the Nauvoo Legion, as the Saints still called the Utah territorial militia, was alerted to hold itself in readiness "to march at the shortest possible notice to any part of the Territory." On August 5, Brigham Young, who had not been officially notified that he was being replaced as governor, declared martial law in the territory with an edict that forbade "all armed forces, of every description, from coming into this Territory, under any pretence whatever." And later in the month, Young recalled the Saints from the "outer cordon" of colonies and urged the Nevada Saints in Carson Valley, "Buy all the powder, Lead, and Caps you possibly can. . . ."† And like the colonists,

---

* "The Mormon War began formally on the 18th of July with the departure of the Tenth Regiment from Fort Leavenworth," Norman F. Furniss wrote in *The Mormon Conflict, 1850–1859.*

† Back in Utah, Orson Hyde, leader of the Carson Valley colony, tried to collect twenty thousand dollars from the Gentiles who had taken over his sawmill. In

missionaries in the states and abroad were called home to help defend Zion from the Gentile invaders.

The prospect of an army bearing down on them caused a considerable amount of hysteria among the Saints. To the Mormons who had been in Missouri and Nauvoo, the situation seemed alarmingly familiar, and historian Juanita Brooks wrote, "From one end of the territory to the other, the people of Utah retold and relived their past sufferings, the mobbings and burnings and final expulsion from Nauvoo." The *Deseret News* ran a series on the life of Joseph Smith that emphasized the suffering and persecution the Mormons had endured. Several spirited hymns, one titled "Up, Awake, Ye Defenders of Zion," were penned to rally the faithful, and Mormon leaders engaged in an orgy of jingoistic sermonizing and speechmaking.* George A. Smith, who was sent south from Salt Lake City with orders for local commanders, was a stirring preacher who told the settlers on one occasion that "in case of invasion it might be necessary to set fire to our property and hide in the mountains, and leave our enemies to do the best they could." On his return to Salt Lake City, Smith reported finding among the southern colonists a desire for "vengeance for the cruelties that had been inflicted upon us in the States. They did feel that they hated to owe a debt and not be able to pay it."

The Mormons took steps to enlist the aid of their only ally— the Indians of the Great Basin—in their struggle against the Gentiles. Mormon policy had always had a dual, somewhat conflicted

---

this he was unsuccessful, even after he threatened them, in an open letter that he read before the Utah legislature, "with thunder and with earthquakes and with famine until your names are not known among men."

* Up, awake, ye defenders of Zion,
The foe's at the door of your homes
Let each heart be the heart of a lion
Unyielding and proud as he roams.
Remember the wrongs of Missouri
Forget not the fate of Nauvoo
When the God-hating foe is before you
Stand firm and be faithful and true.

purpose: to pacify the Indians, on the one hand, so that they would become, in the Mormon's aforementioned peculiar vision, "a white and delightsome people" and, on the other, to be sure that they were ready to fight on the side of the Mormons in case of trouble. Now that the enemy was almost at the door, Brigham Young wrote Jacob Hamlin, president of the southern Utah Indian Mission, advising him, "Continue the conciliatory policy towards the Indians, which I have ever recommended, . . . for they must learn that they have either got to help us or the United States will kill us both."* In late August, Hamlin took ten or twelve Indian chiefs to Salt Lake City, where, on September 1, they met with Brigham Young, who presumably told them that they and the Mormons had to stand firm against a common enemy.

Massacre at Mountain Meadows

As anti-Gentile fervor and war hysteria spread throughout Utah, westward-bound emigrant parties continued to pass through Salt Lake City on their way to California via the Highway of the West, the Humboldt River. In early August 1857, a particularly large party, some 140 emigrants, arrived in Salt Lake City. The Fancher party, so called after Richard Fancher, one of its leaders, consisted of both families from Arkansas and a rough group of frontiersmen, many of them Mormon-baiters from the hated state of Missouri. Because it was late in the season, the party decided to take the southern route to California, a longer but warmer route. When it left Salt Lake City is uncertain, but Hamlin reported meeting it near Fillmore on August 25; he might have advised

* As Furniss pointed out, the Gentile press was aware of and typically exaggerated the danger to the Utah expedition posed by the Great Basin Indians. In 1857 the *New York Times*, Furniss wrote, "accused Brigham Young of teaching these savages both the techniques of farming and the arts of war." A West Coast newspaper declared that the Mormons could count on the support of two hundred thousand Indians "for a desperate and sanguinary struggle with the 'Gentiles.' "

Samuel Bowles (lower right), early Great Basin traveler, and companions (from *Our New West* by Bowles)

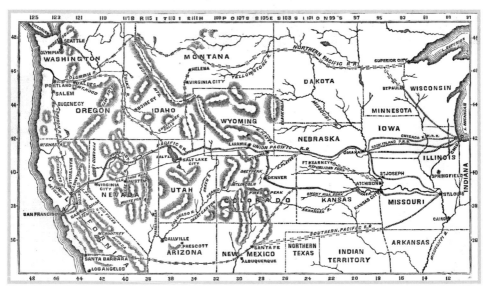

Map to accompany Bowles's *Our New West* (from *Our New West* by Bowles)

William F. Cody (from *Last of the Great Scouts: The Life Story of Col. William F. Cody*, as told by his sister Helen Cody Wetmore)

A representative mining town, Austin, Nevada (from *Our New West* by Bowles)

Washing for gold (from *Our New West* by Bowles)

Laying the track of the Pacific Railroad (from *Our New West* by Bowles)

Old Elk and his squaw, Utah Indians (from *An Expedition to the Valley of the Great Salt Lake* by Stansbury)

West side of promontory, Flat Rock Point (from *An Expedition to the Valley of the Great Salt Lake* by Stansbury)

Early Virginia City (courtesy Nevada Tourism)

Old mining camp scene (courtesy Nevada Tourism)

A miner and his family, Berlin, Nevada (courtesy Nevada Tourism)

Brigham Young in his last
years (from *Brigham Young*
by Werner)

Joseph Smith Sphinx, Garden of Gilgal, Salt Lake City (all photographs in this section by the author)

This Is The Place Monument, Salt Lake City

Restored 1865–66 cotton mill, Washington, Utah

Brigham Young Forest Farmhouse (c.1850s), Pioneer Trail State Park, Salt Lake City, Utah

Wilford Woodruff home, 1871

Territorial Statehouse, Fillmore, Utah, capital of Utah Territory

Cove Fort, built in 1867 to protect the Deseret Telegraph line from Indians

Pioneer cabin, built in 1851 as part of the Iron Mission; now located at the Iron Mission State Park/Museum, Cedar City, Utah

Charcoal oven, Old Irontown, Utah

Pine Valley Ward Chapel, 1868

A pioneer-era ghost-town church, southern Utah

Wagon wheel collection, Iron Mission State Park/Museum, Cedar City, Utah

Mormon handcart, Hurricane, Utah

Monument honoring
the "Noble Pioneers"
of Hurricane, Utah

them about stopping places, particularly Mountain Meadows, the six-mile-long grazing area noted for its clear water and lush grasses near Hamlin's home in Santa Clara right on the southern rim of the Great Basin.

The tragic fate of the Fancher party at Mountain Meadows is a story within a story, a massacre in a war that produced no other bloodshed, and, wrote the gifted Mormon historian Juanita Brooks, a classic example of mob psychology at its very worst. The Mountain Meadows Massacre can be regarded as an isolated, shameful episode in the Mormon past, but historians agree that it is inconceivable that the killing of some 120 defenseless men, women, and children could have ever occurred if Utah had not been caught up in the hysteria of an impending war.

The emigrants were heading into difficult territory. The Mormons had been told not to trade with Gentiles passing through Utah; this was sure to make life difficult for such a large wagon train that trailed some nine hundred head of cattle behind it. Indians, who began harassing the train when it reached Fillmore, were another problem. To make matters worse, the Indians were convinced (rightly or not, it hardly matters) that the Fancher party had poisoned a well, killing several Indians. As the train lumbered south, the Indians, "happy in the sense of Mormon approval," wrote Mrs. Brooks, harassed the emigrants, and "sent out runners to other bands for reinforcements in this exciting and thrilling game." In ordinary times, the Mormons could have used their influence to stop the attacks, and, indeed, some Mormons wanted to do this, but others believed that letting the Indians have their way with the Fancher party would make them all the more loyal to the Mormon cause. (As Juanita Brooks pointed out, the Mormons in southern Utah were outnumbered four to one by Indians and depended on their friendship and goodwill for their survival.)

For their part, members of the Fancher train were doing their best to antagonize the Mormons. Some of the Missourians bragged that they had taken part in the 1838 Haun's Mill Massacre in Missouri when a mob killed seventeen defenseless Mormons and wounded twelve. Another, who claimed to have been part of the mob that killed Joseph Smith, was supposedly heard to say: "I would like to go back and take a pop at Old Brig before I leave the territory." The emigrants took a malicious delight in naming their oxen Brigham Young or Heber Kimball and whipping and abusing them as they passed through Mormon settlements. They also told the Mormons that, once they reached California, they were going to come back with an army, a threat that played on Mormon fears of being attacked simultaneously from the west and the east.

The Fancher train also had the bad fortune to arrive in Utah Territory just after the Mormons had learned that their beloved Apostle, Parley Pratt, had been murdered in Arkansas, where many of the emigrants were from. The murderer, Hector Mc-Lean, was an outraged husband whose estranged wife had been so taken with Pratt that she converted to Mormonism and then became one of his many polygamous wives.* In the East, public opinion supported the murderer, an alleged wife-abuser and heavy drinker, which made the Mormons back in Utah feel all the more isolated, threatened, and misunderstood.

Most Mormon writers have argued that what happened next to the Fancher party could never have occurred under normal circumstances, that only the tension caused by the impending Utah War caused otherwise God-fearing and righteous men to act like cold-blooded killers. Other factors must be figured in: For one, the Mormons in this period had an almost fanatical respect for authority; any order from a higher-up carried the weight of both church and state and, to their way of thinking, must be obeyed. Juanita Brooks suggested that Mormons participating in the attack might have felt they were avenging the death of Joseph Smith, a

---

* Juanita Brooks wrote: "Many Mormon writers, among them B. H. Roberts and Leland H. Creer, have insisted that the word of Pratt's death was not known in southern Utah at this time, and hence could not have had any influence upon the feelings of the people. This is a mistaken idea, for word had gone out immediately." In her authoritative book, *The Mountain Meadows Massacre*, Mrs. Brooks offered ample proof of her statement.

man whom they loved "with an intensity almost past understanding." Vengeance, in fact, was always in the forefront of Mormon thought and rhetoric in pioneer times. "So the wind grew into the whirlwind," Mrs. Brooks wrote. "Exaggeration, misrepresentation, ungrounded fears, unreasoning hate, desire for revenge, yes, even the lust for the property of the emigrants, all combined to give justification which, once the crime was done, looked inadequate and flimsy indeed."

As the Fancher train settled down in Mountain Meadows to prepare for the long dry crossing to California, the Mormons in Cedar City and the surrounding region debated what to do about the intruders. By this time, the southern Mormons had come to regard the Fancher party as more of a vanguard of the Utah Expedition than what it really was—an inconsequential, if irritating, party of passers-through. In the emergency meetings held in and about Cedar City, all past resentments against Gentiles were dredged up and directed at the pioneer party at Mountain Meadows. Elder Isaac Haight's words, on September 6, reflected the feelings of many Mormons:

> They [the Gentiles] drove us out to starve. When we pled for mercy, Haun's Mill was the answer, and when we asked for bread they gave us a stone. . . . They have followed us and hounded us. They come among us asking us to trade with them, and in the name of humanity to feed them. All of these we have done and now they are sending an army to exterminate us. . . . I have been driven from my home for the last time, I am prepared to feed to the Gentiles the same bread they fed to us.

In one of their calmer moments, the southern leadership dispatched a messenger to Salt Lake City to ask for Brigham Young's instructions on the matter. This brings up a question that has been raised many times in the past: Did Brigham Young authorize or order an attack on the Fancher train? The facts, as laid out in

Juanita Brooks's painstaking account, indicate he did not, that his orders to the southern Saints were to let the wagon train pass in peace, and that these instructions arrived too late to prevent the massacre. These instructions are contained in a letter to Haight, which Brooks believed is genuine. It read: "In regard to the emigration trains passing through our settlements, we must not interfere with them until they are first notified to keep away. You must not meddle with them. The Indians we expect will do as they please but you should try and preserve good feelings with them." But more than the letter or other testimony, it seems incredible that Young would authorize or approve an act that would gain them nothing and reflect so poorly on the Mormon cause.

As the southern Mormons waited for Young's reply, the Indians stepped up their attacks on the Fancher party at Mountain Meadows; they had even lost a few warriors to the emigrants, who were putting up a good fight. When Mormon leader John D. Lee went to the meadows with some of his militiamen to try to restrain them, he reported back to Cedar City that the Indians were outraged by their own losses and told him, as he later wrote, "unless they could kill all the *'Mericats,'* as they called them, they would declare war against the Mormons and kill everyone in the settlements." The situation deteriorated further when three emigrants tried to escape to seek help and were killed by Mormons and Indians. Apparently the other Fancher emigrants witnessed the killings, for the Mormons were now afraid that, should the emigrants take word of Mormon guilt to California, a force would surely return to punish them. In their fervid minds, there was not time to wait for instructions from Brigham Young. So they decided to kill all the emigrants except for children too young to comprehend or report what happened.

The trap the Mormons set for the emigrants was thorough, premeditated, and cold-blooded. On the morning of September 11, Lee, showing a white flag, offered the emigrants safe passage under armed escort to Cedar City. Leaving the weapons, livestock, and wagons behind, Lee explained, would appease the

Indians. After some deliberation, the emigrants accepted the terms and laid down their weapons. From there on in, "it all worked out according to plan," Mrs. Brooks wrote. First the youngest children were loaded into a wagon and sent on ahead. Next the women and older children were escorted down the road. Then came the men, each one walking beside an armed Mormon escort. At the command "Halt! Do your duty!" the slaughter began. Each escort shot the man beside him, while the Indians, Brooks wrote, "leaped from the brush on both sides of the road at once and, stimulated by the shrieks and screams, fell upon their victims with knives and hatchets and soon quieted them."

Between 120 and 150 men, women, and children died in the Mountain Meadows Massacre. Seventeen very young children were spared and eventually were taken back to Arkansas. At first the Mormons blamed the Indians for the killings; then, as it became evident that whites were involved, the accusations began, with each man trying to lay the blame on another. Their conflicting stories produced such a tangle of fact and falsehood that even the date of the massacre is uncertain, although Mrs. Brooks made a good case that it occurred on September 11. Only one man was ever convicted for crimes committed during the massacre, and that only as a sop to national outrage over the episode. John D. Lee, respected Mormon leader and pioneer, was executed by a firing squad on the site of the massacre on March 23, 1877, almost twenty years after the fact.* After that, the Mormons set out to erase the Mountain Meadows Massacre from their collective memory.

The Mountain Meadows Massacre produced, belatedly, one hero: Juanita Brooks. Born in 1898, Mrs. Brooks knew nothing of

---

* Few Mormons of the time had better credentials than Lee. He was baptized into the faith in Far West, Missouri, in 1838; he was also a bodyguard for Joseph Smith in Nauvoo, and, in Utah, a member of the Council of Fifty. He also had eighteen wives and sixty children. On April 20, 1961, the Council of the Twelve Apostles, acknowledging that Lee was no more guilty than others in the massacre, authorized "the reinstatement to membership and former blessing of John D. Lee."

the event as a girl growing up in a small Mormon town in southern Nevada. When she was a twenty-year-old schoolteacher, she encountered a dying old man with a troubled conscience who told her "my eyes have witnessed things that my tongue has never uttered." Although he died before he could tell her his story, she made inquiries and, from what other old-timers told her, gradually began to piece together an account of the massacre, which included the unsettling possibility that her own grandfather might have taken part in the bloodshed. Her book on the massacre, originally published in 1950, was not well received by the LDS hierarchy, but her research was so thorough, no one could easily dispute her facts, interpretations, or conclusions. As she wrote—a bit disingenuously—in her introduction: "I feel sure that nothing but the truth can be good enough for the church to which I belong."

Juanita Brooks's *Mountain Meadows Massacre* taught twentieth-century Mormons about this stain on their pioneer past. It also began a process of reconciliation that continues to this day. In September 1955, the descendents of Richard Fancher and other families invited Mrs. Brooks to speak at the dedication of a memorial at Harrison, Arkansas, where the Fancher emigrant train originated almost a century before. In her brief remarks, she called the massacre "one of the most despicable mass murders of history." Mormons and Arkansans came together again in 1992 at Mountain Meadows to dedicate a new granite memorial at the site of the massacre.* In a ceremony, a Fancher descendent read from the Book of Mormon: "I, the Lord, will forgive whom I will forgive, But of you it is required to forgive all men."

---

* The inscription on the new Mountain Meadows memorial, which reads that the wagon train was "attacked while en route to California," does not mention the actual massacre. When I visited the site in 1992, a graffitist had inserted above the word *attacked*: "By white Mormons from Cedar City and New Harmony and 'Danites' from SLC. The party surrendered after four days and all but small children were executed."

PREPARATIONS FOR WAR

At the time of the massacre, the church had not yet decided how to respond to the threat posed by the advancing Utah expedition. Their choices were to stay and fight, to submit without resisting, or to retreat into the mountains and wage guerilla warfare. Then, on September 8, a representative of the U.S. Army, a young captain named Stewart Van Vliet, arrived in Salt Lake City. From the Mormon point of view, his mission was presumptuous: to arrange for the billeting and provisioning of the U.S. Army when it arrived in Salt Lake City. They greeted Van Vliet cordially, but in private meetings Brigham Young took a tough stance, explaining that the Mormons regarded the army as just another mob bent on persecution and destruction, and he vowed that the Saints would vigorously defend their homeland.* Brigham Young might have been bluffing, but Van Vliet believed what he was told. He reported back to the Army that the Mormons would fight to the death, and he strongly recommended that the U.S. forces winter at Fort Bridger rather than proceed directly to Salt Lake City.

Van Vliet's recommendation was taken seriously. Until early September, when the able Albert Sidney Johnston, then a colonel, had taken over command, the Utah expedition had been essentially leaderless, and, with the Army disorganized and spread out over the plains, it seemed an inauspicious time to attempt the well-guarded mountain passes that would take it directly into Salt Lake City. Also, the Mormons had begun a series of aggressive guerrilla attacks and raids that gave weight to Van Vliet's warning that the Saints were prepared to fight to the death if the Army tried to approach Salt Lake City. On October 3, the Mormons burned Fort Bridger, and two days later nearby Fort Supply, and set fire to the grass around the forts that the Army would need for

* Since Washington had never officially informed Brigham Young that he was being replaced as governor of Utah, the Mormon leader took the legal position that he was still the chief executive of the territory and that the approaching army was just an undisciplined mob.

grazing. And, in a busy two days, a small band of raiders led by Major Lot Smith and Porter Rockwell, the Destroying Angel of Mormondom, now turned guerrilla fighter, burned three wagon trains—seventy-two wagons containing some three hundred thousand pounds of supplies—on the Green River and Big Sandy.*

The winter camp the Army set up to house nearly two thousand regulars stretched from the ruins of Fort Bridger several miles up Black's Fork, a settlement they named Camp Scott. The gubernatorial appointee, Alfred Cumming, arrived with his vivacious wife, Elizabeth; on November 21, he issued a proclamation, "To the People of Utah Territory," declaring himself governor, and sent a letter to Brigham Young accusing him of "violent and treasonable acts."† In early December, Delana R. Eckels, the new chief justice of Utah who was also with the Army at Camp Scott, impaneled an all-Gentile grand jury and indicted Brigham Young, Porter Rockwell, William Hickman, and other prominent—and absent—Mormons for having "wickedly, maliciously and traitorously levied war against the United States." And, back in Washington, in his first annual address to Congress, President Buchanan made it clear that the Utah expedition, despite its unpromising start, would go forward. "This is the first rebellion

---

* Not every Mormon raid was successful. In his biography of Rockwell, Harold Schindler included a delightful account of "a comedy of errors" that played out before dawn on September 25. Intercepting a column of infantry at Pacific Springs, Rockwell and five men, in a surprise attack, managed to run off a large herd of mules. However, the stampede came to a sudden halt when the rope trailing from the lead, or bell, mule became tangled in sagebrush. At that very point, the Army bugler sounded the Stable Call, and the entire herd turned and raced back to the Army camp to "an expected bag of oats." With it went the six mounts of the Mormon raiders who had dismounted, confident that their raid had been successful. The Mormons were forced to skulk around on foot all the next day until, after nightfall, they could sneak up on the Army and retrieve their horses. It was, Schindler wrote, "the first Mormon action against the United States government."

† Most men on the Utah expedition were charmed by the loquacious Mrs. Cumming and her collection of "pleasing anecdotes," although one young Army captain described her as "one of the most intolerable talkers on earth." She was the granddaughter of Revolutionary War leader and agitator Samuel Adams.

which has existed in our Territories," he said, "and humanity itself requires that we should put it down in a manner that it shall be the last."

Enter Colonel Kane

All the tough talk notwithstanding, Buchanan took one tentative step to avoid all-out war. As 1857 was ending with his Army stuck at Camp Scott, he commissioned Colonel Thomas L. Kane, a longtime friend of the Mormons, to mediate the dispute. Kane had become interested in Mormonism in 1846 and later that year caught up with the Saints on their trek westward in Iowa. There he helped them secure the government's permission to winter over on Indian lands, and, after the Mormon arrival in the Great Basin in 1847, continued to advise them on governmental matters. After accepting the job from Buchanan, Kane, traveling under the name of a friend, Dr. Osborne, sailed to San Francisco via the Isthmus of Panama and arrived, frail and sickly, in Salt Lake City on February 25, 1858. His health must have been a real concern, for Brigham Young supposedly assured him: "Friend Thomas, the Lord sent you here and he will not let you die. . . . You have done a great work and you will do a greater work still."

In Salt Lake City, Kane met secretly with Young and other leaders. His goal was to avoid bloodshed through negotiation by arranging for the peaceful movement of the troops into Utah; earlier he had written his father: "The day may be, and probably is past to make peace, but not to save our poor fellows." On March 8, he left Salt Lake City, arriving, so tired he could not get off his horse, at Camp Scott on the twelfth. Kane somehow antagonized Johnston, recently made a brevet general, who wanted no part of a peacemaking effort, but he convinced the new governor, Cumming, to try negotiating with the Saints before force was used. Much to Johnston's annoyance, Cumming and Kane left for Salt Lake City on April 5 without a military escort.

Meanwhile, both sides continued to prepare for war. The

administration more than doubled the expedition until it totaled 5,606 men and officers. Six million dollars was spent acquiring forty-five hundred wagons, fifty thousand oxen, four thousand mules, "and to employ about 5,000 teamsters, blacksmiths, and others," wrote Arrington in his economic history, adding: "It was the magnitude of the contracts let in the spring of 1858 that led administration opponents to refer to the Utah expedition as a 'Contractors' War." At Camp Scott, Johnston and his officers were itching for a fight. To them, Cumming's willingness to negotiate before sending in the Army was a sure sign that he was going soft on Mormonism.

The "Move South"

For their part, the Mormons did not have much faith that Kane could stave off an invasion of Utah. On March 18, while Kane was still at Camp Scott, the Mormons decided, finally, on a strategy: that they were going to go "into the desert and not war with the people [of the United States], but let them destroy themselves." The "Move South," as it is known in Mormon history, called for the removal of thirty thousand people living north of Provo to the southern and southwestern reaches of Utah Territory. By the end of March, five hundred selected families, picked for the move because they were relative newcomers to Utah who had never been driven from their homes before, were on their way south, and on April 1, Young, Heber Kimball, and other leaders, their goods piled high in wagons, moved out to Provo.

The contents of graneries in northern Utah were also moved south to feed the Mormon refugees but also to keep the grain out of the hands of the enemy. In Salt Lake City the Saints covered over the foundation of the temple, then four years under way, so that it would look to enemy eyes like a plowed field. As a contingency, the Mormons also made plans to exercise what Brigham Young called "the privilege of laying waste our improvements"— preparing to burn buildings, fields, and supplies in advance of the enemy. In another statement, Young elaborated on the "scorched earth" policy:

Before I will again suffer as I have in times gone by there shall not be one building, nor one foot of lumber, nor a fence, nor a tree, nor a particle of grass or hay, that will burn, be left in reach of our enemies. I am sworn if driven to extremity to utterly lay waste this land in the name of Israel's God, and our enemies shall find it as barren as when we came here.

The Move South was predicated on Brigham Young's belief that extensive oases existed in the southwestern part of the territory to which the Saints could retreat and where they could exist, indefinitely if necessary, in relative comfort and safety. How he could have thought this ten years after the Mormon arrival in the Great Basin—given their determination to explore "every inch" of their new homeland—is perplexing. An exploring party sent to the region, which is now southern Nevada, in 1854 failed to find this garden in the desert, and two more, dispatched at the last minute in early 1858, actually established a short-lived settlement (at present-day Panacca, Nevada) but otherwise found nothing resembling the country of Brigham Young's imagination. By the time they returned to report their failure, the Move South was already in progress.

Meanwhile, Kane and Cumming were making their way to Salt Lake City. En route the new governor saw just what the Mormons wanted him to see: a military presence in Echo Canyon, the pathetic sight of Mormon families leaving their homes, and displays of Mormon patriotism and cordiality as bands playing patriotic airs greeted him at small towns on the road. On his arrival in Salt Lake City on April 12, his first official visitor was Brigham Young, who took him on a tour of the city.

In private meetings, the two men aired grievances but on the whole got along so well that, on April 15, Cumming wrote Johnston, who had warned that the Mormons would probably kill him, that "I have been everywhere recognized as the governor of Utah; and so far from having encountered insults and indignities, I am gratified in being able to state to you that in passing through the settlements, I have been universally greeted with such respectful attentions as are due to the representative of the executive authority of the United States in the territory." Ten days later Young introduced Cumming from the pulpit of the tabernacle, and, in the course of a half-hour speech, Cumming reported to Washington, "the audience of several thousand listened respectfully to all that I had to say, approvingly even, I fancied, when I explained to them what I intended to be the character of my administration. . . . I have observed that the Mormons profess to view the Constitution as the work of inspired men, and respond with readiness to appeals for its support."

Once Cumming saw that the Mormons would accept him as Utah's first non-Mormon governor, he became their defender. He was outraged when he learned that Johnston's army had, on June 4, begun, without his consent, its march to Salt Lake City, a move that could endanger the peace process that was by then well under way. On June 7, peace commissioners, sent by Buchanan to counter growing criticism of the expedition, had arrived in Utah with an offer of "a free pardon to all who will submit themselves to the authority of the federal government." Although some Mormons questioned why they had to be pardoned for crimes they had never committed, Brigham Young, practical as always, accepted its terms, saying: "If a man comes from the moon and says he will pardon me for kicking him in the moon yesterday, I don't care about it, I'll accept his pardon. It doesn't affect me one way or the other." Johnston, in the spirit of the moment, issued a proclamation assuring the citizenry that the Army is "as ready now to assist and protect them as it was to oppose them while it was believed they were resisting the laws of their government," while Cumming, in his own proclamation, rejoiced: "Peace is restored to our territory!"*

* Cumming's wife, Elizabeth, arrived in Salt Lake City from Camp Scott on June 8. In a letter home she described the city as she found it: "I was not prepared for the death like stillness which existed. A large beautiful city, the houses

Not quite. The Army was still advancing on Salt Lake City, and thousands of Mormon refugees camped in the south were not going to return home until they were certain what the soldiers would do. When the Army entered Salt Lake City on June 26, it found a city ready to be destroyed. A small contingent of Mormon men left behind had piled straw around each house and stood ready to set fire to it should the soldiers prove to be aggressive or belligerent. To everyone's relief, it was not necessary to set fire to the city. The peaceful passage of the Army through Salt Lake City that day was described by a newspaper correspondent as "one of the most extraordinary scenes that has occurred in American history." Some found the city eerily beautiful; everyone remarked on the silence broken only by sounds of a marching army, military band, the rumble of wagons, and "the monotonous gurgle of City Creek." The officers kept the men under control, and, as he rode through, Colonel Philip St. George Cooke removed his hat in deference to the men of the Mormon Battalion, whom he had led on the trek to California. Even Brigham Young was satisfied with the Army's discipline: "Not a house, fence, or sidewalk has been infringed upon by any of his [Johnston's] command. . . . he has carried out his promises to the letter."

One of those kept promises was Johnston's guarantee that the Army would pass through the city and keep going. True to its word, the Army camped that night outside the city on the banks of the Jordan River, then moved south to Cedar Valley. Four days later the church announced from its headquarters at Provo: "All who wish to return to their homes in Great Salt Lake City are at liberty to do so." Brigham Young led the return, and the costly, inconclusive Utah War was over.

---

all separate—each with its garden—wide streets, with a pebbly stream running on each side—city capable of containing twenty thousand inhabitants—as level as Augusta, Georgia—houses mostly about two stories high, built of adobes, which are like bricks in shape & size, but a grey stone colour instead of red—the gardens full of flowers & vegetables & promises of fruit—but the doors of all houses closed—not a window to be seen—only boards instead—not a carriage or wagon or mule or horse or man to be seen."

WINNING THE PEACE

As Johnston's Army was marching toward Salt Lake City, the *New York Times* of June 17, 1858, wrote that the story of the Utah War is "crowded by as much ignorance, stupidity and dishonesty, as any Government ever managed to get into the annals of a single year." The truce that followed did little more to inspire. The Army that numbered about twenty-four hundred men and officers camped first at the northern end of Cedar Valley, then moved to a permanent site across from a creek where Fairfield, Utah, is today. The camp they built there became the third-largest city in Utah, "a hot purgatorial spot," one observer noted, "where winter was long and rigorous, summer hot and uncomfortable, a place where alkaline water curdled soap, and dust storms proved almost unendurable." Johnston named it Camp Floyd after Buchanan's secretary of war, John B. Floyd.

Strategically Camp Floyd was well placed about forty miles from both Salt Lake City and Provo, Utah's two largest towns, close enough to be threatening but far enough away to keep Saints and soldiers apart. The isolation of Camp Floyd was a burden on the troops. There was a dramatic society and a school for enlisted men, but the only other distractions were in a nearby settlement of camp followers called Frogtown, to which soldiers could sneak off to imbibe a locally produced whiskey known as Valley Tan and otherwise enjoy themselves.* The troops were also occasionally called upon to build roads, conduct forays against Indians, and guard immigrant trains. One detachment escorted the young survivors of the Mountain Meadows Massacre to Fort Leavenworth.

In his book on the Utah War, Furniss gave Johnston credit for keeping his troops under control. When trouble did occur, he pointed out, it was the fault of anti-Mormon federal judges, who were determined to punish the Mormons for treason, despite Buchanan's pardon for this alleged crime. In March, Judge John Cradlebaugh, a federal appointee, called eight hundred soldiers to

---

* Valley Tan was also the name taken by a newspaper published during the occupation of Utah by anti-Mormon Gentiles.

Provo to guard Mormon prisoners he intended to arrest for a series of murders, including the killing of a Mormon apostate, William Parrish, in March 1857. The appearance of troops in the city convinced many Mormons that the Army was about to occupy the entire territory, and a tense period followed as, Furniss wrote, "excited Mormons poured into the city to protect their leaders from round-up, imprisonment, and execution." Although Cradlebaugh did arrest the mayor of Provo, many of his other suspects simply vanished, and he finally disbanded his court and ended his investigation in frustration.

There were other incidents: A band of off-duty soldiers, on its own, attacked a remote Utah settlement before an officer stopped them. In Salt Lake City, a Mormon shot and killed an Army sergeant (who had earlier injured him in a dispute over grazing rights) and escaped through a crowd of protecting Mormons. For a while, the Mormons were afraid Johnston would use the incident as an excuse to send troops to Salt Lake City, and some even made preparations to reenact the Move South. But Johnston wisely decided against provoking the Mormons; instead he withdrew the few soldiers who were already there—and in danger of their lives—and the crisis passed.

Starting in 1859, the situation grew less tense, as the threat of civil war drew the attention of the Army away from Utah to events back east. Starting in 1860, soldiers were withdrawn until only an insignificant number—seven hundred or so—remained at Camp Floyd, and these were preoccupied with sorting out their own loyalties in the impending conflict. And, in the summer of 1860, the Mormon-friendly and pro-Union officer Philip St. George Cooke was appointed commander of the post, replacing the recently departed Johnston. Cooke, who opposed the pro-Southern policies of Secretary Floyd, changed the name of the post to Fort Crittenden, after J. J. Crittenden of Kentucky, author of a plan to resolve peacefully the North-South conflict.*

* The Virginia-born Floyd had been accused of promoting the Utah War in order to divert troops to the West and to weaken the federal government militarily.

Finally, in July of 1861, following the firing on Fort Sumter in April and the start of the Civil War, the post was evacuated but not before the government conducted what Leonard Arrington called "the largest government surplus sale yet held in history." In one auction alone, the government sold four million dollars' worth of property for about one hundred thousand dollars. Flour, tools, livestock, wagons, and a variety of other equipment and foodstuffs went to the Mormons at bargain prices. Then, when the Army moved out, scavengers moved in, dismantling the buildings piece by piece for the valuable stone and lumber. All along, the Saints had profited by doing business with the Army; now they were making money from the Army's departure as well. So ended, wrote a diarist, "the great Buchanan Utah Expedition, costing the Government millions, and accomplishing nothing, except making many of the Saints comparatively rich and improving the circumstances of most of the people of Utah."

The Utah War did establish a federal presence in the territory and install a non-Mormon governor, but otherwise the diarist was correct: It accomplished nothing. It did not quell a rebellion because the Army did not find a rebellion to quell. It did not destroy Mormonism, as some in the East hoped it would, or put an end to polygamy. President Buchanan and others anticipated that the Mormon people would welcome the troops as liberators from the oppression of their religion and its leaders, but the Saints displayed unity, grit, and determination to survive that even their enemies had to admire. And Brigham Young, although no longer governor, emerged from the war still the undisputed leader of the Mormon people. In a dispatch to his newspaper in Philadelphia, a soldier-correspondent offered this assessment of the Mormon leader:

Some reckless slander, destitute of either honor, honesty or truth says that Brigham Young remains secluded, never leaving his house, but conceals himself from the rage of the Mormons, who can now see his duplicity and falsehood. This is untrue, entirely without foundation. Brigham has been here several times since I came to Camp Floyd and the Mormons show him the utmost respect. . . . He is still their head man, and his word is omnipotent wherever Mormonism has a foothold. My worthy friend, the Bishop . . . introduced me to him, adding that I was a printer. "Ah!" said Brigham, "then I presume you have often put in type our own correspondents' accounts of affairs out here. Now do you take me for the terrible, treasonable, anathematizing, many-wived, law-resisting rascal I have been represented?" And, of a truth I should say, no. He has an open, pleasant countenance, that speaks of benevolence, humanity and frankness; there is nothing in his appearance to indicate the bold bad man that the race of Drummonds have represented him to be. I am not much of a physiognomist but I take it that Brigham Young is one of the *best abused men* we have within our large domain. . . . He is no longer governor nor is he vested with any civil authority; but Young's moral powers remain unaltered and unweakened with the Mormon settlers of Utah.

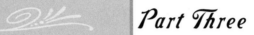

Part Three

THE WORLD
INTRUDES

Chapter Twelve

ROADS INTO

THE GREAT BASIN

The coming of white men into the Salt Lake Valley in 1847—and the rapid spread of Mormon settlers throughout the Great Basin—did not put an end to the exploration of the region. On the contrary, curiosity about the Great Basin only increased with settlement. It was also clear that the Great Basin, although inhospitable to man, was increasingly important as a link in the trail west and that more must be learned and understood about the dry, mountainous region if the country was to fulfill its destiny as a continental power.

The explorers who came after the Mormons were not pathfinders like John C. Frémont, nor were they motivated, like the trapper Jedediah Smith, "to be the first to view a country on which the eyes of a white man had never gazed . . ." Their missions were more precisely defined: to gather scientific information about this new land and to chart, survey, and evaluate routes for future wagon roads and railroads across the West. Many of these explorers were bright young officers with the Corps of Topological Engineers, a branch of the Army founded in 1838 to explore the West and, in the service of an expanding nation, to record scientifically its discoveries. To lead these expeditions, the men had to be adventurers with a scientific bent; the Army's James Hervey Simpson, for example, crossed the Great Basin in 1859 with a geologist, a taxidermist, a meteorologist, and an artist in tow and produced a 489-page report that ended with nineteen appendixes on astronomical, geological, botanical, ichthyological, and various other scientific observations. Two of these explorers, Howard Stansbury and John W. Gunnison, were called upon to be sociologists as well, since their orders specified that they study both the Indian tribes of the eastern Great Basin and the newly arrived Mormon people spreading out from Salt Lake City.

While earlier explorers found only wilderness and Indians, these expeditions often came across settlers and other whites going about their routine business in the country that was being explored. In 1853 and again in the winter of 1854, two parties of explorers descended from the Wasatch Mountains into the Mormon town of Parowan in southwestern Utah. The second party, which was close to succumbing to cold, fatigue, and hunger, was led by none other than the Pathfinder himself, John Charles Frémont, on his fifth and last expedition. Other explorers also encountered non-Indians who had gotten there before them. In 1858, James Hervey Simpson's proposed route across the Great Basin was used to carry the mail by the stagecoach operator George Chorpenning before Simpson had even explored it. The brilliant Clarence King, a civilian, passed coolies laying railroad track as he led his scientific expedition over the Sierra Nevada and into the Great Basin in 1867. And, over the winter of 1849–1850, while Howard Stansbury was living among the Mormons in Salt Lake City, settlers were dismantling his surveying stations for firewood, a serious inconvenience since the lumber for the stations had to be hauled, he noted, "upward of thirty miles."

"Porphyry, Geiss, Dark Slaty Shales . . ."

Howard Stansbury, the first officer in the Army Corps of Topological Engineers to appear in the Great Basin, was under orders to survey the Great Salt Lake Valley, study the natural resources of the area, scout a route from the valley to the Oregon Trail, and study both the Indian tribes and the valley's more recent inhabitants, the Mormon people. Stansbury also had to calm the fears of the Mormons who assumed, with paranoia based on twenty years of persecution, that his only purpose must be to harass them and perhaps drive them from their new home. Their suspicions seemed to be confirmed when the new Indian agent for California, a troublemaker named Wilson, spread the word that he had been authorized by the president to expel the Mormons if he thought it necessary, and, Stansbury later wrote, the Saints "very naturally supposed from such a declaration that there must be some connection between General Wilson and myself; and that the arrival of the two parties so nearly together was the result of a concerted and combined movement for the ulterior purpose of breaking up and destroying their colony."

Once reassured—or, as Stansbury put it, "undeceived"—that he was there only to explore and survey, the Saints were hospitable and cooperative. Brigham Young "laid the subject matter before the council called for the purpose," and informed Stansbury, the explorer later wrote, that they "were much pleased that the exploration was to be made; that they themselves had contemplated something of the kind, but did not yet feel able to incur the expense, but that any assistance they could render to facilitate our operations would be most cheerfuly furnished . . ." The Mormons provided Stansbury with provisions, manpower, and the services of a capable Mormon scientist, Albert Carrington, a Dartmouth graduate. The following July the Saints invited the Army explorers to be guests of honor at their annual Pioneer Day celebration.

Leaving the surveying task in the charge of his second-in-command, Lieutenant Gunnison, Stansbury and a small party headed north to reconnoiter a road directly from Fort Hall to Salt Lake City. After fording the Bear River, the group left the main emigrant road and followed the valley of the Malade River northward, a route that Stansbury described as "extremely level, free from underbrush, with very little artemisia, and affords ground for an excellent wagon-road."

On October 19, Stansbury set out to circumnavigate, by land, the Great Salt Lake, with five men and sixteen mules, despite warnings about hostile Indians, a lack of game and water, and the winter weather soon to close in. His four-week trip is not one of the epic journeys of the Great Basin, but the scarcity of water and some nasty weather caused both man and mule to suffer. Stansbury also proved himself to be an astute observer and interpreter of geological phenomena and a lively writer whose concern with human detail produced a readable narrative. In his entry for October 23, as "rocks observed," he listed "porphyry, geiss, dark slaty shales, and metamorphic sandstone, dipping to the northeast," while adding in the same paragraph: "and at the spring where we nooned, a small jointed cane trailed on the ground, in some instances to a distance of more than thirty feet. The men made excellent pipe stems of this material."

The trip provided Stansbury and his men with memorable sights. There were "thousands of acres, as far as the eye could reach," covered with wild geese and ducks, but the desolation of the lake and landscape had a depressing effect. Camped on a high promontory, Stansbury could see islands that "shot up from the bosom of the waters, their summits appearing to reach the clouds." He continued:

> The stillness of the grave seemed to pervade both air and water; and, excepting here and there a solitary wild-duck floating motionless on the bosom of the lake, not a living thing was to be seen. The night proved perfectly serene, and a young moon shed its tremulous light upon a sea of profound, unbroken silence. I was surprised to find, although so

near a body of the saltiest water, none of that feeling of invigorating freshness which is always experienced when in the vicinity of the ocean. The bleak and naked shores, without a single tree to relieve the eye, presented a scene so different from what I had pictured in my imagination of the beauties of this far-famed spot, that my disappointment was extreme.

Stansbury's expedition took the small party out across the desert to Frémont's Pilot Peak and back around the southern end of Great Salt Lake, across the Jordan River and back to Salt Lake City on the afternoon of November 7, thereby becoming, in Stansbury's own words, "the first party of white men that ever succeeded in making the entire circuit of the lake by land." From his observations, Stansbury was able to conclude that the Great Salt Lake was once part of "a vast *inland* sea, extending for hundreds of miles; and the isolated mountains which now tower from the flats, forming its western and south-western shores, were doubtless huge islands, similar to those which now rise from the diminished waters of the lake." The desert west of the lake was, Stansbury concluded, "entirely worthless" for human habitation, but he did have the imagination to envision one possible use for it: "its extent, and perfectly level surface, would furnish a desirable space on which to measure a degree of the meridian."

"An Anomaly So Very Peculiar"

After his return to Salt Lake City, Stansbury rejoined Gunnison in his surveying tasks until winter weather forced them to return to Salt Lake City. Stansbury devoted the next chapter of his report to observations of the Mormons, since "the founding, within the space of three years, of a large and flourishing community, upon a spot so remote from the abodes of man, so completely shut out by natural barriers from the rest of the world, so entirely unconnected by watercourse with either of the oceans that wash the shores of this continent—a country offering no advantages of inland navigation or of foreign commerce, but, on the contrary, isolated by vast uninhabitable deserts, and only to be reached by long, painful, and often hazardous journeys by land—presents an anomaly so very peculiar, that it deserves more than a passing notice."

Stansbury thought well of the Mormons. Even polygamy was given a sympathetic airing, although Stansbury was aware that, as "an 'outsider' and a 'gentile,' it is not to be supposed that I should have been permitted to view more than the surface of what is in fact as yet but an experiment, the details of which are sedulously veiled from public view." Stansbury also delved into Mormon history, testified to the "prodigious productiveness" of Utah soil, wrote admiringly of the Saints' missionary zeal and educational system, extolled their patriotism: "a more loyal and patriotic people cannot be found within the limits of the Union," but astutely pointed out that "a stern determination exists among them to submit to no repetition of the outrages to which they were subjected in Illinois and Missouri." Brigham Young was praised as a man possessed of "a personal reputation I believe to be above reproach"; Stansbury expressed his opinion that "the appointment of any other man to the office of governor would have been regarded by the whole people, not only as a sanction, but as in some sort a renewal . . . of that series of persecutions to which they had already been subjected. . . ." Among his conclusions, Stansbury included a prediction that holds up well even today:

When what is now but a Territory shall have become a sovereign State, with the uncontrolled power of making its own laws, . . . we shall then see in our midst a State as different from the rest of the Union in faith, manners, and customs, as it is widely separated by the vast plains and inhospitable deserts that surround it. That such a State will soon be formed, no reflecting man can well doubt, who has witnessed the indomitable energy, the unity and concentration of action, together with the enthusiastic spirit of proselytism which seems to possess the entire Mormon community.*

After wintering in Salt Lake City, Stansbury set out in early April to survey the Great Salt Lake and its islands. In two days they were on an island that Frémont had called Disappointment Island but that Stansbury "deemed it but due" to name Frémont Island after "the first adventurous explorer of this distant region." Although spring was in the air as the party set out around the lake, it also had to battle blizzards, gales, and other challenges posed by the mercurial climate, as well as thirst and other hardships. On May 20 Stansbury noted that a year had passed since they had left Fort Leavenworth and that of the original party "only four now remained: the rest having broken their engagements and gone to the gold-mines." On July 16 he reported, the survey and the triangulation of the lake having been completed: "To-day we took a final leave of this singular lake," concluding that "the necessity of transporting, by means totally inadequate, every pound of provisions and every drop of water needed for the daily consumption of a large party of men . . . made this survey one of unusually arduous and protracted toil."

But Stansbury was an unusually positive person and he ended with the cheerful observation that the "salubrity of the climate is such that . . . not a man was seriously unwell, and most of the party were in the uninterrupted enjoyment of robust health." He also praised the "constant kindness and generous hospitality" of the Mormon community, and summed up the accomplishments of the expedition, which included the "selection and measurement of a base line, six miles in length," the construction of "twenty-four principal triangulation stations," and surveys of the Great

---

* Stansbury's prediction of "a State as different from the rest of the Union in faith, manners, and customs . . ." anticipated a mid-twentieth-century view of the Latter-day Saints as not just a sect but a distinct people or a "near nation," as Thomas O'Dea put it in *The Mormons*.

Salt Lake and its islands, Utah Lake, and the Jordan River and some of its tributaries.

His homeward trek took him directly east from the Jordan to the Weber River and then to Fort Bridger via Muddy Creek and the Bear and Muddy Rivers. Jim Bridger himself guided the party to Fort Laramie, not through South Pass, as they had come, but further south through Bridger's Pass, the Medicine Bow Mountain, Laramie Basin, and Cheyenne Pass, "a practicable route . . ," Stansbury noted in his report, "through the chain of the Rocky Mountains, at a point 60 miles south of that now pursued." William Goetzmann in his *Army Exploration in the American West* called "the return trail blazed by the Stansbury-Gunnison party . . . one of its most important achievements, for it was the most direct and efficient route located thus far to the Salt Lake." Stansbury was injured falling from a horse, an accident that abruptly ended the expedition and Stansbury's days as an explorer. He died in 1863 from a heart condition brought on, his obituary read, by the "over-exertions and hardships" of his Salt Lake expedition.

"Central Route" to the Pacific

By the early 1850s, the focus of exploration had shifted from wagon roads to railroads. Selecting a transcontinental route had been bogged down in sectional bickering and politics ever since a New York merchant, Asa Whitney, proposed to Congress in 1845 that a railroad be built from Chicago, through South Pass, to the West Coast. The problem was that only one railroad, at first, would be built, and every section of the country wanted it. In 1853, Congress authorized the Corps of Topographical Engineers to send out four expeditions. The so-called Pacific Railroad Surveys were supposed to determine the best route across the country, but their real purpose was to appease the various regional interests. Senator Thomas Hart Benton, "the Missouri warhorse," vigorously promoted the central route that stretched from St.

Louis roughly along the thirty-eighth parallel and across the Great Basin, but the real power lay with Secretary of War Jefferson Davis, a southerner, who openly favored the most southern route of them all, one that followed the thirty-second parallel. "If the section of which I am a citizen has the best route," Davis queried the Senate in late 1858, "I ask who that looks to the interest of the country has a right to deny it the road?"*

The central route lost an ardent advocate in Congress when Benton was defeated in the election of 1850, but Benton, elected to the Missouri legislature the next year, stayed in the fight. In a twenty-four-page pamphlet distributed in 1853 as a "Letter from Col. Benton to the People of Missouri," Benton extolled the advantages of the central route with "enthusiasm and fervor" (and hyberbole) that carried him, wrote editor LeRoy Hafen, "far from the facts":

> Central to the Union, and embracing the business centres of the Atlantic and Pacific, and the Mississippi valley States— on a straight line with San Francisco and St. Louis, and connecting at this latter point with the concentrated steamboat navigation of the Great West, and with the entire railroad system, from the Mississippi to the Atlantic—straight and smooth—not a mountain to be climbed, a river or swamp to be crossed, a hill to be tunnelled—wood, water, and soil for continuous settlement . . . the whole traversable in winter . . . such is the character of the CENTRAL route, and which

---

* In addition to the central route that went directly across the Great Basin, the other three routes under consideration were the northern route, between the forty-seventh and forty-ninth parallels; the Albuquerque route on the thirty-fifth parallel; and the southern route on the thirty-second latitude. Lieutenant Amiel Weeks Whipple, assigned to the thirty-fifth parallel expedition, crossed the Colorado at the Needles, where he passed briefly into the Great Basin. In *Army Exploration in the American West, 1803–1863*, author William H. Goetzmann pointed out that Whipple "solved" the last mystery of the Great Basin by showing "that it did not terminate at the Mojave River, since the Mojave had no connection with the Colorado. Instead, the Basin area continued south to the Gulf of California as if through a vast lagoon at its southern end."

now claims a share of the public attention, and of the Congress appropriation. I shall ask for it that justice, and that it may be examined by some practical man whom I can commend, and who will have a stomach to the work, and do it without talk or delay.

The first "practical man" to explore the central route at Benton's behest was the adventuresome naval lieutenant Edward F. Beale, who, in 1853, was authorized to return to his post as superintendent of Indian affairs in California by the central route. Beale was accompanied by his cousin, Gwinn Harris Heap, an eastern journalist, and together they produced a highly favorable report about the route. Beale and his party left Westport, Missouri, on May 10, 1853. By June 23 they were at the Grand River (now the Colorado), a fearful obstacle that proved the absurdity of Benton's claim of not a river to be crossed on the central route. "It flowed with a loud and angry current," Heap wrote, "its amber-colored waters roaring sullenly past, laden with the wrecks of trees uprooted by their fury." The losses they sustained trying to cross the unfordable river by canoe and raft resulted in a sixteen-day delay while Heap led a party to Taos, New Mexico, to renew their provisions and supplies.

In the Great Basin, they arrived in the pioneer iron-producing town of Paragonah at the start of the troubles between Indian chief Walker and the Mormons known as the Walker War. Here they found the residents, whom Brigham Young had ordered to nearby Parowan for their protection, in the process of destroying their town. "It was to us a strange sight," Heap wrote, "to witness the alacrity with which these people obeyed an order which compelled them to destroy in an instant, the fruits of two years' labor."*

---

* Heap described Chief Walker as "a man of great subtlety, and indomitable energy." Perhaps he had a sense of humor as well, for, while the expedition was at Parowan, Walker sent a message to the local militia commander "telling him that 'the Mormons were d——d fools for abandoning their houses and towns, for he did not intend to molest them there, as it was his intention to confine his depredations to their cattle, and that he advised them to return and mind their

At Parowan (Parawan, in Heap's spelling), a community of about one hundred houses, the party observed "an excellent system of irrigation," which produced "wheat and corn . . . as fine as any that we had seen in the States." Heap also observed that there was at least one Indian child living with most Mormon families; the whites had apparently purchased them in accord with Brigham Young's belief that it was better for the Mormons to buy Indian children than have them sold into slavery elsewhere. Heap wrote that the children "were treated with kindness, and even tenderness; were taught to call their protectors 'father' and 'mother,' and instructed in the rudiments of education." Heap could not leave the Mormon settlements without commenting on "the odious practice of polygamy which these people have engrafted on their religion," although he had to admit that he would not have been aware of it "had not a 'Saint' voluntarily informed us that he was 'one of those Mormons who believed in a plurality of wives,' and added 'for my part I have six . . .' "

Heap and his men left Cedar City and Mountain Meadows in early August to follow the Mormon wagon road to San Bernardino. The party experienced some anxious moments with Pah-Utah Indians, to Heap "the greatest horse thieves on the continent." Heap described how the Indians, who used the horses and mules they stole for food, trailed the party hoping to snag any animal lagging behind and how, at night, they would "lurk around the camp and concealing themselves behind rocks and bushes, they communicate with each other by imitating the sounds of birds and animals." Further on in his report, he described the arduous crossing of the Mojave Desert in vivid detail:

August 16. The heat increased as we advanced into the desert, and most of the party had divested themselves of the greater part of their clothing. The guns, which we carried

---

crops, for, if they neglected them, they would starve, and be obliged to leave the country, which was not what he desired, for then there would be no cattle for him to take.' "

across the pummels of our saddles, were hot to the touch; and, to add to our annoyance and suffering, the wind, ladened with an impalpable sand, blew fiercely from the southward, feeling as if issuing from the mouth of a furnace, and obliterating in many places all traces of the road. The mules, already jaded by travelling across the sandy plain, went slowly along, their heads drooping to the ground. The pale moon, occasionally overshadowed by clouds, threw a ghastly light over the desert, and skeletons of animals glistening in her beams, strewed the way, adding horror to the scene.

The Beale/Heap party arrived in Los Angeles on August 22, having covered 1,852 miles in exactly one hundred days. Benton praised him in a letter: "Your expedition has been filling the U.S. during all the summer, and has fixed the character of the central route," adding, "The Government expeditions seem to be forgotten." Heap's account of the trip was published in serial form in the *National Intelligencer* and as a book in 1854.

MASSACRE ON THE SEVIER

The next venture along the central route into the Great Basin was led by Lieutenant John W. Gunnison, who had been Stansbury's second-in-command during the expedition of 1849–1850.* Gunnison's central route expedition was one of the four surveying parties the U.S. Army Corps of Topological Engineers sent out in 1853 and 1854 and the only one that went directly over the Rockies and across the Great Basin. Leaving St. Louis on June 23, 1853, Gunnison proceeded along the Arkansas River to Bent's

---

* In 1852, Gunnison published a book, *The Mormons*, that he described as a "treatise on the faith and condition of the Mormons [resulting] from a careful observation of that strange and interesting people during more than a year's residence among them in an official capacity." His purpose in writing it, Gunnison wrote, "is not 'to shoot folly as it flies,' but to let folly tire on its own pinions." Historian H. H. Bancroft wrote of the book: "Unlike most writers on the subject [the Mormons], Mr. Gunnison appears to have given the subject some thought."

Fort, through Colorado's Cochetopa Pass, and then across the Grand (the Colorado) and Green Rivers, and finally through the Wasatch Mountains into the Great Basin, arriving in Manti, Utah, on October 18.

Gunnison had been warned that the Utah Indians were up in arms, but he apparently believed—because his relations with them on the Stansbury expedition were so good—that they would recognize him as a friend. This probably explains why his party did not take adequate steps to protect themselves when they set up camp on the Sevier River. When the Indians attacked on the morning of October 26, 1853, Gunnison was killed as he rushed from his tent trying to assure the Indians of his goodwill. Six others died in the massacre, including the topographer R. H. Kern and the German biologist Frederick Creuzefeldt. Four others escaped and joined Lieutenant E. G. Beckwith, Gunnison's second-in-command, and those men who had separated from Gunnison days earlier to scout a route northward from the Sevier to Salt Lake City.

Beckwith led the survivors to Salt Lake City for the winter, and in the spring he took the Stansbury route to and from Fort Bridger and declared the Weber and Timpanogos Canyons suitable for railroads. And since he and Gunnison had already concluded that the central route across the mountains was impossible for a railroad, he asked for and received permission to survey farther north, along the forty-first parallel, to California. His route via Pilot Peak and the Humboldt River was a familiar one, but the forty-first parallel took him away from the river to Mud Lake, beyond which he discovered two more passes through the Sierra Nevada. His report touted the forty-first parallel route, but, because he was not an engineer, his recommendations were largely ignored.

To test the central route in winter and put to rest the belief that snow made the mountains impassable, Benton turned to son-in-law Frémont, who, Benton wrote in a letter, "is not afraid of snow in the mountains where there are valleys and passes and wood . . . He means to stand in the most elevated passes on the Central Route in

January next. He will have with him Indians and mountainmen who are no more afraid of snow than himself." Now forty years old and recovering from an illness, Frémont was an explorer past his prime who admitted in a poignant letter to his wife that a wet saddle no longer made a good pillow. But, when his party became bogged down in heavy snows in the Wasatch Mountains, Frémont rallied like the Pathfinder of old and guided his starving and frozen men to Parowan, Utah, where Beale and Heap had been just six months before. When they arrived on February 8, 1854, they had been without food for two days.* Frémont proceeded on west until he reached the Sierras at about the thirty-seventh parallel and followed the range south until they were able to make an easy crossing at a point that Allan Nevins, his biographer, put at "a little south of Walker's Pass." Frémont never wrote a report on the expedition, but a letter he circulated to newspapers recommending the central route ended with a plea that politicians stop their bickering and get on with the job of building a railroad:

> It seems a treason against mankind and the spirit of progress which marks the age to refuse to put this one completing link to our national prosperity and the civilization of the world. Europe still lies between Asia and America; build this railroad and things will have revolved about; America will lie between Asia and Europe—the golden vein which runs through the history of the world will follow the iron track to San Francisco.

Wagon Roads West

Even more pressing than a railroad route was the country's need for roads. California, in particular, was calling for roads to link

---

* Although he opposed polygamy as a presidential candidate in 1856, Frémont remained grateful for the hospitality the Mormon settlers showed his expedition. Allan Nevins, his biographer, tells how Frémont once refused to introduce the anti-Mormon lecturer Kate Field "on the ground that 'the Mormons saved me and mine from death by starvation in '54.' "

them with the rest of the country, specifically a central route that would pass directly through the Great Basin from Carson Valley to Salt Lake City, bypassing the more circuitous northern road along the Humboldt River. As already noted, the Army sent Lieutenant Colonel Edward J. Steptoe in 1854 to work on the Cedar City road, and also to investigate the Gunnison massacre, particularly charges that the Mormons were somehow involved.* The next major wagon-road exploration came in the wake of the Utah War. Captain James H. Simpson, stationed at Camp Floyd, in 1858 scouted a wagon route from that base through the Timpanogos Canyon to Fort Bridger. On his return, he made a tentative probe west of Camp Floyd of a possible route to California, but soon decided to return to Camp Floyd for the winter.

In the spring, Simpson again headed west, through a pass in Humboldt Mountains and on across the Great Basin, in the belief, expressed in a proposal to the War Department, "that a direct route from this post [Camp Floyd] to Carson Valley, in Utah, can be obtained, which would avoid the detour by the Humboldt to the right, and that by the Las Vegas and Los Angeles route to the left, and that it could be obtained so as to make the distance hence to San Francisco less than 800 miles; that is, that a route could be found in this direction 260 miles shorter than the Humboldt River route and 390 miles shorter than the Los Angeles route."

A week out, the party encountered a band of peaceful but destitute "Go-shoots," dressed almost entirely in capes made of rabbit skins, whom Simpson regarded as "the most wretched-looking creatures . . . I have ever seen." Simpson also described how a Go-shoot woman gutted a rat, then "pressing out the offal, she threw the animal, entrails and all, into the pot." The natives' taste for rodents both repelled and fascinated Simpson. In his journal,

---

* Steptoe found no evidence of Mormon complicity. Right after the massacre, the Mormon-owned *Deseret News* lamented the death of Gunnison, "who was endeared to us by a former and fondly cherished acquaintanceship in 1849–50, while he was engaged with Captain Howard Stansbury in the survey of the Great Salt and Utah Lakes." Also, a Mormon guide was among those killed.

Simpson recounted how his guide, John Reese, while scouting ahead alone, became lost and close to starving, some Indians offered him "three fat rats, but as they had been roasted with entrails and offal unremoved, he said he did not feel hungry enough to accept their generous hospitality."*

Simpson reached the Walker River in the western Great Basin on June 7; almost simultaneously word of his approach reached San Francisco via the telegraph that by then extended as far as Genoa. On the three-day trip from the river to Genoa, the party encountered a grisly sign that a rough form of justice was beginning to prevail among the miners of the Sierra Nevada—the body of William "Lucky Bill" Thorrington, a horse-thief and murderer whom vigilantes had strung up almost a year before. The sight moved Simpson to astonishment "that the relic of such a season of popular agitation and excitement should be left to be harped upon by every passer-by." Genoa, which Simpson put at between 150 and 200 people, fired off a thirteen-gun salute and ran up the American flag as the men paraded into town.

Simpson proceeded on alone to Placerville and Sacramento, and from there by steamboat to San Francisco. On his way up the Sierras from Genoa, he met at the Lake Valley mail station the celebrated "Snowshoe Thompson," famous for delivering the mail on skis and snowshoes over the Sierras in winter, a skill he learned as a child in Norway. On Simpson's return, he was treated to a hair-raising ride down from Lake Valley with a driver "so drunk as not to know what to do, and yet as obstinate as a mule," an experience that caused him in his report to deplore the condition of the twelve miles of road from Lake Valley to Carson Canyon and express his astonishment, "considering this is a portion of the great emigration route over the continent, that Congress has not done something about it."

---

* John Reese, a Mormon and former Salt Lake City merchant, was one of the first residents of Mormon Station, later renamed Genoa. On the way west, Simpson named Reese Valley and River after him because, he wrote, "Mr. Reese has been of considerable service, and discovers very laudable zeal in examining the country ahead in our explorations."

Simpson, departing Genoa on June 24, led his party back to Camp Floyd by a route that ran some forty miles south of the one he had taken west.* By the time he reached Camp Floyd, emigrants were already using his route across the Great Basin to reach California. The route he pioneered cut some 200 miles off the Humboldt road from Salt Lake City to Genoa (and shortened the road from Camp Floyd to Genoa by 283 miles).

He also pointed out that his return, or more southerly, route was the longer of the two by twenty-nine miles, but "in grade, grass, and extent of cultivable soil, it is better." In assessing Simpson's "brilliant career as an Army explorer," Goetzmann noted that he

> remained a wagon-road man, and believed (like Benton, curiously enough) that the government should first build local roads and postal routes, then populate the country and develop its resources before attempting to construct a transcontinental railroad. In practical terms he had done his part to bring this about. The Pony Express followed his northern route. The Chorpenning Mail Company used his southern route. The telegraph also followed close to this line. Russell, Majors, and Waddell drove their wagons and stock over it, and emigrants passed over it every day on their way to California.

"THE BEST AND BRIGHTEST"

The Great Basin's last exploration of the pioneer era was unlike any of the others. For one, it moved from west to east, which by then, 1867, was the direction taken by the telegraph, the soon-to-be-completed transcontinental railroad, and the miners coming

---

* In his *Report of Explorations across the Great Basin of the Territory of Utah*, Simpson claimed to be the first to cross the Great Basin directly. "Some individuals," he wrote, "more venturous than others, had made a less circuitous bend than the old route by the Humboldt River, but yet a direct journey across no one had effected." In writing this, he seemed to be unaware of Jedediah Smith's desperate trek, west to east, across the Great Basin in 1827.

from California into the Great Basin. It also was the first expedition that focused not on roads or unknown parts but on the mineral resources of the region. And it was not led by a mountain man or soldier. Instead it was both inspired and directed by a brilliant twenty-five-year-old Yale-educated aesthete and geologist named Clarence King.*

King's exploration and survey started at the eastern base of the Sierra Nevada and proceeded over two seasons back and forth across the Great Basin ending, in 1872, in the Great Plains east of the Rockies. King's orders, which he wrote, clearly stated the goals he set for himself:

> The object of the exploration is to examine and describe the geological structure, geographical condition and natural resources of a belt of country extending from the 120th meridian eastward to the 105th meridian, along the 40th parallel of latitude with sufficient expansion north and south to include the line of the "Central" and "Union Pacific" railroads.... The exploration ... should examine all rock formations, mountain ranges, detrital plains, coal deposits, soils, minerals, ores, saline and alkaline deposits ... collect ... material for a topographical map ... conduct barometric and thermometric observations [and] make collections in botany and zoology with a view to a memoir on these subjects, illustrating the occurrence and distribution of plants and animals.

King manned his expedition with an array of young but capable scientists—biologists, botanists, geologists, topographers, ornithologists, and a noted photographer, Timothy O'Sullivan, one of Mathew Brady's stars during the Civil War. The expedition had a rousing send-off with a dinner party at Yale University before it

---

* With King's Fortieth Parallel Survey, civilian scientists took over the exploration of the West from the soldiers of the U.S. Army Corps of Engineers. This transfer was formalized when the U.S. Geological Survey was formed in 1879— with Clarence King as its first director.

shipped out to San Francisco via the Isthmus of Panama and made its way across the Sierras to a base camp in Glendale, Nevada, near the site of modern Reno, where twenty cavalrymen joined the expedition to protect it against Indians. By mid-July, the exploration was under way, with the party splitting up in different directions, including one that attempted, unsuccessfully, to run the rapids of the Truckee River into Pyramid Lake. Soon, however, the entire expedition was in jeopardy as malaria struck down one man after another. King led them to higher ground in the Sierra, in hopes that cooler temperatures would improve their health. Once the ailing men were settled, King led the healthy few on an expedition to the Stillwater Mountains, one of the Great Basin's distinctive north-south ranges on the eastern edge of the Carson Sink. There, on September 22, atop a mountain fittingly called Job's Peak, King was adjusting a theodolite when he was struck by lightning. He took a week to recover from the shock; then it was back to the field to salvage what was left of the season.

King wintered in comfortable quarters in Virginia City. There "King dressed the part of a dandy" in doeskin trousers and lemon-colored gloves, with "a low-crowned wide-awake [a low-crowned felt hat, apparently so-called because it had no nap] topping his ensemble," according to his biographer, Thurman Wilkins. In Virginia City, King, two geologists, and photographer O'Sullivan explored the maze of underground tunnels of the Comstock mine. While observing the smelting process, the men noticed that a great deal of ore was being wasted. King assigned James D. Hague to figure out a new ore-reduction process, and eventually King was able to report that "by a slight variation of the chemical condition we have succeeded in raising the percentage of yield from 64 and 66 percent to 93 and 95 percent." King also concluded that Comstock reserves went deeper and were correspondingly richer than most experts thought: "The examples of other great veins . . . rather favor the idea of a continued silver occurrence in depth." And, in 1876, the strike known as the Big Bonanza proved him right.

The next season, the party pushed practically all the way across the Great Basin to the Great Salt Lake. There was a diversion when a soldier deserted, and King, afraid that a successful escape would inspire other troopers to do the same, gave chase, "trailing him like a bloodhound," for one hundred miles across northern Nevada. Catching up with him at a pass in the Havilah Mountains, King sneaked up on the fugitive and captured him, he later wrote, "in a hand to hand struggle in which I nearly lost my life." The season ended that year in Salt Lake City; when it resumed the next spring, King led one group eastward out of the Great Basin to the Green River area where he discovered extensive deposits of coal. Another group followed the Bear River to its source and from there made its way to the crest of the Uinta Mountains, the east-west-running range to the east of the Wasatch. The third group resurveyed the Great Salt Lake; the lake had risen nine feet, adding six hundred square miles to its surface, since Stansbury had mapped it a decade before.

King was the first to recognize that the Great Basin, in the Pliocene era, contained two huge inland lakes separated by a high central plateau.* King named the western body of water Lake Lahontan, after the early eighteenth-century French officer whose tall tale about an inland sea in the American West had a major impact on early thinking about the region. In his years remaining in the West, King added to his legend by crawling into a cave and killing a a grizzly with a single shot—a foolhardy feat, Goetzmann pointed out, "no mountain man would have even considered." In 1872, he exposed a diamond fraud in Colorado, a piece of geological detective work that brought him more fame. In Colorado he met the Harvard historian Henry Adams and began a curious friendship that helped, through Adams's writings, keep

---

* The Great Basin's eastern prehistoric lake, Lake Bonneville, of which the Great Salt Lake is a remnant, was named by Grove Karl Gilbert, chief geologist on an expedition that crossed the Great Basin, north to south, in 1872. Gilbert published his findings before King did, although he graciously admitted that King and his colleagues should have had the honor of naming Lake Bonneville, a "literary priority . . . to which they were fairly entitled by priority of investigation."

King's reputation alive. King also discovered the first glacier in the United States, and he proved himself to be no mean writer with the publication, in 1872, of a collection of sketches, *Mountaineering in the Sierra Nevada*.*

Through his own work and that of the brilliant men he gathered around him, King put the exploration of the West on a scientific footing, while still bringing to it much of the adventuresome spirit that marked the Great Basin's earlier investigations. The final reports of the Fortieth Parallel Survey consisted of seven volumes and an atlas, and King's own contribution—volume 1, *Systematic Geology*—remains "a classic in the field of historical geology," wrote Richard A. Bartlett in *Great Surveys of the American West*. King was rewarded for his fieldwork with the directorship of the new U.S. Geological Survey, but he resigned after a year, lured away by private business interests in western cattle and mining. The rest of his life was marked by failure, illness, and a diminution of what a friend called "his astonishing power of diffusing happiness wherever he went." It was as if the gods were punishing him for abandoning the scientific work he did so well. The man whom Henry Adams had called "the best and brightest man of his generation" died, almost forgotten, in 1901 of tuberculosis.

* King dismissed the work as a "slight book of travel," but critics have consistently praised it as being on a par with Washington Irving's *Astoria* or *Captain Bonneville* and Francis Parkman's *Oregon Trail*. "King has a painter's eye . . . ," wrote the critic Van Wyck Brooks.

Chapter Thirteen

OVERLAND TO UTAH

O n October 18, 1861, the telegraph line from the east reached Fort Bridger in Utah Territory. Brigham Young inaugurated the service by sending this unequivocal message eastward: "Utah has not seceded, but is firm for the Constitution and the laws of our once happy country, and is warmly interested in enterprises as the one so far completed."* As elsewhere, the Civil War was a time of change in Utah, but those changes had little to

* Writing in the *Utah Historical Quarterly*, Gaylon Caldwell pointed out that, while the text of Brigham Young's telegram is taught to every Mormon child in Utah, in the East it was the technical achievement of a telegram being sent from faraway Utah—not Brigham Young's vow of loyalty—that interested the newspapers. The *New York Times* did comment skeptically, however, that the Mormon leader "has evidently forgiven the United States Government the war it waged upon him a few years since, or else he fears the South might prove still worse masters than Uncle Sam." Caldwell added: "The celebrated message was sent to Mr. J. H. Wade, president of the Pacific Telegraph Company, and not to President Abraham Lincoln, as is commonly supposed."

do with slavery; the few blacks the Mormons had in bondage were freed without fanfare in 1862 when Congress did away with slavery in the territories. The war did force the Mormons to reassess their relationship with the federal government. Brigham Young's telegraphic vow of loyalty not withstanding, he and other leaders believed that the War Between the States was the country's just punishment for its harsh and uncharitable treatment of the Saints in the past—"The yoke is off our neck and on theirs," Heber Kimball exulted.* Still, the transcontinental telegraph, which linked up in Salt Lake City on October 24, 1861, one week after Brigham Young's telegram, tied the Territory of Utah closer than ever to the United States of America.

The transcontinental telegraph was an enterprise to which the Mormons made a great and willing contribution. Under the terms of contracts signed with the two companies building the line—one eastward from Carson City, Nevada, the other westward from Fort Leavenworth—the Saints supplied men, materials, provisions, and labor for one thousand miles of the line as it stretched east and west across the Great Basin. For his involvement and cooperation, Brigham Young received, for the church, eleven thousand dollars in gold and, personally, ten thousand dollars in stock in the Overland Telegraph Company. The telegraph lines were joined in Salt Lake City on October 24, 1861, one week after he sent his famous telegram. On that same day Young proposed that the Saints build their own telegraph line, one that would run north and south, link the reaches of the Mormon Kingdom, and tie in with the national line at Salt Lake City.

Once the telegraph penetrated the Mormons' "rocky fortress," the Saints could no longer claim to be isolated or independent from the rest of the country. Not that they ever really were. Right

---

* Many Mormons saw the Civil War as a fulfillment of Joseph Smith's divine revelation of December 25, 1832, "concerning the wars that will shortly come to pass, beginning at the rebellion of South Carolina ... For behold the Southern States shall be divided against the Northern States ... " (Doctrine and Covenants, section 87).

from the beginning it was obvious that many roads would pass through Utah. In the 1850s and 1860s, getting the mail from coast to coast, running a telegraph line across the country, and spanning the continent by railroad became matters of pressing concern, and nearly all of the routes under consideration ran across the Great Basin. It was also evident that the Mormons could never be truly self-sufficient. Ever since their arrival in the Great Basin in 1847, they had been dependent on the outside world to fill many of their needs, be it clothing or seeds or materials to start their industries and businesses.

The first non-Mormon merchants arrived in Salt Lake City with wagons full of goods in the fall of 1849. By then the Mormon pioneers needed to replace the clothing and other items they had brought with them, and the crowds pressing to get into the stores were so large that many had to do their dealing through open windows. One of the first Gentiles to profit from this pent-up demand was a flamboyant trader named Benjamin Holladay, who brought supplies to General Kearny's Army of the West during the Mexican War and, when that conflict was over, turned his attention to Salt Lake City. Holladay brought along a letter of recommendation from Colonel Alexander Doniphon, who had proved himself to be a friend of the Mormons during their troubles in the late 1830s in Missouri.* Holladay presented the letter to Brigham Young, who then told his flock that Holladay "can be trusted as an honorable dealer." Holladay's first shipment to Utah, worth seventy thousand dollars, was quickly disposed of at a large profit, and shipments in the years that followed were larger and more lucrative. Finally, as the gold supply decreased in Utah,

---

* When Missouri Governor Lilburn Boggs issued his famous Extermination Order in 1838 (see chapter 7, page 118), he ordered Doniphon, then an officer in the state militia, to expel the Mormons from the state. Doniphon not only ignored the order, but also courageously saved Joseph Smith, then a prisoner, from a mob intent on killing him in October 1838. The Mormons remained grateful. If the U.S. government were to replace him as governor of Utah, Brigham Young once said, "I should as soon General Doniphon would be that man, as any I know of."

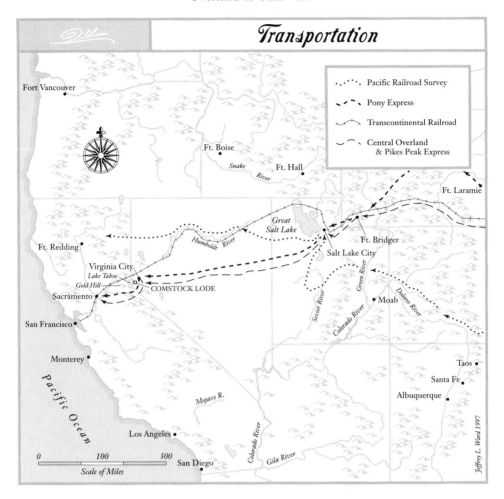

Holladay traded goods for cattle, which he then drove to California and sold at enormous profit. Soon he was established as the leading operator of wagon trains and stagecoaches in the West.

At the same time, the United States government was beginning to award contracts for overland mail service to daring and enterprising individuals willing to take on the challenge of moving mail across deserts and mountains and through hostile Indian territory. Mail to California then went by ship, a system that earned nothing but complaints for being slow and unreliable. In 1850, a freighter named Samuel H. Woodson bid $19,500 to win a contract to carry the mail from Independence, Missouri, to Salt Lake City, but he soon found that it was impossible to meet the contract's stipulation that he complete the trip, one way, in thirty days. To speed things up, he contracted the next year with Feramoz Little, a nephew of Brigham Young, to handle the western end of the route from Salt Lake City to Fort Laramie, but Little kept getting bogged down in the snow, and service hardly improved at all.

To carry the mail west, from Salt Lake City to Sacramento, the government awarded a contract for monthly service to George Chorpenning, a former forty-niner, and his partner, Absalom Woodward, for $14,000. On their first trip, they loaded the mail on a mule and set off for Utah, a trip that took them fifty-three days. In November, Woodward was killed by Indians near the Malade River in northern Nevada, and Chorpenning struggled on alone. Although he never performed to the satisfaction of customers in California, he managed to keep renewing his contract until he was providing weekly service for the grand sum of $130,000 a year. Before his contract was finally canceled in May 1860, Chorpenning had purchased stagecoaches and was carrying both mail and passengers, a combination of services that was beginning to make economic sense to other freighters and expressmen in the West.

In the meantime, Californians were not the only ones chafing under the slow and unreliable delivery of mail and other services. The Mormons too, as they expanded their contacts and business dealings with the outside world, needed better access. Also, letting Gentiles profit from services that the Mormons could provide themselves went against the Mormon policy of controlling everything that went on within their mountain kingdom. If Mormons ran the freighting companies operating in and out of Utah, the reasoning went, they could control the prices of the goods that their people needed and keep them reasonable. If combined with passenger service, a Mormon company also could bring to Utah those Mormon converts affluent enough to pay their own way. And those who still came by wagon train or on foot could be accommodated by the stations along the way that the company would set up.

THE Y. X. COMPANY

The Mormons' opportunity to enter the express business arose in 1856 when the Post Office canceled the contract held by non-Mormons running the mail—slowly and unreliably—between Independence and Salt Lake City. Brigham Young believed that the government would never award him personally—or the Mormon Church—a contract, so, using Heber Kimball as a front, he entered a bid of twenty-three thousand dollars (some thirteen thousand dollars lower than current holders) and was awarded the contract. It covered a four-year period, December 1, 1856, to November 30, 1860, but because of the poor state of communications, the Mormons did not learn that they had obtained the business until mid-January 1857, and this lapse of a month and a half would become significant as this venture developed. The contract itself was immediately transferred to the trustees of the newly formed Brigham Young Express and Carrying Company, which, to de-emphasize Mormon involvement, was known simply as the Y. X. Company.

Because of the urgency involved, the Mormons chose two stalwarts, William Hickman and Porter Rockwell, the reputed leaders of the Danites, to carry the first mails. Hickman left Salt Lake City on February 8, 1857, and arrived in Independence twenty-six days later. From there on in, the two frontiersmen split the route. With Fort Laramie the midpoint, Hickman and his crew covered the route to Independence, Missouri; Rockwell to Salt Lake City.* With better weather and organization, the speed of the mail delivery increased; in June a courier averaging eighty miles a day covered the distance between Salt Lake City and Independence in fifteen days.

---

* Hickman reluctantly took on the assignment only after Brigham Young ordered him: "You are the very man; get your bays and roll out." In his biography of Porter Rockwell, Harold Schindler speculated that the dissatisfaction that eventually caused Hickman's estrangement from the church and Brigham Young started at this time. He was excommunicated in June 1868 and four years later published his hostile autobiography, *Brigham's Destroying Angel.*

Once the mail service was under way, the Mormons put into effect their plan for developing the route with the same dazzling speed and efficiency that they had used to bring emigrants across the country and to colonize the far corners of the Great Basin. Livestock, equipment, and provisions were either purchased or obtained from church members, who were told their contributions were actually investments in the enterprise. Similarly, labor was provided by missionaries "called" to improve the road and establish the stations, starting with improvements to Fort Bridger and Fort Supply on the western side of the South Pass and proceeding eastward until there were stations—to be developed along a typical Mormon grid into mile-square towns—located about every fifty miles. Thus, there would be fresh horses for coaches and wagons and provisions for emigrants negotiating the trail west on foot. In all respects it was a well-thought-out and workable plan. Had it succeeded, it would have extended Mormon influence from Fort Bridger all along the Oregon Trail to the Missouri River, and, wrote historian Arrington, would "have changed the whole structure of Mormon, and perhaps Western, economic development."

That was not to be. When Abraham O. Smoot appeared to pick up the mail bound for Salt Lake City about July 1, 1857, postal authorities informed him that the Mormon mail contract had been canceled, ostensibly because they had failed to begin service on December 1 as the contract called for, although, later, there were accusations that the Mormons had tampered with the mail. When Smoot and Rockwell, whom he met east of Fort Laramie, delivered the news to Brigham Young, the Mormon leader called the cancelation of the contract "a great legal and moral outrage," but by this time the Mormons had learned that the Army was on its way to Utah to install a new, non-Mormon governor and perhaps arrest Brigham Young for treason and rebellion. Brigham Young responded to the threat by closing and dismantling the stations the Mormons were in the process of establishing between Salt Lake City and Independence and by recalling the Mormons he had sent there, in an effort to consolidate his Kingdom before the Army arrived.

The ensuing Utah—or Mormon—War turned out to be so profitable for freighters hauling supplies and other firms doing business with the U.S. Army that the nonshooting conflict became known as the Contractors' War. The firm doing the lion's share of the freighting business was Russell, Majors, and Waddell, a partnership headquartered in Leavenworth, Kansas. In 1857, two years after it was founded, the firm won an Army contract to haul five million pounds of goods and supplies to Army posts throughout the West, and the following year it contracted to haul twice that amount to Utah alone. By one count, supplying the Utah expeditionary force was a massive enterprise that required thirty-five hundred wagons, forty thousand oxen, one thousand mules, and four thousand men.

THE PONY EXPRESS

The spark plug of the firm was a Vermont-born promoter and wheeler-dealer named William H. Russell. One of Russell's many ambitions was to secure a government contract to carry the mail from the Missouri River to California over a central route that would pass through Salt Lake City and cut directly across the Great Basin. In the late 1850s the mail to California was—to the great frustration of Californians—delivered slowly by the Butterfield Overland Mail Company, founded in 1857 by New Yorker John Butterfield, via a long, looping southern route that began in Missouri and swung south through Texas, Arizona, and New Mexico to southern California, then north to San Francisco. It was still widely believed at the time that the central overland route, which crossed both the Wasatch and Sierra Nevada Ranges, was impassable in winter, but Russell was sure he knew otherwise.* To prove his point and thereby, he hoped, obtain the mail contract,

---

* As Russell well knew, the experience of Johnston's Utah expedition, which monthly sent express riders back and forth from Camp Scott and Fort Leavenworth, proved that the route could be negotiated in the winter, wrote Raymond W. and Mary Lund Settle in their *War Drums and Wagon Wheels: The Story of Russell, Majors, and Waddell.*

Russell came up with a scheme—the fabled Pony Express—that would succeed brilliantly, in its short life, in delivering the mail speedily back and forth to California, prove beyond a doubt the viability of the central route even in winter, and provide the country with a historical episode so chock-full of romance and derring-do that it still has a hold on our collective imagination. The Pony Express would also be the financial undoing of Russell and his partners.

Russell's idea of sending horses and riders at full gallop over the entire nineteen-hundred-mile route from St. Joseph, Missouri, to Sacramento, California—whence the mail was taken by river steamer to San Francisco—seems all the more daring in face of the fact that the firm of Russell, Majors, and Waddell was in serious financial straits, if not actually bankrupt, at the time he came up with the idea. Although the firm had been the Army's major contractor for the Utah War, Mormon raiders had caused them losses of some $495,000, for which, as it turned out, they would never be compensated.

The Pony Express was all part of Russell's grand plan to put the company back on its feet, a plan that began to unfold in February 1859, when he formed a freighting company, the Leavenworth & Pike's Peak Express Company, to run between Leavenworth, Kansas, and Denver, a city that Russell helped found as a processing center for gold from Pike's Peak. Three months later he acquired John Hockaday's government contract to deliver mail from St. Joseph, Missouri, to Salt Lake City, which put him into the Great Basin and gave him control of about two-thirds of the central route to California. But as business grew, so did his problems. The Colorado gold fields were a disappointment and never attracted the express business he had hoped for, and the costs of developing Leavenworth & Pike's Peak were more than he anticipated. So, before year's end in 1859 he turned to his more conservative partners, William B. Waddell and Alexander Majors, to bail him out. Which they did—only because they feared, if Russell failed, they would, too. Together they formed a new company, whose lengthy name reflected Russell's ambitions: the Central Overland California & Pike's Peak Express Company. It was the C.O.C. & P.P., as it was known, that became the parent of the Pony Express.

Majors and Waddell were even less enthusiastic about Russell's Pony Express; to these seasoned businessmen, the numbers did not add up, and there was no way the service could pay for itself, let alone make a profit. At first they refused to back him, but Russell was uncommonly persuasive, and he had some convincing arguments on his side. For one, Californians were demanding faster mail service; the route taken by the Overland Mail Company was twenty-eight hundred miles long and took twenty-five days to travel in coaches and wagons that carried both passengers and mail. His route was more than eight hundred miles shorter, and he proposed making the trip in ten days, well under half the time taken by the Overland Mail Company. Furthermore, he had the support of U.S. Senator William M. Gwinn of California; once Russell proved that the express would work, Gwinn would try to get a subsidy from Congress for the line. Besides, Russell told Majors and Waddell, he had already committed them to the plan. Once his partners learned that, they reluctantly agreed to go along. Otherwise they would be putting the prestige of their already shaky firm at risk.

Russell publicly announced the plan in a telegram to his son: "Have determined to establish a Pony Express to Sacramento, California, commencing 3d of April. Time ten days." From then on, through its short, eighteen-month existence, the Pony Express was a sensation in the press. The April 3 date, which Russell apparently picked at random, left only sixty-five days to get ready. Russell turned the job over to one of his companies, Jones, Russell & Co. In that short time, its employees managed, while completing countless other tasks, to purchase five hundred horses (one advertisement specified "grey mares, from four to seven years old . . . with black hoofs") and sign up eighty riders, many of them attracted by ads calling for horsemen who were young and light and fearless. One hundred and ninety stations, which had to be stocked with men, horses, and supplies, were located every ten to fifteen miles along the route from St. Joseph, Missouri, west along the Platte, through South Pass and Fort Bridger to Salt Lake City, and then out across the central Great Basin, the Sierras, and into Sacramento. Twenty-five of the stations were "home" stations, where one rider took over from another. The rest were "swing" stations: Here the rider paused no more than two minutes to get a fresh mount. The 1,996-mile route was divided into five sections, one of which was completely within the Great Basin—from Salt Lake City to Roberts Creek in central Nevada; two more fell, on the east and west, partly within its boundaries.

On April 3, at 7:15 P.M., in St. Joseph, a brass cannon boomed and a rider named Johnny Fry leapt on a bay mare and rode aboard a boat that ferried him across the Missouri River. Fry galloped westward, changing mounts three times, until at 11:30 P.M., he reached Granada, Kansas, a home station, and turned the mail over to the waiting rider. William Hamilton, the final rider of thirty on the first run, brought the mail into Sacramento at 5:25 P.M. on April 14, making the total time for the trip just under ten days.* Seven hours later Hamilton and his horse arrived by steamer to a hero's welcome in San Francisco. The first westbound packet consisted of forty-nine letters, some newspapers printed on lightweight paper, a few telegrams, and various news items for California newspapers. The mail was carried in the four pouches of a specially designed leather saddle-covering. Called a *mochila* (Spanish for "rucksack") and designed to fit over the horn and cantle of the saddle, it could be yanked off one horse and transferred to another in seconds. The rate for sending items via the Pony Express was five dollars a half ounce, high but not nearly

---

* Fry is usually credited with being the first westward rider, and James Randall the first to leave San Francisco—at 4 P.M. (Pacific time) on the first leg of the eastward journey on the same day, April 3. Raymond and Mary Settle, however, wrote: "The identity of these first two riders has never been definitely established, although there are a number of nominations for the honor in each case."

enough to cover the expenses for the run, let alone make a dent in the heavy investment that Russell had already sunk into the venture.

The bold venture, which the dean of Pony Express historians, Arthur Chapman, described as "a veritable telegraph line of flesh and blood," soon came to represent both the romantic myth and the hard reality of the Wild West. From the ranks of the riders came none other than William F. "Buffalo Bill" Cody, who, by featuring Pony Express riders in his Wild West show, helped to keep the legend alive. Cody boasted that, as a skinny fifteen-year-old Pony Express rider, he once rode 384 miles without stopping and that "this stands on the record as being the longest Pony Express journey ever made."* Buffalo Bill's claim, however, has been disputed by historians who give that honor to either Jack Keetley, who rode continuously for thirty-one hours, covering 340 miles, or to Robert "Pony Bob" Haslam, who covered 380 miles through the Great Basin in about thirty-six hours but who, unlike Keetley, stopped midway for an eight-hour nap.

The Pony Expressmen became celebrities in their own right; people along the route turned out just to watch them ride by and disappear in the distance "like," Mark Twain wrote, "the belated fragment of a storm." After his successful maiden ride, Johnny Fry was especially popular; when a young woman was lucky enough to tear off a piece of his shirttail as he raced by, she paid him the honor of sewing it into a patchwork quilt. Riders at the start and end of the ride were required to wear an elaborate uniform, but otherwise dress was ragtag. Originally the horsemen carried a bugle to alert the next station as they approached, but their clock-like schedule and the sound of pounding hoofs proved to be enough to herald their arrival.

---

* Cody was also a teamster for Russell, Majors, and Waddell during the Mormon War; he was working one of the three wagon trains that Major Lot Smith, the Mormon raider, captured on October 4, 1857, according to Henry Pickering Walker, author of *The Wagonmasters*. Smith released Cody and the other men, then burned the wagon trains and three hundred thousand pounds of supplies.

Almost certainly the riders also dispensed with the special leather-bound, lightweight Bible that the company had printed for their wagon-train crews. Alexander Majors in particular was a stickler about religious observance; his book, *Rules and Regulations for the Government of Russell, Majors, and Waddell Outfit*, stipulated: "We expect our trains to observe the Sabbath, and whenever an opportunity occurs to hear preaching, embrace it." Experience also reduced the heavy arsenal of weapons the riders carried at first to just one pistol. The best defense against Indians, they soon learned, was a fast horse. After one rider was ambushed by Indians, he attributed his escape to his horse's "grain-fed muscles." He explained: "Their grass-fed ponies couldn't keep long within gunshot."

WAR ON PYRAMID LAKE

Pony Bob Haslam's long ride was made in the midst of a period of Indian conflict within the Great Basin known as the Paiute— or Pyramid Lake—War. Violence erupted after the Comstock Lode discovery in 1859 brought miners into western Nevada (then still Utah Territory), displacing the Indians and threatening their hunting grounds. In spring 1860, Paiutes and Bannocks were meeting at Pyramid Lake to discuss the situation when, on May 7, a band of Indian renegades attacked and burned the Pony Express stop known as Williams Station and killed three white men. The miners and settlers in the region hastily formed a posse of 105 volunteers who gleefully—since, to them, punishing Indians promised to be great sport—headed for Pyramid Lake.* On May 12, the posse spotted some Indians on a ridge and rushed after them and into what turned out to be a shrewdly conceived ambush. In the fighting, 79 whites were killed and many others wounded. It was the worst defeat for whites in Great Basin history.

* Fed by the Truckee River but, in true Great Basin fashion, having no outlet, Pyramid Lake with its curious rock formation was named by John C. Frémont when his expedition came across it in January 1844.

The bloodshed at Pyramid Lake spread panic through Carson Valley; women and children were herded together for their protection, and the alarmed citizens of Silver City even tried to construct a cannon out of wood. Soon a force of over 700 men, including 207 regulars from California, gathered on the Truckee, and on May 31 met, defeated, and dispersed the Paiute in a short battle. The soldiers moved from there to the Carson River, where they established Fort Churchill, which soon became the terminus of the telegraph from California and an important Pony Express station.

During the Pyramid Lake War, the Pony Express suspended service for a month, the only interruption in its short history. But before it resumed, Russell made an announcement that again put the operation in the headlines: Instead of running weekly, as it had for the eight weeks prior to the Pyramid Lake War, it would now run twice a week. It was a brilliant promotional coup for Russell, but it did little to help the fortunes of the Pony Express, which, for all its glamor, was turning out to be a dismal business failure.

Financial stress was causing dissension within the firm of Russell, Majors, and Waddell. Together and separately, the partners had expanded into stagecoaching and retail stores until they were so overextended that their businesses were competing with one another. In the winter of 1859–1860, the company lost over three thousand head of cattle stranded by blizzards, a loss of $150,000. Russell himself had serious legal problems stemming from his reckless attempt to use government Indian Trust Fund Bonds as collateral on loans.*

The Civil War held out some hope. After the South seceded and Confederates in southern Missouri, Texas, and Arizona cut the service of the Overland Mail Company, Congress suddenly

---

* On Christmas Eve 1860, Russell was arrested in his New York office and charged with receiving stolen property and conspiring to defraud the government. He was taken to Washington and jailed for a few days before being released on three hundred thousand dollars' bail. In late January 1861, he went to trial but his case was dismissed on a technicality.

saw the advantages of the central route. This, of course, was what Russell had wanted all along, but his shady dealings with government bonds ruled him out as a contractor. Besides, the job, which required coaches to run six days a week and the Pony Express semi-weekly, was too big for Russell or the other contender, the Butter-field Overland Mail. In the end, the two companies split the one-million-dollar-a-year route: The Overland Mail became the prime contractor on March 2, 1861, with Russell's Central Overland California & Pike's Peak Express Company subcontracting for the eastern half, from Salt Lake City to the Missouri River.

Although his company was only a subcontractor on the central overland route, Russell, ever an optimist, was encouraged; he finally had the government subsidy that he had been angling for all along. But the Civil War turned out to be bad for business, and the company continued to lose money and sink more deeply in debt. When employees stopped receiving regular paychecks, a terminal symptom in any company, they nicknamed the C.O.C. & P.P. the "Clean Out of Cash and Poor Pay." Ben Holladay, who had become associated with the company in 1858, tried to reorganize it and, when this did not better its situation, drove it into bankruptcy. At an auction on March 7, 1862, Holladay himself purchased the company for one hundred thousand dollars.*

By the time Holladay took over the company, the Pony Express was gone. It was never intended to last beyond the completion of the transcontinental telegraph line, and the day after that connec-

* After the sale of the company, Russell went into the express business and mining in Colorado in an unsuccessful attempt to recoup his fortune and reputation. His debts when he filed for bankruptcy on April 3, 1868 (eight years to the day after the inaugural run of the Pony Express) were more than $2.5 million. On his return to New York, he was reduced to selling a patent medicine, Tic Sano, a neuralgia cure. He died at his son's home in Palmyra, Missouri, on September 10, 1872. The National Pony Express Centennial Association placed a monument at his grave in 1962. Partner Waddell retired from business after the C.O.C. & P.P. bankruptcy and also died in 1872. Majors lived until 1900, although that same bankruptcy ended his career. Years later "Buffalo Bill" Cody, whom Majors had hired for the Pony Express, arranged to have his memoirs published as *Seventy Years on the Frontier*.

tion was made at Salt Lake City on October 24, 1861, ads announcing the Pony Express's demise appeared in newspapers. A few solitary riders still on the trail with mail to deliver kept riding in true Pony Express tradition; one arrived in San Francisco on November 4 with 103 letters in his *mochila*. The Pony Express had lasted just over eighteen months; in that time its riders made 308 runs each way—a total of 616,000 miles—from St. Joseph, Missouri, to San Francisco and carried 34,753 pieces of mail. Its reliability through desert, snow-clogged mountains, and hostile Indian territory was extraordinary. It also lost huge amounts of money; some estimates put its net losses between $300,000 and $500,000. Its total receipts of $90,141 hardly covered what it paid for horses. Alexander Majors, Russell's reluctant partner, later wrote that "the amount of business transacted over this line was not sufficient to pay one tenth of the expenses to say nothing about the amount of capital invested."

Still, the Pony Express accomplished much. To William Russell's credit, it proved the superiority of the central overland route across the Great Basin, a route that, with some variation, both the transcontinental telegraph and railroad would take. At a time of national crisis, it tied a splintered country east to west, and, historians say, by speeding word of Fort Sumter to California, helped keep that state in the Union. Of course, it was an anachronism from the start: by the time it began, telegraphs and railroads were operating in much of the country and it was only a matter of time before they would cross the continent. When the Pony Express died, its obituaries were nostalgic. The *Sacramento Bee* lamented the fact that the Pony Express had been replaced by the telegraph, "a senseless, soulless thing that eats not, sleeps not and tires not, and knows not the difference between a rod of ground and the circumference of the globe." Similarly, the editor of the *California Pacific* waxed eloquent but said it well:

Goodbye, Pony! No proud and star-caparisoned charger in the war field has ever done so great, so true and so good a work as thine. No pampered and world-famed racer of the turf will ever win from you the proud fame of the fleet courser of the continent. You came to us with tidings that made your feet beautiful on the tops of the mountains; tidings of the world's great life, of nations rising for liberty and winning the day of battles, and nations' defeats and reverses. We have looked to you as those who wait for the morning, and how seldom did you fail us! When days were months and hours weeks, how you thrilled us out of pain and suspense, to know the best or know the worst. You have served us well!

Napoléon of the West II

It was a sign of the changing times that William Russell, who had such an impact on transportation in the West, never set foot within the Great Basin, while Benjamin Holladay, his successor in the express business and inheritor of his title Napoléon of the West, essentially operated out of offices in either New York, San Francisco, or Washington, D.C. (By contrast, Brigham Young, the Great Basin's greatest historical figure, never left Utah Territory after he arrived there in 1847.) When Holladay was starting in business, he asked Russell for a loan and was turned down. But when Russell was in trouble, Holladay was more accommodating and loaned him money for his troubled Pony Express and other ventures. In the end, Holladay forced Russell, Majors, and Waddell into bankruptcy and ended up the sole owner of their C.O.C. & P.P.

Holladay was one of the most vivid and colorful entrepreneurs to appear in the American West. The son of a poor Kentucky farmer, he left home at sixteen and by age twenty-one was a prosperous businessman in Missouri. Holladay was boisterous, uncouth, fond of drinking and gambling, smarter than any of his competitors, and far more ruthless. He dressed like a dandy—the ruby stick-pin he wore in his cravat was worth thousands of dollars—and he traveled in a gilded coach suited to royalty, but

Holladay had the temperament of a frontier infighter. Typically he would undercut competitors' prices until he drove them out of business, then gouge his customers by charging more than ever. Holladay undercut one rival by charging passengers $2.50 (as opposed to his competitor's reasonable $25 fare) to ride in brand-new Concord coaches. Once the man folded, Holladay raised the fare to $37.50, took the coaches off the line, and began hauling customers in wagons.

Holladay built mansions on Fifth Avenue in New York City and Washington, D.C., where he lavishly entertained the politicians who were the source of government business.* (In five years he received nearly two million dollars in postal contracts.) He also built a palatial estate outside New York City, which he named Ophir after the Nevada silver mine in which he had an interest. Holladay left the social climbing to his wife; he spent most of his time in his offices or on the road inspecting his vast empire and pulling off stunts like running his personal coach from San Francisco to Atchison, Kansas, in a record twelve days.

At the height of his power and influence in the mid-1860s, the Holladay Overland Mail & Express was grossing as much as two hundred thousand dollars a month from hauling cargo and passengers and had contracts with Wells, Fargo; American Express; and United States Express for their business. But Indian attacks, which Holladay claimed cost him half a million dollars, and, after the Civil War, a depression in mining hurt his business just as the trancontinental railroad was beginning to stretch across the country. Then, in 1865, an upstart named David Butterfield (no kin to John Butterfield of the Overland Mail) challenged Holladay on the Missouri-to-Denver run. Butterfield, as it turned out, had powerful backers—Wells, Fargo, American Express, and United

---

* When Holladay shifted his business interests to the Northwest in the early 1870s, he wanted to run for U.S. senator from Oregon but found it more practical to put his own man in the office. His candidate, John H. Mitchell, who won in 1872, was quoted in a newspaper as saying: "Whatever is Ben Holladay's politics is my politics, and whatever Ben Holladay wants, I want."

States Express, who informed Holladay that they would no longer pay the high rates he charged and even threatened to start their own line between Denver and Salt Lake City.

Holladay was not intimidated. Indians began attacking Butterfield's line with devastating effect, while Holladay's coaches and wagons were left alone. This created some suspicion that he had something to do with the attacks, although it is possible that his tough and seasoned crew of drivers and escorts, which included regular Army troops, might have been enough to discourage the Indians. When his spies told him that the rival line was in trouble, Holladay imperiously called in Butterfield's New York banker and made an offer he could not refuse. Then, once the line was his, he raised rates across the board. In less than a year, however, he sold out to Wells, Fargo for almost two million dollars and went into railroads and steamboats in the Northwest.

"Almost a Miracle": The Deseret Telegraph

Just as Ben Holladay was abandoning at great profit his freighting and stagecoach interests, the Mormons were starting work on the telegraph line that would link the most distant part of their kingdom with Salt Lake City and, from there via the transcontinental telegraph, with the rest of the world. As related earlier in this chapter, Brigham Young announced that the Mormons would build their own line on the very day—October 24, 1861—that the transcontinental line was joined in Salt Lake City. However, shortages of materials during the Civil War made it impossible to go ahead with the plan. Four years later, with peace, the Mormons were ready to proceed.

The Deseret Telegraph Company was a typical Mormon enterprise, vastly different from the Gentile-run enterprises—express companies, the transcontinental telegraph, and the railroad—that were beginning to open up the Great Basin to the rest of the country. Whereas Holladay, Russell, and other entrepreneurs went to bankers for their financing, Brigham Young turned to the people, and, in the winter of 1865–1866, contributions amounting to fifty-six thousand dollars in cash were collected from the citizens of Utah. Communities all over the territory sent wagons and supplies for a church wagon train that left in the spring of 1866 for the Missouri River and returned the following October with eighty-four tons of wire and other material essential to the line. In the meantime, young people, many of them women, were "called" on missions to attend telegraphers' school in Salt Lake City.

Like its preparation, the construction of the line was a cooperative venture. Each town on the line was responsible for that portion of its construction. During the winter of 1865–1866, men began cutting poles and surveying the line, and even with a break to plant crops in the spring of 1866, the crews were ready to start stringing wire by the time the wagon train arrived in October. Less than two months later, by December 1, 1866, there was a working line between Ogden and Salt Lake City; by mid-February of the following year, the five-hundred-mile line running from Logan in the north through Salt Lake City to St. George in the south was in operation. In a statement, the director of the project, a Western Union employee on leave, pointed out: "Not a man on this line ever worked a telegraph line before, the line was strung and put into operation in the middle of winter, it is about five hundred miles in length; taking all into consideration please permit me as an old operator to say that I think the working of the same almost a miracle."

Brigham Young dedicated the line to the Lord God of Israel with a message that combined theology with technology, "praying that this and all other improvements may contribute to our benefit, and the glory of our God; until we can waft ourselves by the power of the Almighty from world to world to our fullest satisfaction." Following a pattern set by other Mormon enterprises, Brigham Young was named president of the Deseret Telegraph Company when the territorial legislature incorporated it in 1867 with church officials in all other posts. The same year, to protect a particularly vulnerable section of the line during the Black Hawk

War, the longest and most violent conflict between Indians and Mormons, the church built Cove Fort, a fortress two hundred miles south of Salt Lake City in the middle of a stretch of unsettled territory.*

The Deseret Telegraph was not built to make money; tithing revenues made up the line's deficits until the line was sold to Western Union in 1900. The church paid nothing to use the line; personal messages from individual Mormons were transmitted at minimal charge. The operator/missionaries were paid and supported by contributions from their own communities. The only significant source of revenue came from extending the service to non-Mormon mining communities, which paid full rate. By 1880, the line, which had extended into Idaho, Arizona, and Nevada, was more than one thousand miles long, more than twice its original length.

By knitting the Mormon world together, the line provided both convenience and protection. After it opened, an aging Brigham Young was able to spend the winters in St. George, the heart of Utah's Dixie, and conduct church business over the wires. The Deseret Telegraph allowed the Mormons to keep track of their enemies—Indians whenever they became troublesome and, later, after the pioneer era ended, federal agents on the trail of polygamists.† It might be thought that such a radical advance in communications as the telegraph would lead "to a greater cosmopolitanism in thought and action," but, as Leonard Arrington concluded in his *Great Basin Kingdom*, "it is doubtful that it

---

* The Black Hawk War began on April 9, 1865, when a drunken Mormon pulled a Ute Indian off his horse during a parley over some stolen cattle near Manti. The offended Indians, led by a Ute named Black Hawk, vowed revenge and, over the next five days, killed five Mormons and stole hundreds of cattle. Black Hawk then led factions of Utes, Paiutes, and Navajos in a series of destructive raids on the Mormons. Black Hawk made peace with the Mormons in 1867, but violence continued until 1872 when troops were called in.

† Word of Custer's defeat at the Battle of Little Big Horn was relayed to the outside world via the Deseret Telegraph. A horseman reached Franklin, Idaho, with the news, and a Mormon telegraph operator transmitted it to the East.

had such an influence among the Mormons." More likely, by bringing them closer together, it made them more resistant to change. Arrington, who was at his best when writing about Mormon enterprises, believed the telegraph improved Mormon morale: "it made them proud of themselves, their religion, and their Zion." And it prepared Mormon leaders for the next challenge—in Arrington's words, for "the problems which would be faced when the transcontinental railroad was completed in 1869."

Chapter Fourteen

THE RUSH

TO WASHOE

In 1859, Nevada was not; and its mineral wealth was unknown." So the newspaper editor Samuel Bowles described the western Great Basin of the late 1850s—a desolate expanse of desert and mountains with no good prospects for the future.* But, as Bowles explained, that was about to change. In the spring itinerant prospectors discovered a fabulous underground repository of silver and gold—the Comstock Lode—that, literally and figuratively, put Nevada on the map. The Comstock made Nevada wealthy and attracted enough people so that it qualified, within a few years, for statehood, although political factors also contributed to its rise to legitimacy. And almost overnight the Comstock created the legendary metropolis Virginia City, "the

---

* Samuel Bowles's *Our New West* (1869) is "Records of Travel" of two western trips that Bowles made in 1865 and 1868 with Schuyler Colfax, who was Speaker of the House, 1863–1869, and vice president of the United States, 1869–1873. Bowles's earlier book, *Across the Continent*, is an account of the first trip.

'livest' town, for its age and population, that America ever produced," wrote Mark Twain, its most famous resident.*

Trappers and mountain men, Army explorers, forty-niners, and California-bound pioneers all crossed the inhospitable mountains and deserts that became Nevada, many of them following the well-traveled "highway" west, the Humboldt River. The Mormons included the western Great Basin in its State of Deseret, and Congress made it part of Utah when it created that territory in 1850. That June the Mormons established a trading post at Mormon Station in the Carson Valley, and a year later a Salt Lake City merchant named John Reese built the first permanent trading establishment in that part of the Great Basin. Reese and his brother Enoch brought merchandise from Salt Lake City to sell to overlanders, and they supplemented these offerings with corn, wheat, barley, turnips, and watermelons that they grew in the fields nearby. By November, there were about one hundred people in the Carson Valley, enough for them to begin thinking about their own interests and to petition the United States government for "a distinct Territorial Government" to govern their slice of the western Great Basin.

There had been inklings of gold in the area ever since May 1850, when a California-bound emigrant named William Prouse panned a few specks not far from the California border. Prouse continued on with the wagon train. Once the news was reported in California, a few miners did move east over the Sierra Nevada, but not enough of them to constitute a proper gold rush. It is believed that in the mid-1850s the Grosh brothers, Hosea and Ethan Allan, discovered silver in the vicinity of the Comstock Lode, but both died in 1857—one from blood poisoning after piercing his foot with a pick and the other in a blizzard—without revealing its whereabouts.

---

* Samuel Langhorne Clemens was in Virginia City as a reporter for the *Territorial Enterprise* during the first rush on the Comstock—from September 1862 to May 1864. (The second, larger boom—the Big Bonanza—occurred in 1874–1875 and is outside the period covered by this book.) Clemens signed his pen name, Mark Twain, to a newspaper article for the first time on February 3, 1863.

The next five years produced a tug-of-war between the settlers and the Mormon authorities in Salt Lake City. First and foremost, the settlers wanted the territorial government of Utah to establish law and order in the western Great Basin. When this was not forthcoming, the citizens of Carson Valley petitioned their nearest neighbor, California, to annex them. This maneuver moved the Mormons to organize the western fringe of their territory into a political and judicial entity called Carson County. The residents, however, were still unsatisfied and the next year, 1854, drew up their own constitution "in order to secure the blessings of tranquillity and of free government, . . . until provision is made for our government and protection by other proper authorities." Again the Mormons responded, this time by dispatching Orson Hyde, one of the church's Twelve Apostles, and thirty-six colonists to Mormon Station. Hyde held elections—with Mormons winning all but one of the county offices—set up a court, built a sawmill, and renamed the settlement Genoa. Carson County was also allowed to send one representative to the Utah territorial legislature.

The structure that Hyde and the Mormons gave to Carson County was short-lived. Hyde was recalled to Salt Lake City in November 1856; soon afterward the Utah legislature brought back the court to Salt Lake City and sent the county's lone legislator home. In short order, Carson County was back where it started, unrepresented and ungoverned. The situation was destabilized further the following September when Brigham Young called back all Mormons to the Salt Lake Valley to defend Mormondom from the U.S. Army then advancing on Utah. A wagon train, 123 wagons and about 450 people, under orders not to reveal its true destination to Gentiles, left for Salt Lake City on September 26 while spreading the word that they were actually bound for the Salmon River.

With the Mormons gone, the remaining Gentiles were able to take over the Saints' property and renew their push for separation from Mormon-controlled Utah. A squatters' committee meeting in Genoa once again petitioned Congress for territorial status. This time they succeeded in getting a favorable bill reported out of the Committee on Territories, only to have it die, unacted upon, when Congress adjourned. In early 1859, with the Mormon War behind them, the Utah legislators restored Carson County and sent a judge to preside over it.

"Old Virginny" and "Old Pancake"

Ten days later, during a January thaw, four men, including James "Old Virginny" Finney, working on an outcropping on Mt. Davidson (then called Sun Mountain) in the Virginia Range of the Sierra Nevada, came up with enough gold to persuade them to set up camp and begin mining in earnest. Soon they were pulling out about twelve dollars a day for each miner.

It was mining custom that prospectors could stake out only a claim that they could expect to work, so soon other miners had set up camps nearby. Some of these sank shafts that proved that there was gold to be found well under the surface. In April the local *Territorial Enterprise* reported that "the diggings are in depth from 3 to 20 feet, and prospects from 5 to 25 cents to the pan, from the surface to the bedrock." Mining, which previously looked as if it were petering out in the area, suddenly became a full-time occupation, so much so, it was written in the *Enterprise*, that "the miners are generally temperate and industrious, and whiskey has, therefore, become a drug in the market. . . ." A lower price for liquor might have pleased James Finney, whose place in history is tied to his taste for whiskey. It was about this time, or so legend has it, that Finney was stumbling home one night when he dropped and broke his bottle and, not wanting the whiskey to go entirely to waste, declared that he was christening the town in honor of his native Virginia. True or not, it is a fact that the settlement was named Virginia City soon afterward, and, as an explanation, it is as good as any we have for the name.

Finney's discovery focused attention on the area but the real strike was several months away. In early June 1859, two Irishmen, Patrick McLaughlin and Peter O'Riley, moved up to a site with a good spring at the head of Six Mile Canyon on the northern slope of Mt. Davidson. There they discovered encouraging quantities of gold in an unusual black dirt. As they dug deeper, Rodman Paul explained in his *Mining Frontiers of the Far West, 1848–1880*, they discovered their claim was not just surface pickings but "the decomposed outcropping of a vein . . . By this time the miners, still with no thought of any mineral save gold, were irritably throwing away quantities of heavy bluish sand and blue-gray quartz—what they peevishly called that 'blasted blue stuff.' " Also, the gold they did retrieve had a palish cast that indicated that the nuggets were an amalgam of gold and some other metal, which they assumed was worthless. McLaughlin and O'Riley were winding up work when a veteran miner, Henry "Old Pancake" Comstock, rode up. The savvy Comstock instantly recognized the potential of the site, whereupon he informed the men that he had filed a prior claim to it. And they soon agreed to take him and his cohort, Immanuel Penrod, on as partners.*

For the moment, Finney's site lower on the mountain—with none of the pesky black rock—was considered the more promising of the two finds. The men working the McLaughlin-Riley claim were extracting the gold and simply letting the black earth or "blue stuff" roll down the mountain. Then Judge James Walsh of Grass Valley, California, gave some samples of the unwanted rock

---

* Historian Ronald M. James has speculated on why Riley and McLaughlin did not resist Comstock's demand that he and Penrod be made partners. First, he pointed out, it was "a reasonable possibility" that Comstock, an experienced miner, might have actually claimed the site. Also, miners at the time often preferred to recognize conflicting claims rather than undergo legal battles. Finally "the assumption in the 1850s, that mineral wealth was diffuse and not concentrated, meant that it was not much of a concession to admit Comstock to the site. Additional partners, after all, meant that more feet could be claimed, according to regional mining custom." In fact the foursome soon took on two more partners in return for building two arrastras, crude mills for crushing the black rock. James made these points in a well-reasoned article, "Drunks, Fools, and Lunatics: History and Folklore of the Early Comstock."

to an assayer in nearby Placerville, who, on June 27, analyzed it and came up with some surprising results. A ton of it, he reported, would yield $876 in gold, rich at a time when $100 a ton was considered good, but there was more: that black rock was loaded with silver, $3,000 to the ton. Walsh and two partners rushed back to Mt. Davidson determined to cash in by keeping the ore's high silver content a secret. But, as the Comstock's foremost chronicler, William Wright, pen-named Dan De Quille, wrote in his western classic *History of the Big Bonanza*, "Each man had intimate friends in whom he had the utmost confidence . . . and those bosom friends soon knew that a silver-mine of wonderful richness had been discovered over in Washoe country. These again had their friends."

Encouraged by bystanders along the way calling out "Go Washoe!" fortune seekers from California were soon crossing the Sierra Nevada and pouring into the district. The name Washoe was a tribute to the Washo, the Indian tribe of that region; it was also the name of a valley, "which is some twenty-five miles distant and in no way connected with the mines," the *San Francisco Bulletin* explained in late 1859. The lode itself came to be known as the Comstock, because, wrote De Quille, Old Pancake,

did all the talking and none of the working, and was always ready to tell strangers about the mine. When visitors came it was always *my* mine and *my* everything. Thus people came to talk of Comstock's mine and Comstock's vein—as persons making locations asserted they were on the same vein as Comstock, *i.e.*, the Comstock vein—and in that way the name of Comstock became fastened upon the whole lode. As the first claim was called the Ophir, that would have been a more fitting name for the whole vein than the one it now bears.* For a long time Comstock no more appreciated the

* From the Old Testament, 1 Kings 9:28: "And they came to Ophir, and fetched from thence gold, four hundred and twenty talents, and brought it to king Solomon."

heavy black material that accompanied the gold . . . than did O'Riley and McLaughlin.

Soon after the uncovering of the Comstock Lode in 1859, the mining community took steps to impose order on chaos. On June 11, the miners established the Gold Hill Mining District—Gold Hill being the name of the settlement that was growing up around Finney's original claim—and adopted "rules and laws for our government" in a document that began: "Whereas, the isolated position we occupy, far from all legal tribunals, and cut off from those fountains of justice which every American citizen should enjoy, renders it necessary that we organize in body politic for our mutual protection against the lawless, and for meting out justice between man and man, . . ." The rules covered murder, theft, and other crimes—expulsion from the district being the surprisingly harsh penalty for gambling—but mainly they tried to impose order on the recording and sale of mining claims. Not that rules did much to regulate anything; the first book of records was kept behind the bar of a saloon, and miners could insert or delete entries at will.

About four thousand miners arrived in the newly named Virginia City before a heavy snow closed mountain passes. The next year ten thousand came, an infusion of population that virtually created the State of Nevada. These would-be miners came from everywhere, but mostly from California; many of them were forty-niners who had passed right over the Comstock a decade before. The Comstock Lode extended for two and a half miles on the eastern side of Mt. Davidson, under the towns of both Gold Hill and Virginia City. When he was working on the *Territorial Enterprise*, Twain wrote: "Often we felt our chairs jar, and heard the faint boom of a blast down in the bowels of the earth under the office." Seventeen thousand claims were eventually filed on it, most of them worthless. In 1876, its best year, its production was a record thirty-eight million dollars, and, although it is famous for its stupendous production of silver, the Comstock yielded almost as much gold. Eventually there were nearly two hundred miles of tunnels, some of which extended three thousand feet.

"The Wondrous City of Virginia"

There was nothing cosmopolitan about the Virginia City on the Comstock. Food was scarce, the water undrinkable unless laced with whiskey, and lodging was so poor that miners slept in shanties, tents, wagons, or caves dug into the side of the mountain—in one description, "coyote holes in the mountain side forcibly seized and held by men." The only hotel, grandly named the International, was, wrote De Quille, "a little frame structure, capable of accommodating only a small number of persons, and those in the roughest style imaginable." A San Francisco writer, Frank Soule, deplored everything about the place: "I have been through one hundred degrees of latitude, north and south, but never have found so inhospitable, miserable, God-forsaken a spot as this same Virginia City."

Speculators and other shady characters far outnumbered the miners. The practice of buying and selling shares in dubious claims was rampant. One miner thought he had seen signs of silver under his domicile and claimed the entire street of shanties and tents. When claims overlapped, violence was the most convenient way of settling a dispute. Wrote De Quille in *A History of the Comstock Silver Lode & Mines*: "At one time the nightly killings were so frequent that residents expected each morning to hear there was 'a man for breakfast.' " An Indian uprising on Pyramid Lake in May 1860 temporarily dampened the speculative boom, and prices of Washoe stock fell in San Francisco. Still, it had been quite a spring, much sound and fury but little in the way of payoff. Of the four thousand claims filed, only three hundred had been actually mined, and only twenty of those were actually paying off.

The mining boom quickly resumed, as did the transformation of Virginia City into a town of architectural substance and, by frontier standards, sophistication. What Twain called "the flush times" began six months after he took the job on the *Territorial Enterprise* in the fall of 1862, "and they continued with unabated splendor for three years." As Virginia City grew, "large fire-proof buildings were going up in every direction," he wrote, "and the wooden suburbs were spreading out in all directions." The settlement's architecture included banks, hotels, theaters, "hurdy-gurdy houses," gambling palaces, "a whiskey mill every fifteen steps," breweries, and jails. Twain wrote that there was "even some talk of building a church."

The traveler and writer John Ross Browne described "the wondrous city of Virginia" located on "a slope of mountain speckled with snow, sagebrushes, and mounds of upturned earth, without any apparent beginning or end, congruity or regard for the eternal fitness of things. . . ." Figuring the city's population was a guessing game at best, Mark Twain put it at fifteen to eighteen thousand during "flush times." When newspaperman Bowles got there in summer 1865, the "fast and fascinating times of 1862–63" were over. Still, he observed, the "exceedingly well-built" city had an "air of permanence and of profit, and contains a population of seven or eight thousand, besides the adjoining town or extension of Gold Hill, which has about three thousand more." In these numbers, men outnumbered women about two to one.

Most of the miners on the Comstock were plain prospectors, called placer miners, who knew how to get gold from the surface with pans and rockers, but who lacked the expertise and the capital that mining on the Comstock called for. Many prospectors were more interested in discovering claims and selling them than actually working them. The original discoverers of the Comstock, for example, assumed that their claims would soon give out, as had all the others in their experience. So, to their everlasting discredit, they soon sold out their interests for pittances to men who would become wealthy on their discoveries.

McLaughlin, for instance, was the first to sell his interest—for thirty-five hundred dollars. Comstock's partner, Manny Penrod, did two and a half times better by holding out for a few days.

Henry Comstock received eleven thousand dollars for his share and later depicted himself as a victim of "the intrigues of civilized rascality." Finney sold out for a bottle of whiskey and an Indian pony, a story that has been reprinted so many times that it has a ring of truth. Alvah Gould, who gave his name to the famous Gould and Curry mine, relinquished his claim, according to Mark Twain, "for a pair of second-hand government blankets and a bottle of whiskey that killed nine men in three hours . . . an unoffending stranger that smelled the cork was disabled for life."*

Many of the stories about the men of the Comstock were either invented or perpetuated by Comstock historian De Quille, who was both a first-rate mining reporter and an inventor of tall tales. De Quille was the first to print the story about James Finney's naming Virginia City with spilled whiskey, and he explained that Comstock's sobriquet, "Old Pancake," was given him because he was always too busy to make bread. ("Even as, with spoon in one hand, he stirred up his pancake batter, it is said that he kept one eye on the top of some distant peak, and was lost in speculations in regard to the wealth in gold and silver that might rest somewhere beneath its rocky crest.") In most of the stories, the early miners came to hard and penniless ends. James Finney, so it was reported, was drunk when he was thrown from a bucking horse and killed. Gould ended up operating a peanut stand in Reno. Comstock, who was, according to De Quille, "a man flighty in his imagining," went mad and killed himself. Lemuel "Sandy" Bowers, an illiterate Irishman, and his wife, Eilley Orrum, a Scottish

---

* In his article, Ronald James made the case that Finney, Comstock, and others were "hard-working, locally prominent miners," who deserve more credit than they have received for the Comstock. Also, the men only "understood gold"; silver was something outside their experience. And they knew that most gold rushes died quickly. "To resist a willing buyer offering thousands of dollars for a claim to a vein that might pinch out a few feet from the pit's bottom would have been reckless gambling," James argued. And, since they had neither the money nor the experience to mount an elaborate mining operation, James concluded that "they made the rational best choice." However, to the more sophisticated miners who came after them and who developed the legends about them, they appeared either "mad, lazy, drunken, and unimaginative or incredibly unlucky."

282 • *The World Intrudes*

boardinghouse keeper, held on to their claims and became so rich that Bowers proclaimed, "I've got money to throw to the birds," at a party he hosted at the International Hotel before they left on an extravagant three-year tour of Europe.* On their return, they settled into the palatial home they had built in the valley, but they lived so carelessly that, after Sandy died in 1868, Eilley, deeply in debt, had to support herself telling fortunes and giving tours of the mansion.

Among those on the Comstock after the first discoveries were certain men with the money and know-how to exploit the lode. Judge Walsh was one of this new breed. In September 1859, he transported nearly forty tons of ore to San Francisco. "Although it cost $512 per ton to transport and mill," James wrote, "The $114,000 it produced more than offset the expense." George Hearst, a hard-rock miner from California, purchased a one-sixth share in the Ophir mine and the first winter managed to pack out thirty-eight tons of the "blue stuff" to San Francisco, which, after smelting, earned him and his partners a profit of $91,000. It was the start of a fortune that Hearst would bequeath to his son, William Randolph. Irish-born John W. Mackay was a hard-working but mostly unsuccessful placer miner until he came to the Comstock. He and his three Irish partners—James G. Fair, James C. Flood, and William S. O'Brien—parlayed moderate success with their first mine into ownership of the Consolidated Virginia, which turned out to be the Big Bonanza of 1874 and which made the four "bonanza kings" among the richest men in the world.

Banking opportunities on the Comstock inspired William C. Ralston, founder of the Bank of California, to monopolize the

---

* Eilley Orrum lived through much Great Basin history. In 1850, she migrated from Scotland to Salt Lake City with her first husband, a Mormon, but left him when he became a polygamist. She and her second husband went as colonists to the Carson Valley with Orson Hyde in 1855, but she stayed behind to operate her boardinghouse when he and the other Mormons were recalled to Salt Lake City in 1857. She married Bowers the next year. "When it became known what lay underneath their claims," wrote H. H. Bancroft, "the Bowers became famous alike for their riches and their ignorance of the uses of wealth."

Comstock's mills, build a railroad to haul ore from Virginia City to the mills on the Carson River, invest in the main water company serving the mines, and acquire a substantial share in the Comstock's most productive mines. Ralston, who operated through his agent, William Sharon, came in late, after the Comstock went into its first decline in the latter half of the 1860s, but he was in an enviable position to profit when the Comstock went into bonanza in the 1870s.* But Ralston was overextended in other ventures and his bank folded on August 26, 1875. The next day Ralston's body was found in San Francisco Bay, the cause of his death unknown.

Other newcomers provided the technical expertise needed to mine the Comstock, which presented problems even the most experienced hard-rock miners had not encountered before. At a depth of 175 feet on the incline, the Ophir widened out until it was 45 to 65 feet across, and the vein and the earth around it became so soft and unstable that the tunnels began collapsing on the men, making it too dangerous to proceed. The company called in a German mining engineer, Philip Deidesheimer, who devised a system of interlocking cubes—the so-called "square set" method of shoring up a mine—that enabled miners to drill in any direction without a cave-in. Legend has it that Deidesheimer was stumped by the problem until he emerged from the mine one day and, discouraged, stretched out in the sagebrush. From that vantage point he began watching bees construct a hive, and suddenly he had it. That night he did his sketches, and three days later timbers for the square sets, which became giant underground pillars when they were filled with rock, were being lowered into the Ophir. Deidesheimer passed up his chance to become wealthy: he never patented the square set method that was eventually used around the world.

Another innovator, Almarin B. Paul, a friend of Hearst's, came

Bonanza is a Spanish word meaning "prosperity"; a mine said to be "in bonanza" is producing rich ore. Conversely, a mine "in borrasca" (storm) is not paying off. Paul wrote that the words are a tribute to the Spanish, "one of the world's great mining peoples."

to Virginia City to solve the problem of how to process silver and gold. In sixty days he transported an entire stamping mill across the Sierra, and he had it up and operating on the same day his contract with mine owners was to expire. Paul also developed the important "Washoe pan process" that quickly and chemically separated the silver from rock. Deidesheimer's square sets and Paul's Washoe pan process, Paul wrote, "were fundamental, in that without them the [Comstock] mines could not have been developed at all . . ."

A. S. Hallidie, an innovator responsible for the San Francisco cable car, and another German, Adolph Sutro, also tackled problems on the Comstock. Hallidie devised a flat, woven-wire cable for hauling up ore from great depths that was stronger than rope and easier to handle than round steel cable. It was Hallidie's cable that made the San Francisco cable cars possible. Sutro came to the Comstock in 1864 to build a three- to four-mile-long tunnel from the mines to Carson Valley. At the time flooding was slowing work on the Comstock, and temperatures were so brutally high that miners sometimes could work only fifteen minutes at a time. Sutro believed the tunnel would drain the mines, cool them by providing adequate ventilation, provide a way of hauling ore to mills in the Carson Valley, and perhaps, in the building, uncover new sources of gold and silver. It took Sutro more than a dozen years to finance and build his tunnel; by then the Comstock boom was over and the tunnel never earned back the four million–plus dollars it took to build.

Mining in the western Great Basin was not limited to Virginia City and its neighbor, Gold Hill. In his account, Bowles described mining districts at Humboldt, Austin, Belmont, Aurora, Silver Peak, Egan Canyon, Pahranagat, Cortez, and Palmetto "scattered freely all through the central belt of the State to the California line, . . . [where] numerous mining camps are established, and more or less machinery, carted all the way from California at ten to thirty cents a pound, is pounding away on hopeful silver ores." The rush to the White Pines district in west central Nevada came close to matching the rush to Washoe in intensity. It began in early 1868, after an Indian directed resident prospectors to promising silver deposits atop the nine-thousand-foot-high Treasure Hill. The mountain attracted so many miners that it came close to Virginia City in population. But the boom was fleeting: The diggings turned out to be shallow—no vein ran deep into the earth as on the Comstock—and the two million dollars it produced in 1870 was its best effort. By 1875, only one mine was being worked.

THE ROAD TO STATEHOOD

The allure of the Comstock almost depopulated Carson Valley communities such as Genoa and Carson City. When the provisional legislature convened in Genoa in December 1859, only four representatives appeared—the rest were in the hills looking for gold and silver—and it had to adjourn for want of a quorum. In Washington, the process of separating Nevada from Utah was going ahead in spite of its distracted citizenry. The first secessions of southern states had removed the obstacle in Congress to adding nonslave territories to the Union. One of President Buchanan's last acts in office was to sign a bill, on March 2, 1861, creating the Territory of Nevada out of Utah, the territory that had humiliated him by resisting his authority during the Utah War. By early July Nevada's newly appointed governor, a New Yorker named James Warren Nye, had arrived in Carson City. A month later, his secretary, Orion Clemens, and his secretary's brother, Samuel (soon to be better known as Mark Twain), disembarked at Carson City from an overland stage. In his travel classic, *Roughing It*, Twain, who would try his hand at prospecting before settling down to newspaper work, described the city as a "wooden" town, population two thousand, "in the shadow of a grim range of mountains overlooking it, whose summits seemed lifted clear out of companionship and consciousness of earthly things."

The bill making Nevada a territory put its western boundary at the "dividing ridge separating the waters of Carson Valley from those that flow into the Pacific"; in other words, the boundary of the Great Basin itself. The bill included the curious proviso that California must approve this boundary, and that state, afraid that it might give away valuable mineral resources, refused to recognize the line. The impasse left several areas in limbo. At Honey Lake north of Carson City several people were wounded when lawmen from both sides tried to settle whether it was in California or Nevada. Also in dispute was the mining town of Aurora, where citizens voted in both California and Nevada elections—and elected its citizens to each legislature—before a boundary commission finally settled the matter by giving Honey Lake to California and putting Aurora three miles within Nevada.*

By the time Samuel Bowles passed through in 1868, Nevada was a state. While most people in the Nevada Territory were distracted by the promise of riches, the process of admitting Nevada—now that the territory had both wealth and population—to the Union was proceeding apace. There was another consideration: President Lincoln was trying to pass the Thirteenth Amendment abolishing slavery and might need Nevada to garner the necessary two-thirds vote in each congressional house. And there were Republicans who feared that the election of 1864 might be so close that it would be thrown into the House of Representatives, in which case Nevada's votes would help reelect Lincoln.

On December 11, 1863, thirty-nine delegates produced a constitution, a necessary first step toward statehood. The document included a three-million-dollar subsidy for the first company to build a railroad from Nevada to the navigable waters of the

---

* As he wrote in *Roughing It*, Aurora was the last place in which Mark Twain tried his hand at mining; after giving himself up to "solid misery" there, he opened a letter and, "Eureka! [I never did know what Eureka meant, but it seems to be as proper a word to heave in as any when no other that sounds pretty offers]. It was a deliberate offer to me of Twenty-Five Dollars a week to come up to Virginia and be city editor of the *Enterprise*."

Pacific. The constitution also levied a tax on Nevada's mines and mining property, and it was this provision that doomed it to defeat by popular vote (8,851 to 2,157). There were also those who thought Nevada would be better off remaining a territory; the *Humboldt Register* came out against statehood in a feisty editorial that declared: "The Humboldt world is dead-set against engaging to help support any more lunk-heads till times get better. . . . If we have a State Government we'll have more fat-headed officers to support; and if we undertake to support them without taxing the mines, we'll run hopelessly into debt. If we do tax them, we'll stop development of them."

The fight against the constitution was led by an aggressive mining lawyer, William Stewart, who fit right in with the rough-and-tumble society of the mining camp despite his eastern upbringing, schoolteacher background, and a stint at Yale College. Stewart's local fame was assured when he faced down a notorious gunman in a Genoa courtroom, forced the man at gunpoint onto the witness stand, and, after eliciting testimony that helped win his case, escorted him out of the courthouse.* Stewart railed against the proposed levy on the "poor miner's shafts and drifts and bed-rock tunnels," but it must have been fairly obvious to everyone that it was the rich miner whose interests he had at heart.

Stewart wanted statehood for Nevada; he simply opposed any tax that might hurt mining. Over the next several months, Stewart led the movement for a new constitution in what Robert Laxalt in *Nevada: A Bicentennial History* has called the "most frenzied period in Nevada's political history." Railroads were again an issue at the second constitutional convention called in July 1864. On the thirteenth of that month Leland Stanford, governor of California and president of the Central Pacific Railroad, appeared before the

---

* The gunman was "Fighting" Sam Brown, who had reputedly killed thirteen men in Texas and California before arriving in Virginia City. After Stewart humiliated him, Brown took a shot at an innkeeper named Henry Van Sickle, who retaliated by killing him with a blast from a shotgun. A coroner's jury in Virginia City acquitted Van Sickle with the words, "It served him [Brown] right."

convention to argue that a subsidy should go to his railroad only, not to some competitor who might get tracks into Nevada before he did. Although Nevada obviously would benefit from a railroad, there was considerable opposition, particularly from the owners of toll roads and freighting companies whose huge profits from Nevada's mining boom would disappear if a railroad came into the state. In the end, the convention produced a document that gave no railroad subsidies and taxed mines on their net proceeds only. It also determined that the new state would be called Nevada, meaning "snow-covered" in Spanish, and not Humboldt or Washoe, as some citizens wanted. The constitution easily won popular approval, but by now it was late October and the presidential election was drawing near. So the document was sent to Washington by the fastest means available—the telegraph. At the time it was the longest message ever sent, and it cost a stupendous $3,416.77. Lincoln signed the bill making Nevada the thirty-sixth state on October 31, 1864.*

Nevada soon paid its debt to President Lincoln. On election day, November 8, it elected a Republican legislature, which then chose Nye and Stewart as the new state's United States senators. Together with Nevada's one popularly elected representative, the men left at once for Washington, arriving there in time to vote for the Thirteenth Amendment to the constitution, which ended slavery. The Nevada legislature ratified the Thirteenth Amendment on February 16, 1865.

Nevada had gone from desert wasteland to state of the Union in just five years. Ironically, Nevada was created out of Utah, a territory that had first applied for statehood fifteen years before and that would have to wait another thirty-two years—until 1896— before it attained that goal. The act of Congress conferring state-

---

* David Herbert Donald, in the biography *Lincoln* (1995), wrote that the president "showed little interest in the legislation admitting the new state [i.e., Nevada] and did not try to rush the admission of other states in order to gain their electoral votes in the election of 1864." At the time Lincoln told a visiting delegation, "Except it be to give protection against violence, I decline to interfere in any way with any presidential election."

hood on Nevada gave it all land west of the 116th meridian to the California border, but Nevada would get larger still, mostly at Utah's expense. In two more actions, one in 1862 and again after statehood in 1866, Congress added sizeable strips of western Utah to eastern Nevada. In 1867, the triangular piece of Arizona Territory below the thirty-seventh parallel, a parcel containing Las Vegas, was given to Nevada. These additions were mining land, Nevada argued successfully, and should belong to a mining state.

The state seal, adopted with Nevada's constitution in 1864, left no doubt that this was a mining state: On one side, an ore-car leaves a mine entrance; on the other, there is a picture of a quartz mill, its chimney belching smoke. In the mountainous background, a railroad crosses a trestle bridge, and beyond the distant peaks, a rising sun.

"Crazy" Judah's Railroad

The fact that the Nevada seal showed a railroad was significant, too, for the transcontinental railroad left a permanent mark on Nevada and created communities that turned out to be more permanent and prosperous than those that owed their existence to the vagaries of mining. In May 1868, for example, landowner Myron C. Lake donated large tracts north of the Truckee River to the Central Pacific in return for the railroad's agreement to build a station there. So the city of Reno was born, named by Charles Crocker, the railroad's chief of construction, for Union General Jesse L. Reno. The town became a major depot for the Comstock, and its prosperity only increased when the Virginia & Truckee Railroad reached there in 1872.

By the time Nevada became a state, the railroad from California was already on its way. The Pacific Railroad Act of 1862—which guaranteed whoever built the railroad generous land grants, rights of way, and substantial loans in the form of government bonds—made the transcontinental railroad inevitable. The western portion of the railway, which had to meet the challenge of passing over and through the Sierra Nevada before it reached Nevada and the Great Basin, was the result of the vision and engineering genius of one man, Theodore Dehone Judah, who had gone to California in 1854 to supervise the construction of the Sacramento Valley Railroad, the first operating line in the state.

Judah became so obsessed with the idea of building a railroad across the Sierra Nevada that he was known as "Crazy" Judah. But his conviction that the job could be done was contagious. In the summer of 1861 he obtained the backing of two hardware merchants, a grocer, and a retailer—the future "Big Four" of the Central Pacific Railroad: Collis P. Huntington, Mark Hopkins, Leland Stanford, and Charles Crocker—to conduct a survey in the mountains and locate a feasible route. After completing the survey, Judah went to Washington to lobby for the railroad; his efforts helped pass the Pacific Railroad Act.

On June 28, 1861, the Central Pacific was legally incorporated with Stanford as president, Huntington vice president, Hopkins treasurer, Judah chief engineer, and Crocker a director. A year and a half later, on January 8, 1863, Leland Stanford, now governor of California, wielded a silver-plated shovel to break ground for the start of the Central Pacific in Sacramento, an event that began the march of the railroad over the Sierras. In September, Judah, who had fallen out with his partners, left for New York to try to raise money to buy them out. Crossing the Isthmus of Panama, he contracted yellow fever and died in New York in November.

With Judah gone, the Big Four themselves had to build the railroad. Among the immediate problems was a labor shortage in California. To fill his manpower needs, Crocker, the line's construction chief, proposed hiring Chinese workers. It was a radical idea at the time. The Chinese, slight of build and, with long pigtails and baggy clothes, eccentric in appearance, were widely considered inferior to whites. But, as Crocker suspected, they turned out to be skilled, hardworking, and uncomplaining. They were also healthier and more sober than their white counterparts. Crocker started small, with a crew of fifty Celestials, as the Chinese were called (because they referred to their homeland as the Celestial Kingdom); eventually almost twelve thousand Chinese workers labored on the Central Pacific. It was the Chinese who bore the brunt of the incredibly hazardous and difficult work in the Sierras, especially the building of snow sheds to conquer avalanches and snow slides and the boring of the Summit Tunnel.

On May 4, 1868, the Central Pacific line reached the Truckee River on the California-Nevada border. For the eastward-moving railroad, that meant the hardest part of the job was over. It had taken the Central Pacific five years to cross the Sierras and reach Nevada, a feat that one writer compared with Hannibal crossing the Alps. (The comparison does not do the railroad justice; no engineering crew in history had accomplished so much in so little time.) Just boring the sixteen-hundred-foot Summit tunnel was a two-year job during which daily progress was measured in inches. By comparison, the laying of track across Nevada, although not without its challenges, seemed uneventful. In less than a year and a half the railroad crossed all of Nevada and most of Utah to the final meeting point at Promontory, Utah.

Somewhere in the desert, the advanced grading crews of the two railroads met—and continued right on past each other, the Central Pacific to the east, the Union Pacific to the west. Both lines were convinced that the railroad that laid the most track would gain the most in the way of land grants and government subsidies. Working literally side by side but moving in opposite directions, the crews were too close for comfort or safety. Each side, one Irish, the other Chinese, set off blasts without warning, raining debris down on the rival crews. Several workers of both lines were killed in the foolishness. Under government pressure to settle the matter, the Central Pacific's Huntington and the Union Pacific's chief engineer, Grenville M. Dodge, met in the capital and agreed, in April 1869, that the railroads would join at Promontory Point, Utah, 690 miles from Sacramento and 1,084 from Omaha. The agreement ended the railroad race across the Great Basin and set the stage for the joining of the transcontinental railroad at Promontory Point, Utah, on May 10, 1869.

Chapter Fifteen

GETTING READY

FOR THE

RAILROAD

The 1860s were yet another time of trial for the Mormons. There was a measure of disappointment, maybe even disillusionment, when the nation did not destroy itself during the Civil War, as Joseph Smith had prophesied and Brigham Young had confidently predicted. Not only did the federal government survive, but it grew increasingly hostile to Mormonism. All through the decade, for example, Congress sheared off large chunks of Utah Territory and gave them to neighboring Nevada, Colorado, and Wyoming, until Utah was reduced to its present size in 1868. Even the departure of the U.S. Army from Camp Floyd in 1861 did not permanently rid Utah of the irritating presence of federal troops. In October 1862, an Army officer with his own plan for destroying Mormondom was assigned to Utah. He stationed his men in the hills east of Salt Lake City and trained his artillery on the City of the Saints below.

Eighteen sixty-two was a particularly bad year. Early on, Congress unceremoniously rejected yet another bid by Utah for statehood. Utah Territory did not have enough population for statehood, Congress said, but the real reason was opposition to Mormonism, especially polygamy. On July 8, President Abraham Lincoln, despite his avowed intention to leave the Mormons alone—or, as he folksily put it, "to plow around" them—signed an anti-polygamy law, the Morrill Anti-Bigamy Act, the first of several legal attempts to destroy the now-sacred institution of plural marriage. And then there was the transcontinental railroad. On July, 1, 1862, Congress passed the Pacific Railroad Act. This served notice on the Saints that within the near future the transcontinental railroad would run through Utah and the Great Basin, bringing with it all the unsavory influences that the Saints associated with the world outside the Great Basin, a world that they called, with a delightful sense of irony, "civilization."

And, in the same year, there was trouble—and bloodshed—in Zion. A Welsh convert named Joseph Morris, who had migrated to Utah in 1853, had established a following of about five hundred people and was preaching his own version of Mormonism based on his personal revelations from God. Morris's words challenged the authority of Brigham Young and questioned the rectitude of polygamy. His revelations also told him that he was the seventh angel of the Apocalypse and that Christ's Second Coming was imminent, even giving the precise day.

In 1860, Morris walked forty miles from his home in South Weber in the Cache Valley to Salt Lake City to inform Brigham Young that he must repent in order to be saved—and accept Morris as a prophet—but he was rebuffed with what he described as a "brief and filthy response." On his return home, Morris established his own branch of the Mormon Church and gathered adherents around him. In February 1862, Brigham Young sent Wilford Woodruff and John Taylor to South Weber to investigate. They found the Morrisites guilty of apostasy and excommunicated the leader and sixteen of his followers. The Morrisites retreated into their compound, which they called Kingston Fort, and, with the Second Coming so close, Morris persuaded many to consecrate their property to his church. That spring, the Morrisites did very little planting—with the end of the world so near, what was the point?—and, to dramatize their faith in the approaching end, went out into their fields and trampled down whatever was growing there.

Like all doomsayers, Morris faced a huge credibility problem when Reckoning Day came and went with the world still intact. Some of his followers asked for their property back. Morris refused their request and locked up several who tried to leave the community. When word of this reached Salt Lake City, a judge friendly to the Mormons, John F. Kinney, issued a writ for their release, which the Morrisites arrogantly burned when it was served. The Mormons then sent a posse of over five hundred men to the compound in South Weber to arrest Morris. On arrival, the marshal in charge, Robert T. Burton, placed his men strategically around the fort and sent in a demand for Morris to surrender. When Morris delayed waiting for word from God, Burton ordered a warning shot fired into the fort. The bullet ricocheted through the gathering inside the fort, killing and wounding several. In returning the fire, the Morrisites killed a deputy, and the siege was on.

To observers of religious cults in the late twentieth century, the situation at Morris's Fort Kingston will seem familiar: a charismatic leader with a direct line to God, devoted followers convinced of the impending end of the world and willing to die for the faith, a standoff with authorities, and, finally, an assault that turns deadly. The siege lasted three days—until the Morrisites displayed a flag of surrender. When the posse entered the fort, Burton asked Morris to surrender, and, in a confused mêlée that followed his defiant "Never!" the marshal shot and killed him and two others. About ninety of the cultists were arrested and taken to Salt Lake City. In March of 1863, they were tried, with seven convicted of second-degree murder and sixty-six convicted of resistance, but all were later pardoned by the governor of Utah.

"That Thing . . . That Calls Himself Governor"

In a society based on conformity and obedience to authority, any dissent has significance, but the Morrisites never really threatened Brigham Young's leadership; to Wilford Woodruff, whose excommunication of Morris led to the final tragedy, the "whole Concern shows to what Extent fals Prophets & fanaticism will go." But Brigham Young had bigger problems to deal with. Since he was no longer governor, he had to contend with a series of federal appointees to that and other posts, men of varying abilities and attitudes toward the Mormons.* Alfred Cumming, Utah's first Gentile governor, who replaced Brigham Young at the start of the Utah War in 1857, had worked in relative harmony with the Mormons. When Cumming left in May 1857, Lincoln appointed an anti-Mormon hack named John W. Dawson, who outraged the Saints by his persistent and unwanted advances to a Mormon widow, whom he then tried to bribe into keeping quiet. Dawson fled Salt Lake City when the situation became public and, not far from the city, was overtaken and beaten by persons unknown. He predictably blamed Brigham Young who, just as predictably, denied all knowledge of the incident.

Dawson, who served less than a year, was succeeded by Stephen S. Harding, who became more and more suspicious of the Mormons over the two years he served, an attitude reflected in his petition to Congress to give federal appointees in Utah the power to appoint all jurors and local militia officers. The proposal was very unpopular with the Mormons; Brigham Young venomously called him "that thing that is here that calls himself Governor . . . If you were to fill a sack with cow shit, it would be the best thing you could do for an imitation and that would be just as good." Finally, the Mormons protested Harding's actions at a mass meeting, and Lincoln removed him in 1863. The Mormons

* The territorial officers, all presidential appointees confirmed by the Senate, were governor, secretary, three judges, marshal, and attorney. Although the salaries were notoriously low, the offices did attract some capable men who probably saw the positions as stepping-stones to other opportunities.

considered his successor, James D. Doty, a vast improvement, but, as a rule, M. R. Werner, Brigham Young's 1925 biographer, observed, the federal appointees in Utah behaved like "soldiers in foreign wars," who "were addicted in private to the acts which they so strenuously deplored as vices in public . . . They were far away from home and from neighbors whose opinions they considered it advisable to respect, . . . with the usual result in that situation of a complete exercise of the freedom of their natural impulses. To the Mormons, who coated their impulses with sanctity, the personal acts of the federal officials seemed outrageous and degenerate."

DISCOURAGING POLYGAMY

The Mormons viewed Lincoln with an unsentimental eye. Brigham Young said the "feeling of Abe Lincoln is that Buchanan tried to destroy the mormons & Could not. Now I will try my hand at it." The Anti-Bigamy Act of 1862, which bore the name of its sponsor, Representative Justin Morrill of Vermont, might have done some damage to the Mormon Church if the federal government, its attention diverted by the Civil War, had had the time or the inclination to enforce it. The law prohibited plural marriage in the territories and made polygamy punishable by a five-hundred-dollar fine and up to five years in prison. It also disincorporated the Mormon Church, restricted the church's ownership of property to fifty thousand dollars, and nullified all past legislation regarding polygamy passed by the Utah territorial legislature. For their part, the Mormons ignored the law or circumvented its provisions; most of the church's property was transferred to church leaders, particularly Brigham Young, an act that made the church leader an extraordinarily wealthy man, at least on paper. And, no matter what the law, the Mormons always argued that any legislation directed against polygamy violated the First Amendment stipulation that "Congress shall make no law respecting an establishment of religion or prohibiting the free exercise thereof."

In 1867, with the Civil War behind the country, the Mormons asked Congress to repeal the Morrill Anti-Bigamy Act. The act was dying of neglect, they argued, or, in the petition's words: "The judiciary of the Territory has not up to the present time, tried any case under said law though repeatedly asked to do so by those who have been anxious to test its constitutionality." In retrospect, it seems like a naive gesture and a misreading of the postwar mood of Congress. The House Judiciary Committee, instead of acting on the petition, inquired why the bill had not been enforced. Soon thereafter, the Cullom bill, a piece of legislation designed to strengthen the Morrill Act, was introduced. Under its terms, the governor of Utah would have the power to appoint local judges and sheriffs, supporters of polygamy would be barred from jury duty on polygamy-related cases, probate courts would no longer hear criminal cases, wives could testify against husbands, and polygamists could not vote, hold office, or become citizens. The Cullom bill did not become law—eventually most of its provisions would be included in other laws—but the message it sent to the Mormons was clear: The fight against polygamy in Congress was just beginning.

The next major assault on the institution was made in 1869, the last year of the pioneer era, with the introduction of a bill to grant the vote to all women in the territories. The legislation was called "A Bill to Discourage Polygamy in Utah," the thought—so widespread among Gentiles—being that Mormon women hated polygamy and would use the vote to get rid of it. The Mormons, however, saw it differently: To them, enfranchising women was a good idea because it meant more voters behind the institution. And, when Utah's congressional delegate and the Mormon newspaper, the *Deseret News,* both came out in favor of the bill, its sponsors had second thoughts and withdrew it. But the Utah territorial legislature went ahead anyway, and the next year, 1870, enfranchised women of the territory; that is how Utah became the first place in the United States where women could vote.

"To the Saints of Utah: Enough of Your Treason"

At the start of the Civil War the Mormons were assigned the duty of guarding the overland mail routes and telegraph line through the Great Basin to California. It was the only contribution the Mormons were asked to make to the war effort, and Brigham Young gave the task to Utah's territorial militia, the Nauvoo Legion, under the command of Lot Smith, the heroic maurauder of the Utah War. The guard duty turned out to be uneventful and short-lived. In October of the same year, the duty was transferred to an aggressive U.S. Army officer, Patrick Edward Connor, and his contingent of 750 men, the Third California Infantry, or Volunteers, as they were called.

Colonel Connor turned out to be one of the Mormons' most dedicated and able enemies; he threw himself into his self-appointed task of destroying them with vigor and enthusiasm. Connor was forthright about his hostility to "the enormity of Mormonism." In a letter to his superior officer, he described the Saints as "a community of traitors, murderers, fanatics, and whores . . ." Instead of operating from the now-deserted Camp Floyd, forty miles south of Salt Lake City, he marched his men straight through Salt Lake City and bivouacked them on a hillside east of—and overlooking—the city. There he built a permanent installation, which, to add to the insult, he named Camp Douglas, after the recently deceased, anti-Mormon senator from Illinois, Stephen Douglas. "I intend to quietly intrench my position," Connor reported, "and then say to the Saints of Utah, enough of your treason."

At first the skirmishing between Young and Connor was petty. Young established price controls to protect merchants and others doing business with the Army. Connor, for his part, required Mormon suppliers to swear an oath of allegiance to the federal government, a requirement that caused Brigham Young to respond: "Let them come and say 'Will you sell me a bushel of potatoes?' Then comes the answer 'Do you want me to take the oath of allegiance? If you do, go to hell for your potatoes.' "

The Mormons also suspected that Connor intended to arrest Brigham Young and other Mormon leaders on charges of polygamy. When a rumor got out in March 1863 that arrests were imminent, hundreds of armed Mormons surrounded Young's residence, even going so far as to erect scaffolding around the complex so that they could shoot down Connor's men when they tried to take their leader into custody. Two days later, Young had a friendly judge, Chief Justice John F. Kinney, issue a writ for his arrest on charges of bigamy. The case was then bound over to the next session of court and never came to trial. Although there is no evidence that Connor ever intended to arrest the Mormon prophet, Young and others believed that they had outfoxed Connor by preventing him from arresting Young and bringing him to trial before a less sympathetic judge. "Harding [the Utah governor], Connor, & Co. are at present quite crestfallen and apparently at a loss at what to do next," Brigham Young wrote with some satisfaction.

BEAR RIVER MASSACRE

In late January 1863, Connor proved to be of some use to the Mormons when he and some two hundred of his Volunteers marched north to the Bear River to subdue a band of northern Shoshone who had been attacking wagon trains on the overland trail and harassing remote Mormon settlements. In an unusually harsh statement, the *Deseret News* called the Shoshone "that bastard class of humans who play with the lives of . . . peaceable and law abiding citizens." And to help Connor, who was unfamiliar with the terrain, the Mormons gave him the services of their leading frontiersman and scout, Orrin Porter Rockwell.

The clash, the so-called Bear River Massacre, that followed was a bloody incident that many histories of the era overlook or underplay. By sending a small number of infantrymen ahead and holding back his cavalry until the last minute, Connor tricked the

Indians into thinking that only a small force was being sent against them. Therefore, as Connor hoped, they stayed in their winter camp instead of retreating into the hills. The troopers attacked in freezing weather before dawn on January 29 and found the Indians well-fortified within a ravine. Many soldiers fell in their first charge, as Connor struggled to bring the rest of his men across the icy river. The battle raged for several hours until the soldiers caught the Indians in enfilading fire and the tide began to turn. When, after two hours, the Indians ran out of ammunition, the soldiers charged, finishing off most of the remaining warriors with pistols or picking them off as they tried to escape from the ravine. By the time the rampage was over, 250 Indians, including some 90 women and children, were dead.* The troops, 14 of whom lost their lives, then burned the village. A participant later remembered Connor's "cruel order" to his men: "Take no prisoners, fight to the death; nits breed lice." Later, for leading the attack, Connor was promoted to brigadier general. The celebration that followed at Camp Douglas caused some nervousness among the Mormons; when the soldiers fired off a cannon, armed Mormon men, thinking that the city was under attack, rushed to defend Brigham Young's house.

The following September Connor found what he hoped would be the solution to the Mormon problem. Some of his soldiers were helping two Mormons haul logs out of Bingham Canyon in the Oquirrh Mountains when they came across ore containing silver and gold. A few days later officers from Camp Douglas were picnicking with their wives on a mountainside when they found more ore and uncovered a vein. On September 17, 1863, Connor, several of his officers, and a Mormon bishop filed a claim and established the West Mountain Mining District.

---

* Historian Brigham D. Madsen, author of a biography of Connor and a book on the northern Shoshone, wrote in the *Utah History Encyclopedia*: "Of the six major Indian massacres in the Far West from Bear River in 1863 to Wounded Knee in 1890, the Bear River affair resulted in the most victims, an event which today deserves greater attention than the mere sign presently at the site."

Connor encouraged his men to prospect in the hills and mountains around Salt Lake City. He knew Brigham Young hated mining, and he knew why. Connor was a straightforward individual who did not dissemble or attempt to disguise what he was up to. "My policy in this Territory," he wrote, "has been to invite hither a large Gentile and loyal population, sufficient by peaceful means and through the ballot-box to overwhelm the Mormons by mere force of numbers, and to wrest from the church—disloyal and traitorous to the core—the absolute and tyrannical control of temporal and civic affairs. . . ."* He also established an anti-Mormon newspaper, the *Daily Union Vedette*, and did everything he could, including exaggerating the reports of Utah's mineral wealth that he sent back east, to encourage an influx of miners and prospectors into Utah. For his efforts, Connor became known as the "Father of Utah Mining."

Utah's was not fertile soil for prospectors; most of its mineral wealth was argentiferous lead ore that was costly to extract and process. When General Connor left the Army in the spring of 1866, he invested heavily in Utah mines, including smelting operations, and, as mining's father, became a political leader for the growing faction of Gentiles in the territory. To counter the threat Connor posed, Brigham Young exhorted the Saints to stay home, just as he had during the California gold rush of 1849: "Instead of hunting gold, go and raise wheat, barley, oats, get your bread and make gardens and orchards and raise vegetables and fruits that you may have something to sustain yourselves and something to give to the poor and the needy." Still, he permitted Mormons to work in mines for wages, preferring that to having mine owners import non-Mormon labor into Zion.

---

* There was no predicting how Brigham Young would react to the Gentile officials he had to deal with. Of Connor, he once said, "Men have been here before him; to our faces they were our friends; but when they went away they traduced, vilified and abused us. Not so with Connor. We always knew where to find him. That's why I like him."

"Iron Horse Puffing"

By the time Connor left the Army, the transcontinental railroad was well on its way to Utah. A railroad into Utah was something that the Mormon leader both wanted and worried about. He knew that the railroad would bring large numbers of non-Mormons into Utah and, with them, the corrupt "civilization" he dreaded, and before the railroad even arrived he began to take steps to counteract its influences. On the surface, however, Brigham Young was unconcerned, even enthusiastic about the railroad; in a famous remark he opined that Mormonism "must, indeed, be a ——— poor religion, if it cannot withstand one railroad."* And a railroad could bring a lot of Mormons, especially converts arriving on the East Coast from Europe, to Utah. "Hasten the work!" he once said. "We want to hear the iron horse puffing through this valley. What for? To bring our brothers and sisters here."

As a sign of his good faith, Brigham Young invested in the Union Pacific Railroad Company, accepted an appointment as a director, and supplied men and logistical support for the survey that the railroad conducted in the Wasatch Mountains. When the Mormons on the surveying crew struck for better wages Young sent "a severe letter to the boys," reported the Union Pacific's overseer, Samuel Reed, "bidding them, to complete all work I have for them to do before showing themselves in Salt Lake City." Since then, Reed added, "I have not heard a word about pay." On May 21, 1868, Young signed a contract with the Union Pacific to provide Mormon labor for all the grading, tunneling, and

* Young's quote, with adjective deleted, comes from Samuel Bowles's *Our New West* (1869). Bowles, speculating on the future of polygamy, expressed an opinion, contrary to Young's, that the institution would die of its own accord once the railroad started bringing in large numbers of non-Mormons. "What precise form the revolution will take,—where the wedge will be entered that shall split this rotten trunk to pieces, no one can wisely predict . . . ," Bowles wrote. "But come it must and will. To doubt would be to question progress, to deny civilization, to outrage God." Many people, Mark Twain among them, agreed that the coming of the railroad would make the end of polygamy inevitable.

bridge work for about 150 miles of the railroad east of the Great Salt Lake. As the Mormon leader saw it, the contract would put cash—at two dollars a day—in the pockets of Mormon laborers and, for the time being at least, would keep Gentile laborers out of Utah Territory.

As Newell Bringhurst points out in his *Brigham Young and the Expanding American Frontier*, Young had petitioned Congress in 1853 to construct such a railroad. The route he proposed through South Pass into the Great Basin was identical to the road actually taken, with one major exception. Young wanted the railroad to run through Salt Lake City and was disappointed when the decision was made, at almost the last minute, to bypass the city and run the line around the northern end of the Great Salt Lake. Young responded to the decision to bypass Salt Lake City with typical resilience and set about to construct a branch line to connect the Mormon capital with Ogden. This link, which was completed in January 1870, was a first step in a network of Mormon railroads that would eventually tie the entire territory to Salt Lake City and the transcontinental line at Ogden.* Also, Young won a significant victory when, in a meeting with the heads of both railroads in January 1869, he persuaded them to make Ogden the terminal point for both lines, where freight and passengers would transfer. Young was particularly anxious that the railroads not choose the alternative transfer point, Corinne, a boisterous railroad camp twenty-five miles northwest of Ogden, which had, Arrington wrote, "geographic advantages and sentimental attachments to many Gentiles."

SCHOOL OF THE PROPHETS

To help consolidate the Kingdom against "civilizing influences," Brigham Young revived the School of the Prophets, a vaguely

---

* The railroad brought in so many non-Mormons that Gentiles eventually took over the town. In 1889, when Gentiles won every seat on the city council, the headline in the *Utah Daily Union* read: "Ogden Americanized."

defined organization of church leaders and bishops that was involved in a variety of issues, including church doctrine and economic planning. The school helped finance the railroad network that in the 1870s would spread across Utah, founded local manufacturing enterprises to compete with and, they hoped, replace those imported from the East, instituted policies, and made suggestions that the school felt would make Utah's products more competitive with those produced in the East. One particularly naive suggestion, that wages in all trades be drastically reduced to lower costs and prices, taxed even the Mormon's capacity for sacrifice and died aborning.

One change proposed by the School of the Prophets actually took hold: a prohibition against the consumption of alcohol, tobacco, tea, and coffee. The requirement that Mormons abstain from these substances dates from 1833, when Joseph Smith received a revelation in Kirtland, Ohio, known as the Word of Wisdom, but the edict was never enforced.* Like all frontiersmen, the Mormons were heavy drinkers and producers of whiskey. The fearsome Porter Rockwell was famous for his tippling: one writer described him as "well-behaved even when drunk." Brigham Young was a tobacco-chewer until he gave up "this disgraceful practice" in 1860. Now, late in the same decade, he was urging abstinence but for a practical reason: so the Saints could donate the money they saved to the Perpetual Emigrating Fund and help pay the railroad fares for Mormon emigrants to Utah. The reemphasis on the strictures of the Word of Wisdom—whose followers are promised "health in their navel and marrow to their bones"—became an ingrained part of the Mormon faith. Today, abstinence from alcohol and tobacco not only is required for good standing within the church, but is the one practice, above all others, that most non-Mormons today associate with Latter-day Saints.

---

* An introduction to section 89 of the Mormon gospel, Doctrine and Covenants, explains: "As a consequence of the early brethren using tobacco in their meetings, the Prophet was led to ponder upon the matter; consequently he inquired of the Lord concerning it. This revelation, known as the Word of Wisdom, was the result."

At the same time that he resurrected the School of the Prophets, Brigham Young charged Eliza R. Snow, one of his plural wives, with the task of reestablishing the women's Relief Society, a charitable and educational organization that was founded, under Joseph Smith, in Nauvoo, Illinois, in 1842, to provide aid for men working on the Nauvoo Temple. The Relief Society thrived for a while, but the prophet disbanded it when Emma Smith, his strong-willed wife, began using it as a platform from which to protest polygamy. In Utah, under Eliza Snow's able direction, the Relief Society grew rapidly and eventually became a permanent part of Mormon life; today all adult females are automatically members.

The Relief Society's stated purpose was "to visit the sick and the helpless and the needy, and learn their wants, and, under their Bishops, collect the means necessary to relieve them," but its initial function was to help Mormon women resist the temptations that the railroad was sure to bring into Utah. Brigham Young, who considered himself an arbiter of female fashion, particularly loathed seeing them in dress that he deemed "useless, unbecoming, and ridiculous," and spending money that could be better contributed to some worthwhile organizations, such as the Perpetual Emigrating Fund Company. To strengthen the resistance of females too young to join the Relief Society, Young and Snow together founded, in late 1869, the Retrenchment Society, officially the Young Ladies' Department of the Cooperative Retrenchment Association, to promote, in the words of an early member, "a Spartan plainness of dress."

Brigham Young kicked off the movement toward retrenchment in November 1869 by calling together all the women of his family, including Eliza Snow, and explaining, "All Israel are looking to my family and watching the example set by my wives and children." He announced, "We are about to organize a Retrenchment Association, which I want you all to join, and I want you to vote to retrench in your dress, in your tables, in your speech, wherein you have been guilty of silly, extravagant speeches and lightmindedness of thought. Retrench in everything that is bad and worthless, and improve in everything that is good and beautiful." How successful the Young Ladies' Retrenchment Society was in quelling the desire for the frills of fashion is an open question, but the organization, which shifted its emphasis to education and self-improvement, lives on today as the Young Women's Mutual Improvement Association.*

There were other innovations in the late 1860s that helped solidify Mormon life before the coming of the railroad. The University of Deseret, on the drawing board since 1850, opened in 1869 with 230 students, among them 103 women, but the school was informally organized at the start, and the first bachelor's degrees were not awarded until the mid-1880s.† In 1894, the school became the University of Utah. Another familiar institution in operation today also opened in 1869, just two months before the joining of the transcontinental railroad: the Zion Cooperative Mercantile Institution, a cooperative retail and wholesale venture, designed, in Brigham Young's words, "to bring goods here and sell them as low as they can possibly be sold and let the profits be divided with the people at large." Utah mercantile establishments joining the enterprise were allowed to display the seal of approval, a sign reading "Holiness to the Lord." The ZCMI also opened its own stores, and it has been called the country's first department store. The ZCMI was soon profitable, with the money it earned being invested in other, local church-sponsored businesses, such as ironworks and shoe factories.

There was not much open dissent to Brigham Young's policies during the pioneer era. But just as that era was ending in the late 1860s, a small group known as the Godbeites—after their leader, a

* A "typical resolution," quoted in Arrington's *Brigham Young: American Moses*, read: "Resolved, inasmuch as cleanliness is a characteristic of a Saint, and an imperative duty, we shall discard the dragging skirts, and for decency's sake those disgustingly short ones extending no lower than the boot tops."

† For all the emphasis that the Mormons put on education, Brigham Young was opposed to public schools. He believed that parents should pay for their children's education, and that schools should be free of state control, particularly regarding religious instruction.

wealthy Salt Lake City merchant named William Godbe—began to voice some opposition. The Godbeites, whose few members included two British intellectuals, Edward W. Tullidge and E. L. T. Harrison, as well as the British editor T. B. H. Stenhouse and several other prominent Mormon businessmen, did not think the Mormons should strive for self-sufficiency: instead they believed Utah should be integrated into the economic life of the rest of the country. To do this, they believed, Utah had to exploit its main asset—its mineral wealth—and this meant mining. In the most direct challenge—from Mormons—to Brigham Young yet to appear in print, the Godbeites wrote in their publication, the *Utah Magazine*, "The question then arises—Have we a specialty of the kind in this Territory that will bring us the money we need? . . . the answer comes back from all parts of the Territory, that it is in MINERALS!"

The editorial, titled "The True Development of the Territory," concluded:

> Summed up in a few words—we live in a country destitute of the rich advantages of other lands—a country with few natural facilities beyond the great mass of minerals in its bowels. These are its main financial hopes. To this our future factories must look for their life, our farmers, our stock, wool, and cotton raisers for their sale, and our mechanics for suitable wages. Let these resources be developed, and we have a future before us as bright as any country beneath the sun, because we shall be working in harmony with the indications of Nature around us.

Most societies would consider such opinions only mildly dissentful, but the Mormons, who prided themselves on the oneness of their thought, charged Godbe and Harrison with "harboring the spirit of apostasy." On October 25, 1869, in an excommunication procedure, the men came before the church's High Council. At the proceeding, Harrison testified that he was a loyal and

devout Mormon, and a believer in polygamy, among other principles. His only quarrel with the church was over "the infallibility of
the guidance of the Church without any exceptions." "I presume I
see as little fallibility in President Young as in any man," Harrison
testified, "but I see some; I cannot see but there are points where
he appears to miss it. . . . I have differed with him on the mineral
development of the Territory."

The two men were excommunicated, but otherwise the church
took no further action against the movement. The Godbeites,
some of whom adopted the fashionable mid-nineteenth-century
practice of spiritualism, continued into the 1870s but never
attracted more than a few hundred followers. The *Utah Magazine*
became in 1871 the *Salt Lake Tribune*, a newspaper that took
a strong stance for mining and against polygamy. To mount a
political challenge to the Mormons, some of the Godbeites joined
with Gentiles to form the Liberal Party, of which the Mormon
enemy Patrick Edward Connor is considered a founder. While the
Tribune, Salt Lake's leading newspaper, is a legacy, the movement
itself never seriously challenged Mormonism, and Brigham Young
entered the post-pioneer era with his power and his authority
completely intact.

Chapter Sixteen

GREAT BASIN EPILOGUE:

"IT IS DONE"

May 10, 1869, one of the great days in American history, the joining of the rails at Promontory, Utah, was a day that almost did not happen. A tie-cutting crew that had not been paid for months waylaid the train taking the Union Pacific's Thomas Clark Durant to Promontory and chained his private car to the rails. They held him captive for two days until the money arrived; as a result, the ceremony at Promontory, originally scheduled for May 8, had to be delayed.

Leland Stanford, president of the Central Pacific, also had trouble getting to Promontory. As his train from Sacramento passed over the Sierra Nevada, a logging crew skidded a log onto the tracks, damaging his engine in an accident that could have been much more serious. The train limped into Reno, where the damaged engine was replaced with a workaday locomotive, a balloon-stacked wood-burner named *Jupiter*. Neither man, in fact, arrived in Promontory with the same locomotive he set out in. Durant had to abandon his at a washed-out bridge in Wyoming. He arrived at Promontory pulled by a coal-burning engine, No. 119, that was so ordinary, it did not even have a name.

On the morning of May 10, the two engines faced each other across a gap in the rails: Union Pacific versus Central Pacific. Fifteen hundred people "grouped in colorful confusion" were on hand for the ceremony that began as dignitaries detrained, and Stanford and Durant shook hands. The speeches that day were blessedly short; all of them eloquently saluted, in the words of the Arizona governor, "the enterprise that has banded the continent and welded the oceans." By now, the entire nation was poised to celebrate the news from Promontory. In trim, staccato language that was more expressive than any oration, the four telegraphers on duty readied the country:

TO EVERYBODY. KEEP QUIET. WHEN THE LAST SPIKE IS DRIVEN AT PROMONTORY POINT, WE WILL SAY "DONE!" DON'T BREAK THE CIRCUIT, BUT WATCH FOR THE SIGNALS OF THE BLOWS OF THE HAMMER.

The famous last spike, made of gold, and the silver-plated hammer were both wired to the telegraph; when one hit the other, the signal would go out over the line. First the final tie and rails had to be put in place. Construction superintendents together carried the last railroad tie of highly polished laurel from Stanford's private car to the gap in the rails. Two eight-man crews—one Chinese from the Central Pacific, the other Union Pacific Irish—approached, each carrying one of the two last rails. When a photographer yelled to his assistant, "Shoot!" the Chinese, alarmed by the strange camera pointed at them, dropped the rail and fled. This moment of comic relief lasted until the nervous Chinese, without whose compatriots the Central Pacific would never have made it across the Sierra Nevada to Promontory, could be reassured and talked into returning. Then the tie and the two rails were put into place.

ALMOST READY. HATS OFF;
PRAYER IS BEING OFFERED.

That message was received in Washington at 2:27 P.M., eastern time. Soon thereafter a minister from Massachusetts offered thanks to "the God of mercies and blessings" for bringing about "this mighty enterprise, combining the commerce of the east with the gold of the west, to so glorious a completion."

WE HAVE GOT DONE PRAYING;
THE SPIKE IS ABOUT TO BE PRESENTED.

Leland Stanford accepted the golden spike; weighing eighteen ounces and worth $350, it was engraved with the prayer: "May God continue the unity of our country as the railroad unites the two great oceans of the world." Stanford spoke briefly. His remarks, prosaic for an occasion marked by grand sentiments and sweeping vision, concluded on a commercial note: "We hope to do, ultimately, what is now impossible on long lines—transport coarse, heavy and cheap products for all distances at living rates to the trade." Then two more spikes—one of Comstock silver, the other an alloy "ribbed in iron, clad in silver, crowned with gold"— were presented to Durant.

ALL READY NOW. THE SPIKE WILL SOON BE DRIVEN.
THE SIGNAL WILL BE THREE DOTS FOR THE COMMENCEMENT OF
THE BLOWS.

Durant and other guests tapped in the silver spikes; the privilege of driving in the spike of gold was reserved for Stanford. He raised the silver-headed sledge, took aim, and let the hammer fall. He missed, hitting the rail instead. "In any event," wrote John Hoyt Williams, "the iron rail was a better conductor of electricity than the gold would have been, and the signal went out to the world."

IT IS DONE.

The signal went directly to San Francisco, where it set off 220 guns at Fort Point and rang the bell in City Hall. In Philadelphia the Liberty Bell was rung gingerly so as not to crack it further. New York City's stock exchange closed early. A parade in Chicago was five miles long. Even in Salt Lake City, the city that the railroad passed by, Mormons packed the Tabernacle to receive the news. A telegram was sent to President Grant: "The last rail is laid, the last spike driven. The Pacific Railroad is completed."

Meanwhile at Promontory, *Jupiter* and No. 119, unhooked from their trains, inched up to the rail junction until their cow-catchers touched lightly. This maneuver began a curious railroadic ballet that was choreographed to tell the country that the transcontinental railroad was open and ready for business. Each engine then backed up and hooked up again to its cars. As *Jupiter* stayed in place, No. 119 chugged ahead until it rested on Central Pacific track. Then No. 119 went backward, and *Jupiter* came forward until it halted on Union Pacific rails. Then both trains backed off to allow crews to replace the laurel tie and spikes of precious metal with a tie and spikes of ordinary materials. Regular service, Omaha to Sacramento, began five days later.

Few people missed the significance of the event. It was, in every sense of the cliché, the dawn of a new era. But no one giving speeches spoke of what was being lost. The joining of the rails spelled the end of the pioneer era: A trip across the country that once took months of hardship and danger could now be accomplished in relative comfort in days. Within a few years, the frontier would disappear. So would the stagecoach, the buffalo, and, to a large extent, the American Indian, who was driven from his hunting grounds onto reservations. The American dream of limitless opportunity in the West died hard, but it too eventually disappeared as the railroad made the West just another part of the country.

Brigham Young knew that the railroad would bring him more Saints—but also more Gentiles, and he would spend the eight years he had left of life preparing his kingdom for the challenge.

He was not there for the dedication of the transcontinental railroad at Promontory. Perhaps he was miffed that the railroad had bypassed Salt Lake City or annoyed that both railroads owed the Mormons money. Or he was too busy, for he had his own railroad to build.

Two days after Promontory the Mormons broke ground for the Utah Central Railroad, the thirty-seven-mile line between Ogden and Salt Lake City. Like other church enterprises, it was a cooperative venture: Communities furnished volunteer crews to do the grading and bridge-building; property owners were asked to contribute rights of way; track was laid by emigrants repaying the church for their passage to Utah. Stockholders in the railroad were all Mormons. "Is not the Utah Central Railroad in debt?" Brigham Young asked at the dedication ceremony. "Yes, but to none but our own people . . ."

The Utah Central was dedicated on January 10, 1870. Fifteen thousand Mormons, ten times the number of people at Promontory, attended the ceremonies, and Mormon pride in having done it without government aid or subsidy was evident in everything said that day. Brigham Young drove in the last spike, which was engraved with "Holiness to the Lord" and made by Mormon hands of honest Utah iron. And, when the Mormon prophet raised the steel mallet to strike the final blow, we can be sure that, unlike Stanford at Promontory, his hand was steady and his aim was true.

BIBLIOGRAPHY

Alexander, Thomas G. *Things in Heaven and Earth: The Life and Times of Wilford Woodruff, Mormon Prophet.* Salt Lake City, 1991.

Alexander, Thomas G., and James B. Allen. *Mormons and Gentiles: A History of Salt Lake City.* Salt Lake City, 1982.

Allen, James B., and Glenn M. Leonard. *The Story of the Latter-day Saints.* Salt Lake City, 1976.

Alter, J. Cecil. "Father Escalante's Map." *Utah Historical Quarterly* 9 (January, April 1941), 81–108.

———. *James Bridger: A Historical Narrative.* Norman, Okla., 1962.

Ambrose, Stephen. *Undaunted Courage: Meriwether Lewis, Thomas Jefferson, and the Opening of the American West.* New York, 1996.

American Heritage. *The American Heritage Book of Great Adventures of the Old West.* New York, 1969.

Anderson, Nels. *Desert Saints: The Mormon Frontier in Utah.* Chicago, 1942.

Arrington, Leonard J. *Great Basin Kingdom: An Economic History of the Latter-day Saints, 1830–1900.* Cambridge, Mass., 1958.

———. *Brigham Young: American Moses.* New York, 1985.

Arrington, Leonard J., and Davis Bitton. *The Mormon Experience: A History of the Latter-Day Saints.* New York, 1979.

Bancroft, Hubert Howe. *History of Utah, 1540–1886.* San Francisco, 1889.

———. *History of Nevada, Colorado, and Wyoming.* San Francisco, 1890.

Bartlett, Richard A. *Great Surveys of the American West.* Norman, Okla., 1962.

Beadle, J. H. *Life in Utah; or, the Mysteries and Crimes of Mormonism.* Philadelphia, 1870.

Beecher, Maureen Ursenbach. "The Eliza Enigma: The Life and Legend of Eliza R. Snow." *Dialogue* 11, Spring 1978.

Bennett, Richard E. *Mormons at the Missouri, 1846–1852: "And Should We Die . . . "* Norman, Okla., 1987.

Berrett, William E., and Alma P. Burton. *Readings in L.D.S. Church History.* 3 vols. Salt Lake City, 1953–1958.

Billington, Ray Allen. *The Far Western Frontier, 1830–1860.* New York, 1956.

Bitton, Davis, and Maureen Ursenbach Beecher, eds. *New Views of Mormon History: A Collection of Essays in Honor of Leonard J. Arrington.* Salt Lake City, 1987.

Bloom, Harold. *The American Religion: The Emergence of the Post-Christian Nation.* New York, 1992.

Bolton, Herbert Eugene. *Spanish Borderlands.* New Haven, 1921.

———. *Anza's California Expeditions.* Vol 3. Berkeley, Calif., 1930.

———. *Pageant in the Wilderness: The Story of the Escalante Expedition to the Interior Basin, 1776.* Salt Lake City, 1950.

Bowles, Samuel. *Across the Continent: A Summer's Journey to the Rocky Mountains, the Mormons, and the Pacific States.* Springfield, Mass., 1865.

———. *Our New West.* Hartford, 1869.

Brandon, William. "The Wild Freedom of the Mountain Men." *American Heritage,* August 1955, 4–9.

Brebner, John Bartlett. *The Explorers of North America.* 1933; Cleveland, 1955.

Briggs, Walter. *Without Noise of Arms: The 1776 Domínguez-Escalante Search for a Route from Santa Fe to Monterey.* Flagstaff, Ariz., 1976.

Bringhurst, Newell G. *Brigham Young and the Expanding American Frontier.* Boston, 1986.

Brodie, Fawn M. *No Man Knows My History*. New York, 1945.

Brooks, George R., ed. *The Southwest Expedition of Jedediah S. Smith: His Personal Account of the Journey to California, 1826–1827*. Glendale, Calif., 1977.

Brooks, Juanita. *The Mountain Meadows Massacre*. Rev. ed. Norman, Okla., 1962.

———. *John Doyle Lee: Zealot, Pioneer, Builder, Scapegoat*. Glendale, Calif., 1972.

Brown, S. Kent, et al., eds. *Historical Atlas of Mormonism*. New York, 1994.

Buchanan, Frederick Stewart, ed. *A Good Time Coming: Mormon Letters to Scotland*. Salt Lake City, 1988.

Burton, Richard. *The City of the Saints*. London, 1863.

Bushman, Claudia L., ed. *Mormon Sisters, Women in Early Utah*. Salt Lake City, 1976.

Cairncross, John. *After Polygamy Was Made a Sin: The Social History of Christian Polygamy*. London, 1974.

Caldwell, Gaylon L. " 'Utah Has Not Seceded': A Footnote to Local History." *Utah Historical Quarterly* 26 (April 1958), 171–75.

Campbell, Eugene E. *Establishing Zion: The Mormon Church in the American West, 1847–1869*. Salt Lake City, 1988.

Carson, Kit. *Kit Carson's Autobiography*. Lincoln, Nebr., 1966.

Chapman, Arthur. *The Pony Express*. New York, 1932.

Chittenden, Hiram M. *The American Fur Trade of the Far West*. 2 vols. Reprint: Stanford, Calif., 1954.

Clark, James R. "The Kingdom of God, the Council of Fifty and the State of Deseret." *Utah Historical Quarterly* 26 (April 1958), 132–48.

Cleland, Robert G. *This Reckless Breed of Men: Trappers of the Southwest*. New York, 1944.

Cleland, Robert G., and Juanita Brooks, eds. *A Mormon Chronicle: The Diaries of John D. Lee, 1848–1876*. 2 vols. San Marino, Calif., 1955.

Cline, Gloria Griffen. "Peter Skene Ogden's Nevada Explorations." *Nevada Historical Quarterly* 3 (July–September 1960), 3–11.

———. *Exploring the Great Basin.* Norman, Okla., 1963.

Coues, Elliott, ed. *On the Trail of a Spanish Pioneer: The Diary and Itinerary of Francisco Garcés.* New York, 1900.

Crampton, C. Gregory, and Gloria Griffen Cline. "The San Buenaventura, Mythical River of the West." *Pacific Historical Review* 25 (May 1956), 163–71.

Creer, Leland Hargrave. *The Founding of an Empire: The Exploration and Colonization of Utah, 1776–1856.* Salt Lake City, 1947.

Dary, David. *Entrepreneurs of the Old West.* New York, 1986.

Dellenbaugh, Frederick S. *Fremont and '49.* New York, 1913.

De Quille, Dan (William Wright). *History of the Big Bonanza.* 1876; New York, 1969.

———. *A History of the Comstock Silver Lode & Mines.* 1889; New York, 1974.

DeVoto, Bernard. *The Year of Decision: 1846.* Boston, 1943.

———. *The Course of Empire.* Boston, 1952.

Donald, David Herbert. *Lincoln.* New York, 1995.

Driver, Harold E. *Indians of North America.* 2d rev. ed. Chicago, 1969.

Durham, Michael S. *The Desert States.* New York, 1989.

———. "This Is the Place: Retracing the Pioneer Trail in Mormon Utah." *American Heritage,* April 1993, 65–82.

Elliott, Russell R. *History of Nevada.* 2d rev. ed. Lincoln, Nebr., 1987.

England, Eugene. *Brother Brigham.* Salt Lake City, 1980.

Escalante, Francisco Tomas Velez de. See Warner, Ted J., ed.

Fenneman, Nevin Melancthon. *Physiography of the Western United States.* New York, 1931.

Fife, Austin, and Alta. *Saints of Sage and Saddle: Folklore among the Mormons.* Bloomington, Ind., 1956.

Frederick, J. V. *Ben Holladay: The Stagecoach King.* Lincoln, Nebr., 1989.

Frémont, John Charles. For *Reports,* see Jackson, Donald Dean and Mary Lee Spence, eds.

———. *Memoirs of My Life.* New York, 1887.

French, Joseph Lewis, ed. *The Pioneer West: Narratives of the Westward March of Empire.* New York, 1995.

Furniss, Norman F. *The Mormon Conflict, 1850–1859.* New Haven, 1960.

Garcés, Francisco. See Coues, Elliott.

Gilbert, Bil. *Westering Man: The Life of Joseph Walker.* New York, 1983.

Goetzmann, William H. *Army Exploration in the American West, 1803–1863.* New Haven, 1959.

———. *Exploration and Empire: The Explorer and the Scientist in the Winning of the American West.* New York, 1966.

———. "Death Stalked the Grand Reconnaissance." *American Heritage,* October 1972, 44–48, 92–95.

———. *New Lands, New Men: America and the Second Great Age of Discovery.* New York, 1986.

Greeley, Horace. *An Overland Journey from New York to San Francisco in the Summer of 1859.* New York, 1860.

Grinnell, George Bird. *Beyond the Old Frontier: Adventures of Indian-Fighters, Hunters, and Fur-Traders.* Reprint: Williamstown, Mass., 1976.

Hafen, LeRoy R. "Mountain Men before the Mormons." *Utah Historical Quarterly* 26 (October 1958), 307–26.

Hafen, LeRoy R. and Ann W. *The Old Spanish Trail: Santa Fe to Los Angeles.* Glendale, Calif., 1954.

———. *The Utah Expedition, 1857–1858.* Glendale, Calif., 1958.

———. *Handcarts to Zion: The Story of a Unique Western Migration, 1856–1860.* Glendale, Calif., 1960.

———. *Mountain Men and the Fur Trade of the Far West: Biographical Sketches.* 10 vols. Glendale, Calif., 1965–1972.

Hague, Harlen. *The Road to California: The Search for a Southern Overland Route, 1540–1848.* Glendale, Calif., 1978.

Hastings, Lansford. *Emigrants' Guide to Oregon and California.* Cincinnati, 1845.

Hawgood, John A. *America's Western Frontiers: The Story of the*

Explorers and Settlers Who Opened Up the Trans-Mississippi West.
New York, 1967.

Heap, Gwinn Harris. *Central Route to the Pacific.* Edited by LeRoy
R. and Ann W. Hafen. Glendale, Calif., 1957.

Hirshon, Stanley P. *The Lion of the Lord: A Biography of Brigham
Young.* New York, 1969.

Holliday, J. S. *The World Rushed In: The California Gold Rush
Experience.* New York, 1981.

Houghton, Samuel G. *A Trace of Desert Waters: The Great Basin
Story.* Glendale, Calif., 1976.

Hunter, Milton R. *Brigham Young the Colonizer.* Independence,
Mo., 1940.

Irving, Washington. *The Adventures of Captain Bonneville, U.S.A.,
in the Rocky Mountains and the Far West.* New York, 1868.

Jackson, Donald, and Mary Lee Spence, eds. *The Expeditions of
John Charles Frémont, Travels from 1838 to 1844.* Urbana,
Ill., 1970.

Jackson, W. Turrentine. *Wagon Roads West: A Study of Federal
Road Surveys and Construction in the Trans-Mississippi West,
1846–1869.* New Haven, Conn., 1965.

James, Ronald M. "Drunks, Fools, and Lunatics: History and
Folklore of the Early Comstock." *Nevada Historical Society
Quarterly* (Winter 1992), 215–38.

Jeffrey, Julie Roy. *Frontier Women: The Trans-Mississippi West,
1840–1880.* New York, 1979.

Jenson, Andrew. *Latter-day Saint Biographical Encyclopedia.* 4 vols.
Salt Lake City, 1901–1936.

Kane, Elizabeth Wood. *Twelve Mormon Homes.* Salt Lake
City, 1974.

Kelly, Charles. "Jedediah Smith on the Salt Desert Trail." *Utah
Historical Quarterly* 3 (January 1930), 23–27, 35–52.

———. "The Salt Desert Trail." *Utah Historical Quarterly* 3
(April 1930), 34–53.

———. "The Hastings Cutoff." *Utah Historical Quarterly* 3
(July 1930), 66–82.

Kimball, Stanley B. *Discovering Mormon Trails New York to California, 1831–1868.* Salt Lake City, 1979.

———. *Heber C. Kimball: Mormon Patriarch and Pioneer.* Salt Lake City, 1981.

Lamar, Howard R., ed. *The Reader's Encyclopedia of the American West.* New York, 1977.

Langley, Harold D., ed. *To Utah with the Dragoons and Glimpses of Life in Arizona and California, 1858–1859.* Salt Lake City, 1974.

Laxalt, Robert. *Nevada: A Bicentennial History.* New York, 1977.

Lee, John Doyle. *A Mormon Chronicle: The Diaries of John D. Lee, 1848–1876.* Edited by Robert Glass Cleland and Juanita Brooks. Reprint: Salt Lake City, 1983.

Leonard, Zenas. *Narrative of the Adventures of Zenas Leonard.* Edited by Milo Milton Quaife. Chicago, 1934.

Ludlow, Daniel H. *Encyclopedia of Mormonism.* 5 vols. New York, 1992.

Merk, Frederick. *Manifest Destiny and Mission in American History.* New York, 1963.

———. *History of the Westward Movement.* New York, 1978.

Morgan, Dale L. *Jedediah Smith and the Opening of the West.* Reprint: Lincoln, Nebr., 1964.

———. *West from Fort Bridger: The Pioneering of the Immigrant Trails across Utah, 1846–1850.* Logan, Utah, 1994.

———, ed. *Pioneer Atlas of the American West.* 1876. Facsimile ed.: Chicago, 1956.

Mulder, William, and A. Russell Mortensen, eds. *Among the Mormons: Historic Accounts by Contemporary Observers.* New York, 1958.

Nadeau, Remi. "Go it, Washoe!" *American Heritage,* April 1959, 36–43, 106–7.

National Geographic Society. *Trails West.* Washington, D.C., 1979.

Neff, Andrew Love. *History of Utah, 1847 to 1869.* Salt Lake City, 1940.

Neuberger, Richard L. "Bloody Trek to Empire." *American Heritage,* August 1958.

Nevins, Allan. *Frémont: Pathmarker of the West*. New York, 1955.

O'Dea, Thomas F. *The Mormons*. Chicago, 1957.

Paul, Rodman W. *Mining Frontiers of the Far West, 1848–1880*. Albuquerque, 1974.

———. "The Mormons: From Poverty and Persecution to Prosperity and Power." *American Heritage*, June 1977, 74–83.

———. *The Far West and the Great Plains in Transition, 1859–1900*. New York, 1988.

Poll, Richard D., ed. *Utah's History*. Provo, 1978.

Powell, Allan Kent, ed. *Utah History Encyclopedia*. Salt Lake City, 1994.

Quaife, Milo Milton, ed., *Death Valley in '49*. Chicago, 1927.

Quinn, D. Michael. *The Mormon Hierarchy: Origins of Power*. Salt Lake City, 1994.

Rawling, Gerald. *The Pathfinders: The History of America's First Westerners*. New York, 1964.

Rémy, Jules. *A Journey to Great Salt Lake City*. London, 1861.

Rhodes, Richard. "Farther Continent of James Clyman." *American Heritage*, December 1978, 50–59.

Roberts, B. H. *A Comprehensive History of the Church of Jesus Christ of Latter-day Saints*. 6 vols. Salt Lake City, 1930.

Rolle, Andrew. *John Charles Frémont: Character as Destiny*. Norman, Okla., 1991.

Russell, Carl Parcher. *Firearms, Traps, and Tools of the Mountain Men*. Albuquerque, 1977.

Ruxton, George Frederick. *Life in the Far West*. Norman, Okla., 1951.

Sabin, Edwin L. *Kit Carson Days, 1809–1868*. 2 vols. New York, 1935.

Saum, Lewis. *The Fur Trader and the Indian*. Seattle, 1965.

Schindler, Harold. *Orrin Porter Rockwell: Man of God, Son of Thunder*. Salt Lake City, 1983.

Sears, Stephen W. "Trail Blazer of the Far West." *American Heritage*, June 1963, 60–64, 80–83.

Settle, Raymond W. and Mary L. *Saddles and Spurs: The Pony Express Saga*. Lincoln, Nebr., 1955.

———. *War Drums and Wagon Wheels: The Story of Russell, Majors, and Waddell*. Lincoln, Nebr., 1966.

Shipps, Jan. *Mormonism: The Story of a New Religious Tradition*. Chicago, 1985.

Simpson, J. H. *Report of Explorations across the Great Basin of the Territory of Utah for a Direct Wagon-Route from Camp Floyd to Genoa in Carson Valley in 1859*. Washington, D.C., 1876.

Stampp, Kenneth M. *America in 1857: A Nation on the Brink*. New York, 1990.

Stansbury, Howard. *An Expedition to the Valley of the Great Salt Lake of Utah*. Facsimile ed.: Ann Arbor, 1966.

Stegner, Wallace. *Mormon Country*. New York, 1942.

———. *The Gathering of Zion: The Story of the Mormon Trail*. New York, 1964.

Stenhouse, T. B. H. *The Rocky Mountain Saints: A Full and Complete History of the Mormons*. New York, 1873.

Stewart, George R. *Ordeal by Hunger: The Story of the Donner Party*. Boston, 1960.

———. *The California Trail*. New York, 1962.

Stone, Irving. *Men to Match My Mountains*. Garden City, N.Y., 1956.

Sullivan, Maurice S. *The Travels of Jedediah Smith: A Documentary Outline, Including His Journal*. Reprint: Lincoln, Nebr., 1992.

Taylor, Samuel W. *The Kingdom or Nothing: The Life of John Taylor, Militant Mormon*. New York, 1976.

Thwaites, Reuben Gold, ed. *Early Western Travels, 1748–1846*. 32 vols. Cleveland, 1905.

Time-Life Books. *The Trailblazers*. With text by Bil Gilbert. Alexandria, Va., 1973.

Trimble, Stephen. *The Sagebrush Ocean: A Natural History of the Great Basin*. Reno, Nev., 1989.

Twain, Mark. *Roughing It*. Library of America edition. New York, 1984.

Unruh, John. *The Plains Across: The Overland Emigrants and the Trans-Mississippi West, 1840–1860*. Urbana, Ill., 1979.

Utah Writers' Project. *Utah, a Guide to the State.* American Guide Series. New York, 1945.

Utley, Robert M. *The Indian Frontier of the American West, 1846–1890.* Albuquerque, 1984.

Van Wagoner, Richard S. *Mormon Polygamy: A History.* Salt Lake City, 1989.

Vestal, Stanley. *Jim Bridger, Mountain Man.* 1946; Lincoln, Nebr., 1970.

Walker, Henry Pickering. *The Wagonmasters: High Plains Freighting from the Earliest Days of the Santa Fe Trail to 1800* Norman, Okla., 1966.

Wallace, Irving. *The Twenty-seventh Wife.* New York, 1961.

Warner, Ted J., ed. *The Domínguez-Escalante Journal: Their Expedition through Colorado, Utah, Arizona, and New Mexico in 1776.* Translated by Angéllico Chávez. Provo, 1976.

Weber, David J. *The Spanish Frontier in North America 1513–1821.* New Haven, 1992.

Werner, M. R. *Brigham Young.* New York, 1925.

West, Ray B., Jr. *Kingdom of the Saints: The Story of Brigham Young and the Mormons.* New York, 1957.

Wexler, Alan. *Atlas of Westward Expansion.* New York, 1995.

Wheat, Carl. *Mapping the Transmississippi West, 1540–1861.* San Francisco, 1957–63.

Whittaker, David J. *Mormon Americana: A Guide to Sources and Collections in the United States.* Provo, 1995.

Wilkins, Thurman. *Clarence King: A Biography.* New York, 1958.

Williams, John Hoyt. *A Great & Shining Road: The Epic Story of the Transcontinental Railroad.* New York, 1988.

Winther, Oscar O. *The Transportation Frontier: Trans-Mississippi West, 1865–1890.* New York, 1964.

Young, Kimball. *Isn't One Wife Enough?* New York, 1954.

INDEX